Contents

Band History	1
1999	5
2000	24
2001	33
2002	44
Bringing It All Back Home Tour	47
Martin Slattery	53
Scott Shields	67
Pablo Cook	82
Smiley	87
Tymon Dogg	95
Antony Genn	102
Luke Bullen	112
Simon Stafford	118
John Blackburn	127
Jimmy Hogarth	129
Andy Boo	132
Richard Flack	137
Gary Robinson	143
Ben Gooder	150
Nikola Acin	154
Over Land and Sea	161
1999	163
2000	180
2001	193
2002	200
The Last Tour	206
The Saddest Day	211
Tour History	215
Discography	240
Credits	245

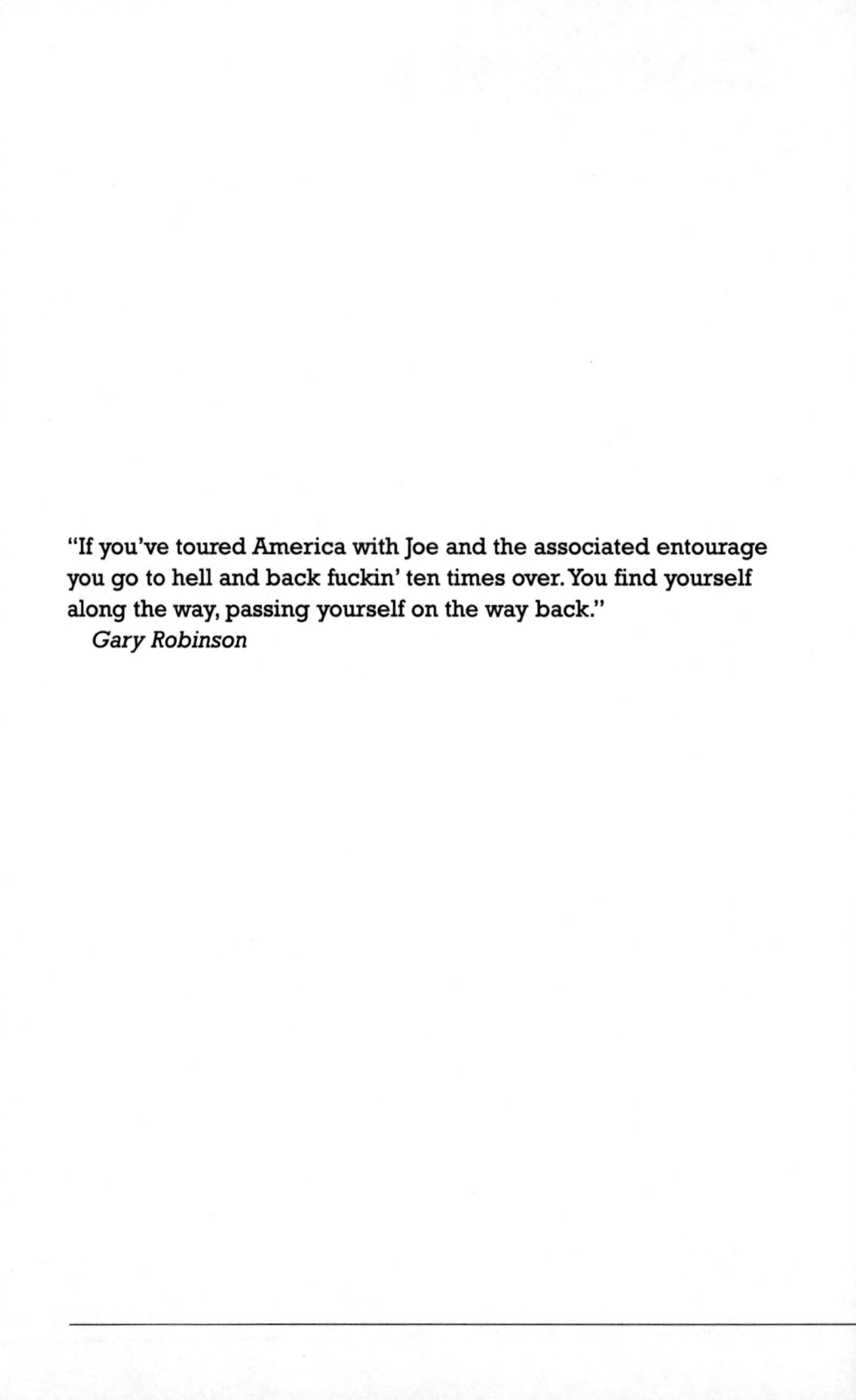

"If you've toured America with Joe and the associated entourage you go to hell and back fuckin' ten times over. You find yourself along the way, passing yourself on the way back."
  Gary Robinson

In Memory of Joe Strummer
1952–2002

VISION OF A HOMELAND

The History of
**Joe Strummer &
The Mescaleros**

Anthony Davie

EFFECTIVE PUBLISHING

Published by:
Effective Publishing
22 Kirby Close, Wootton,
Northampton NN4 6AB
Fax: 01908 261076

First published in Great Britain in 2004

Text copyright © Anthony Davie 2004

© Copyright warning
All rights reserved. No part of this publication may be reproduced or transmitted in any form or by any means without prior permission in writing from the publisher.
Effective Publishing endeavours to ensure that the information is correct but does not accept any liability for error or omission.
If you require any further information on permitted use or a licence to republish any material please contact Effective Publishing.

Copy-editing by Philip Morton
Printed in Great Britain

Cover artwork: Anika Jamieson-Cook and Steve Lea
Front cover photograph: Joe Strummer 2000. Copyright © Dave Maud
Back cover photographs: Joe Strummer & The Mescaleros 2001. Copyright © Anthony Davie
Joe Strummer & The Mescaleros 2000. Copyright © Lucinda Mellor

ISBN 0-9548568-0-5

A CIP catalogue record for this book is available from the British Library

Preface

In compiling this book, I spent many a Saturday at the British Newspaper Library in London, researched hundreds of articles in newspapers and spent endless hours researching on the net.

I also spent many, many happy hours with The Mescaleros and the crew, ranging from interviewing Ant in the car as we drove through London desperate to get to his flat to see an England match on television, sitting in a Mexican restaurant in Hertfordshire in the company of one of the funniest and kindest people it has ever been my pleasure to meet (Gary Robinson), to the peace and tranquility of sitting with Andy Boo and his son Nesta in a Birmingham park.

The whole band and their respective families have been absolutely great in their enthusiasm, help and contributions.

Also the enthusiasm, help and encouragement I have received from so many people, including Richard Flack, Simon "Fozzie" Foster, Dave Maud, John Zimmerman, Bob Gruen, Pat Gilbert and Tresa Redburn, to name but a few, still amazes me.

Of course the book wouldn't have been complete had I not listened to hours of Giuseppe's extensive bootleg collection at his home in the beautiful Italian Alps.

I'm proud to say the hairs still stand up on the back of my neck when I hear *Yalla Yalla*, *X-Ray Style*, *Safe European Home* and everything through to *Johnny Appleseed* and *Coma Girl*.

Those awesome concerts at Olympia Theatre, Astoria, The Roxy, Elysée-Montmartre, Brixton Academy, 100 Club, Acton ... the list is never-ending.

Although having been fortunate enough to have seen 1 in 3 of the bands 160 concerts and become good friends with several members of the band, I still only ever considered myself to be 'at best a punter.'

But to quote Smiley 'you went from a fan to an integral part of the bands life, becoming good friends with the band and crew to running the bands official site.'

I now realise, no one can ever take that away from me.

At times it was only the band and their family's support and encouragement that kept me going.

When you're feeling somewhat at a low ebb, it is amazing how much an email from Ant Genn or Scott, a phone call from Luke Bullen or Kirsty Slattery can lift you and make you even more determined to overcome the numerous obstacles and the confidence sapping responses bordering on apathy that I encountered from one or two people!

How could I have given up? Having experienced the warmth, enthusiasm and sincerity shown to me by Pablo's daughter Anika when she was doing the artwork for the book?

One of the many messages of support I received was from George Binette who simply said 'congratulations on having the determination and intestinal fortitude to bring the project to fruition.'

I will never be able to fully express how important to me everyones support was.

It was these moments of support and kindness shown to me by the band, the crew and so many others plus such great memories that always made me so determined to write and put to print this book about the legendary Joe Strummer and his great band The Mescaleros.

HISTORY OF
Joe Strummer & The Mescaleros

The Mescaleros first came together as a result of Pablo Cook and Joe working with firstly Richard Norris, then Bez from The Happy Mondays. They wrote the soundtrack for two short films, *Tunnel of Love* and *Question of Honour*, in the latter of which Joe, Pablo and Bez also had small acting roles. It starred Eric Cantona and Jake La Motta.

Pablo and Joe also spent many days at a time in the "woodshed" at Joe's house in Hampshire.

They were in the studio writing songs for The Hand of God and Antony Genn walked in one day, listened and said "This is great" – so he joined. They were originally going to be called Longbow, mainly due to the fact that where Joe lived in Somerset was where longbows were manufactured. Then they were going to be called The Hand of God.

Pablo Cook: "Ants came into the studios to pick up some tapes and his enthusiasm was great ... basically me and Joe were knocking about with an idea. It's great to knock about with names of bands and to play around that you might be a band."

Antony Genn recalls: "I just said to him you should be making a record, you're fuckin' Joe Strummer, for fuck's sake. He kinda called my bluff on it and said OK, I'm gonna call you tomorrow, me and you are going to go in the studio."

Pabs adds: "Although *Yalla Yalla* came out of a Strummer, Norris, Cook session, Ants remixed it to its final stage. As soon as Ants and Joe got together it certainly glued everything together because Ants knew how to do it. Plus you've got the added bonus that Ants is a great songwriter."

The band was basically put together over a curry in March 1999.

Scott Shields: "We all met up with Joe and it was just a great vibe. None of us in particular played the right instruments, Martin didn't play guitar, I didn't play bass, Ants didn't really play guitar. I think apart from Smiley, we were all just bluffing it. We were all good musicians and had a good knowledge of musical instruments but we all spent time learning what to play. Over the next couple of months we were in between recording and rehearsing."

Alongside Joe, the original Mescaleros line-up featured Martin Slattery, Scott Shields, Pablo Cook, Antony Genn and Ged Lynch.

After recording most of the first album *Rock Art And The X-Ray Style* at Battery Studios, Ged left to play on a Marianne Faithfull tour. Smiley (aka

Steve Barnard), Robbie Williams' ex-drummer, was brought in. He had been due to team up with The Eurythmics, only to be let down by a last-minute Lennox/Stewart change of plan.

Smiley describes his first meeting in an interview with *www.trakmarx.com*: "It all started bizarrely enough – I was about to embark on a world tour with The Eurythmics. Dates were confirmed, passport details sorted and money negotiated. Then, the dreaded musician's call – the no-real-explanation, confidence-sapping call that only a session musician can experience.

So as I leaned back on my crutch-like Silk Cut to take in the news, the phone rang – a man wanted me to go and play some drums for a Mr Strummer. Now this will probably offend all the borderline fanatic Strummer fans who would give their right hand to have that call but, at that precise time, JS meant practically nothing to me. He used to play for The Clash, who, apart from *Rock the Casbah* being in my Top 10 faves, hadn't really changed my life in any way – now he was going out with his Mescaleros.

"I rocked up to Willesden and sat waiting – as the gates to the studio opened, I pulled in to see Mr S walking towards me. I put out my hand and said, 'Joe, Smiley.' He replied, 'Just off to get a paper.' What a rock 'n' roll moment. Hours later I was playing next to the man, holding down a groove on a track called *Forbidden City*, which I would later record for the *X-Ray Style* album. So, politics, blah blah, I got the job to play as a Mescalero. Now the adventure was about to begin."

Smiley had again met up with Martin Slattery – they had both appeared on Robbie Williams' excellent 1997 debut album *Life Thru a Lens*.

With the Marianne Faithfull tour never materialising, The Mescaleros were left with two drummers – Smiley got the nod and played drums on *Forbidden City* on the *Rock Art* album.

In an interview with *Music Monitor Online*'s Howard Petruziello in December 1999 Joe gave a rough guide to the band's formation: 'Pablo Cook was part of Machine and he also knew Antony from playing sessions with Pulp, Elastica and that scene in London. We both knew Martin Slattery from watching and hanging with him in Black Grape. When Grape split up he was loose and we grabbed him and he brought along Scott Shields and we only had to find a drummer, which you do at the last minute, really. We found a guy called Smiley.'

Joe had also given a similar interview a few months earlier with David Holmes.

In an interview with *The Big Takeover* in December 1999 Joe describes the band's formation to Jack Rabid: "We lucked into Smiley and Scott, they're nice people to hang out with. Very important on the road. We've got cool guys, we've got a happy party going at the moment."

Talking to Adam Rapoport in New York *Time Out*: "I finally met a guy in London, Antony Genn. I knew what he could do, and he said to me, 'C'mon, you're Joe Strummer. You should be making records.' And the moment he said that, I knew we were on."

Joe later told Chris Harris in the *Valley Advocate*: "Working with this new band has been one of the best experiences of his life and has rejuvenated the rocker."

Before the band first took to the road, they were lent a base rig and sample set from Steve Mackey and Jarvis Cocker of Pulp. Also the Manics lent the band some gear. Geoff and Helen at The Depot were very helpful as the rehearsals were normally booked between 10am and 10pm but very rarely started before midnight.

A couple of record executives visited the Depot to watch Joe & The Mescaleros rehearse and play the new songs. The three huddled together whilst the band was playing, and as they finished a song one of them called out to Joe to play *London Calling*. After a few mumbles of discontent, the band played a great version of the Clash classic and the three wise men gave the nod of approval.

Pabs recalls: "Basically Joe was fuckin' with these people. I could understand Joe's point of view, you give them a few new songs. The one thing you don't do is walk up to a great man like Joe Strummer and go: 'Eh mate, can you play *London Calling*?'

You'll get *London Calling* in your own time. There was a vibe there, don't come into Joe's yard and start calling the shots. I think we played *Willesden To Cricklewood* and they shit themselves. I think Joe and Antony took a stand on playing new songs."

In the interim the band moved back to Battery Studios and took the unusual step of using the studio not only to record the new album but also to rehearse for a proposed tour.

Richard Flack was the creative engineer for the *Rock Art* album; he was considered by Joe and the band to be a very important part of the team. He was the seventh Mescalero.

Antony Genn states: "Bill Price got brought in to mix the record. He had mixed *London Calling* and was the engineer for Guy Stevens. He came in, he was a lovely guy but it just didn't work out. The mixes didn't seem to be tough enough for me. He had mixed *Techno D-Day* and *Yalla Yalla* and we weren't really happy. No disrespect to Bill; it was a different thing. I wanted them to be drier, punchier and more aggressive. So we kinda took the reins back and mixed the record ourselves."

In the meantime Pulp were playing at Palazzio Pisani Moretta, Venice Biennale, on 10 June and, realising The Mescaleros still had a lot of their equipment for the four-date British tour, had to rent the missing rig etc so they could still play.

The Pulp connection with The Mescaleros extended not only to Antony Genn being formerly of Pulp but also to Pablo Cook having played with Pulp on a part-time basis. The main core of The Mescaleros' roadcrew, Justin Grealy, Andy Boo and Roger Middlecote, had also worked extensively on tour with Pulp.

Again all the connections had come from Ants: he had got together the engineer, the roadcrew, everything.

1999

Summer tour

Saturday 5 June 1999 saw Joe Strummer & The Mescaleros' first gig at The Leadmill, Sheffield. After support bands Seafood and The Llama Farmers, Joe and his new band came onstage at 10.00pm sharp and opened with *Techno D-Day*. The set that evening also included *London Calling*, *I Fought The Law* and finished with *Tommy Gun*.

Richard Flack: "I went to Sheffield to see the first gig. To be honest it was a bit rough round the edges, but it was so cool seeing Joe and the boys playing live for the first time, it didn't matter. It was a great gig because it was the first and nothing went wrong!"

The following morning the band drove the short distance across the Pennines to Liverpool and that evening took to the Lomax stage at 8.45pm. The Cumberland Street club, with its small capacity of 300, was bursting at the seams. Word had spread that Joe Strummer was in town and everyone was trying to get in.

Dave Simpson reported in *The Guardian*: "Strummer has a clutch of new material and a new skin-tight band. He leaves us with a *Tommy Gun* so startling I drop my can of lager and grown men are seen to weep into the streets."

After the show, an overnight drive to Glasgow arriving at The Stakis Strathclyde with the customary day rooms for showers etc. The roadcrew load-in time was 4.00pm, soundcheck 6.00pm and Joe and the band took to the King Tut's stage at 9.45pm.

An all-night drive back to London followed the show. The first three gigs had gone down a treat. Full houses, great shows, fantastic receptions. After nearly ten years, Joe Strummer was back!

Tuesday 8 June was a day off except for Joe and Ant who went to the Battery Studios to finish off work on the forthcoming single. On Wednesday afternoon the band took the 70-odd-mile trip by minibus to Portsmouth, where a full house awaited them at The Wedgewood Rooms. *Brand New Cadillac* was played for the first time, with Joe having introduced the song to the band during soundcheck only two hours earlier. The set included *London Calling* twice.

Pablo recalls: "Portsmouth was the first night we were approached for sponsorship. A guy was trying to get Joe to wear Adidas, but Joe wasn't having any of that. I think this guy came down on the preconception that Joe was going to dress all in Adidas, baseball hat on back to front etc. I think Joe got pissed off with him.

"We were always jokin' 'cause we had this sort of vision of Joe onstage with his hat on back to front lookin' like somethin' out of The Beastie Boys. Joe said 'I'm not havin' any of that.' The only bad thing was 'cause Joe turned down the sponsorship, none of us could get any gear. I could see Adidas's point, having this really cool geezer – Joe Strummer – wearing your sports gear, but it was completely against everything Joe stood for.''

The band travelled back to London after the show. Pat Gilbert wrote an in-depth review in the following edition of *Mojo*: "'We're making a new form of music,' explains Joe Strummer proudly gesturing to his young backing group, The Mescaleros, with whom he's been cutting his first solo record in eight years. 'It's one part percussionist, one part audience insulting us.' 'Fuck off you old cunt!' shouts a heckler. 'I'm happy to accept that old Portsmouth welcome,' whips back the old man without missing a beat. The audience laughs. Twenty years ago they'd have probably been eating Telecaster sandwich.

"It's been several years since Joe has played live, and clearly he's in his element. Last time he performed in Portsmouth it was to 2,000 people at the Guildhall, with the ill-advised, post-Mick Jones line-up of The Clash; tonight it's to a few hundred curious fans in a small hall up the road and, thanks to the intimacy of the venue, we're treated to what at times seems like Joe Strummer in the round. Looking considerably younger than his 46 years, with intact quiff and Italianate shirt, he's warm, wise and generous, throwing in anecdotes between his band's enthusiastic rampage through The Clash songbook and his new, world-music-meets-punk-techno material.

"'This radio guy asked me what we were playing,' he chuckles. 'You can't say, oh, it's the same old thing... You have to make something up, right? So I came up this word "hip-hopabilly".' And with that the band lurch into a loping, *Sandinista*-type song called *Tony Adams* that's one part bongos, one part audience insult ('Fuck off you old cunt!' becomes a mantra this evening), one part crunching punk-funk. The Mescaleros give it their best shot, ex-Black Grape percussionist Pablo Cook beating out funk rhythms, baby-faced bassist Scott Shields adding booming, nimble bass lines, and former Pulp and Elastica keyboardist Antony Genn chopping away on low-slung, trebly guitar.

"Joe introduces another newie, *Forbidden City*, with a rant about the political situation in Tibet and 'all the other countries fucked over by China'. In the age of rock for rock's sake, it's great to hear the stage as a political platform again, but any feelings of nostalgia for the old days of punkoid activism are quickly allayed by the sheer shock of hearing Joe bashing out old Clash stuff, with a band that, for all their spirit and expertise, aren't The Clash.

"Reports that Strum would only play three old numbers were greatly understated; he plays eight. *London Calling* doesn't quite hit it first time around (it's trotted out as an encore), but *White Man In Hammersmith Palais* – perhaps Strummer's greatest lyrical triumph – hits its scorching punk-reggae crescendo with pace and panache. *I Fought The Law* is played almost impishly fast, Joe seemingly struggling to keep up with the wheeling drum beat of his youthful sticksman; *Tommy Gun* charges along, but sorely misses Mick Jones' inspired lead guitar parts on the coda. *Rock The Casbah* is dedicated to the author of its main piano riff, Topper Headon.

"Which, of course, begs the question, if these songs are deemed relevant and worthwhile, why not get The Clash to play them? Is Strummer undermining The Clash's incomparable integrity in matters of 'meaning something'? And are we guilty in aiding and abetting him by cheering? I'd be a liar if I said I didn't enjoy every minute tonight; but if you're gonna have a plate of beans, it's better to eat Heinz's rather than Somerfield's own brand."

NME's Johnny Cigarettes gave a rave review: "He's got a band to do it justice. *London Calling, Rock The Casbah* and *White Man In Hammersmith Palais* sound as urgent and wiry as the day they were recorded."

Johnny Cigarettes went further when commenting on "Mescaleros stuff" "Best of all, though, is *Yalla Yalla*, a blissful reggae-ish anthem that would have held its own on *Sandinista*."

These first dates had been great for the band, Pablo puts it quite eloquently: "I was playing *London Calling* for fuck's sake, it was so great. We were truly excited about being in a fuckin' great rock 'n' roll band. At the time we were definitely a band, something was definitely happening, we were experimenting all the time. We used to soundcheck for hours, some of the grooves we got into were amazing."

Saturday 12 June, the band met at 11.00pm and took an overnight coach drive to Amsterdam arriving on the Sunday morning for the Tibetan Freedom Concert at Amsterdam's RAI Parkhal. With the band on at 4.00pm they played a 40-minute set, opening with *White Man In Hammersmith Palais*.

An overnight drive to Paris followed, checking in at the hotel in the morning. A capacity 1,400 gave Joe & The Mescaleros a great Parisian welcome when they took to the stage at just before 9.00pm, opening with *Techno D-Day*. Joe dedicated *London Calling* to everyone "who had supported The Clash and when I came here with The Pogues".

"Je Fought The Law and the law fuckin' won" was the intro. The 14-song set finished with Joe declaring "Smiley, do the famous drumroll" and a superb *Tommy Gun*.

This gig was also the first time *Mbube* was used as intro music. Smiley: "Joe had bags and bags of tapes with him all the time; he used to sling them across his bunk every time he got on the bus, with bits of paper, and suddenly *Mbube* was the intro tape. Joe used to give Justin about half an hour's worth of music leading up to us going on."

Tuesday 15th was a day off and a further night's stay in the Place de République Holiday Inn.

At 10.00am next day the band took the four-hour drive to Brussels, loaded in at 2.00pm and came onstage at the Botanique at 9.00pm.

After the show the bus continued its European journey with an overnight drive to Hamburg, which saw Joe return to the Markthalle for the first time since 1980 and the infamous riots which had seen him arrested having allegedly hit someone in the audience with his guitar.

The band opened with *Techno D-Day* at just gone 10.00pm and the gig went without any trouble.

Following a night's stay in Hamburg at the Kempinski Hotel, there was a rest day.

Andy Boo recalls Joe's love of one particular band:

"We were in Germany, it was about 7.00 in the morning. Joe and I were having a smoke and drink and on the telly it came up about The Beach Boys playing in town that night. Joe was going 'The Beach Boys, yeah let's all go and see The Beach Boys.' I just thought, yeah allright! OK Joe, you're having a laugh.

"At lunch time all the band and me went to a Japanese restaurant. The only reason they let me go was Ants looked at me and said 'You look more like a band member than a crew member in your "day off" shirt'. In the restaurant this geezer's only got out the karaoke book. Joe's sitting there tapping his foot as various Mescaleros sang a song. I said to Joe that a good song to do for karaoke is *We Are The World*. 'Look there's seven of us so we can all be somebody, I'll be Michael Jackson and you can be Bruce Springsteen Joe!'

"Joe just sat there and Ants said 'You're not really into this Joe, are you?' Joe said 'No.' So The Mescaleros did this rendition of *We Are The World* with Joe sitting there tapping his fingers on the table.

"After the meal Joe's come up again with this thing about going to see The Beach Boys. I really thought he was joking. But he was serious. So a few went to the Stadtpark, Hamburg, with Joe where they bought the tickets – Joe was never a big blagmeister. At the gig Joe was apparently dancing away, having the time of his life. When they came back to the bus Joe said, 'You're all sacked, you're all sacked. This morning I said we're all going to see The Beach Boys and hardly any of you came.' We were all re-employed the next day!

"When we were in Australia, I was in my room watching telly and there was this history of The Beach Boys programme on. So I rang Joe's room and said, 'What you doing?' He said, 'Nothing, why?' I said, 'Look, there's this programme on telly about The Beach Boys.' He said, 'I know, I'm watching it!'"

The bus drove through the night to arrive on Saturday 19 June at Hultsfred Festival in Sweden. Joe & The Mescaleros were the second-to-top slot behind Suede and came onstage at 10.00pm. The set kicked off with a fantastic intro leading into *Techno D-Day*, included a very short version of *I Fought The Law* and was superbly finished off with Joe hollering "Rock it out

Smiley" at the start of *Tommy Gun*. However, the crowd wouldn't take no for an answer and demanded more with the band finishing the set off with *Bank Robber*. Swedish National Radio recorded this show.

Following the show they took an all-night drive to Stockholm Airport for a morning flight to Vaasa, arriving at Vaasa airport at 11.30 am and taking the 80km drive straight to Provinssi Rock where the band were headlining. They took to the stage at 16.45.

This concert involved a one-off appearance for backline tec Andy Boo who took to the stage on percussion, replacing Pablo Cook who had to fly back to London for a prior contract obligation with Sony regarding a band called Merz.

Andy describes the day: "I was on the bongos and the set had been altered accordingly, Joe attempted to introduce me a couple of times but I hid as I was tucked away right at the back.

A couple of songs later Joe signalled that he was having some problems with his guitar strap and as I came to the front of the stage to help, he grabbed my arm and declared 'Ladies and gentlemen, Rufus on the bongos.'

Monday 21st saw the band fly back to Stockholm where Ant and Joe continued their journey to London by plane to continue work on the new single and everyone else met up with the bus and took the 24-hour drive back to London.

After a few days off the band and crew met up again at Glastonbury on the 26th and came onstage to a super welcome from the 40,000-odd crowd. Joe told the crowd how Tony Blair reminded him of Cliff Richard and therefore the country was being governed by Cliff Richard.

Richard Flack: "The night before Glastonbury, Scott and Ant and myself had stayed up all night doing a remix of *Tony Adams*. (This track later formed the basis for *Cool 'n' Out* on *Global A Go-Go*.) The rest of the band were already there, so we had to drive down (still slightly spannered) and got down there about 7am. When we banged on the tour bus, I think Pabs was already up playing with Titus who was running round like a lunatic."

The BBC filmed some of The Mescaleros' 13-song set, resulting in Joe having an altercation with a camera crew. The band and roadcrew spent the Saturday night at Glastonbury, departing on the Sunday afternoon.

Monday 28th saw the band take a midday flight to Washington for the start of the short American tour, which was sponsored by Von Dutch.

10.00pm Tuesday 29 June at 9.30 Club, on V Street, Washington saw Joe Strummer take to the stage in America for the first time in years. Joe dedicated the show to Bo Diddley and the band opened with *Diggin' The New* which was to be the regular opening song for the foreseeable future.

The *Washington Post*'s Mark Jenkins wrote: "While The Mescaleros provided youthful vigor and versatility – band member Martin Slattery played guitar, keyboards and saxophone – Strummer is still the pub-rocker he always was."

The now regular travel through the night followed the show – next stop: New York. It was during the band's short stay that the *Yalla Yalla* video was shot on the streets of New York.

Smiley: "I remember very clearly that Bob Gruen was there, taking pictures. We went out in the afternoon walking around New York and it was basically us, Ben Gooder and a guy with a camera."

Producer Ben Gooder: "I filmed the band shots by the Flat Iron Building on Broadway just off Times Square. When this was filmed it was raining and we had about 20 minutes to shoot it. It was mad, me squatting down in gutters trying to get interesting angles. We were on the streets totally illegally with no permission, right under the noses of the cops. We just told them, yeah it's all fine, we've got permission from so and so. We got away with it."

Further filming was also shot on the Lower East Side.

That evening another great welcome for the band as they took to the stage at Irving Plaza.

Rob Kemp wrote in New York *Time Out*: "This show will not be as epochal as the Clash's two-week stand at Bonds Casino in 1982, but a long-MIA legend is showing up along with a hot band, promising lots of Clash songs. And that's pretty damn epochal."

Richard Flack: "The original line-up had a real raw energy about them, they had real attitude."

Joe Angio would write some months later, also in New York *Time Out*: "Surrounded by bandmates some 20 years his junior, an energized Strummer ripped into the Clash numbers with gusto. But the evening's true revelation were the new songs: They rocked. The old punk still had it."

In the *New York Times* Ann Powers wrote: "Mr Strummer's new, young band, The Mescaleros, intermingled punk guitar and dance beats in the style of Manchester bands."

Thursday 1 July saw the band leaving New York at lunchtime to start the long-distance journey to the next leg of the tour at Cabaret Metro, Chicago. The band came onstage at the relatively early time of 8.00pm due to the Chicago city ordnance 10.00pm curfew, as it was an all-ages show.

Joshua Klein wrote in the *Chicago Tribune*: "The young faces of Strummer's five bandmates would light up, inspired by the presence of one of their most valued pioneers. Scottish bassist Scott Shields in particular beefed up the reggae-tinged songs, while guitarist Martin Slattery – doubling on keyboards – gleefully pounded out the honky tonk-infused piano part from *Casbah*."

A Friday-night stay in Chicago was followed by a 100-mile trip to Milwaukee where at the Milwaukee Summerfest, Rock Stage, despite early sound problems, the band put in one of their best performances to date including a double playing of *London Calling*.

Blaine Schultz wrote in the *Shepherd Express*: "The real prize in the Crackerjacks this night was how well the group of youngsters in Strummer's new band interpreted the myriad of influences stuffed into some of The Clash's best tunes."

He also commented: "Taking a page from James Brown, Strummer pointed directions to the band behind his back while singing at several points."

After the show the bus headed back to Chicago and the following afternoon the band and crew flew to San Francisco, where Joe's daughters had arrived from London.

Monday was a day off and on Tuesday 6 July Joe Strummer & The Mescaleros played at The Fillmore on Geary Street. It was perhaps their tightest set to date. It is also best remembered for Joe's superb and unique intro to songs in the set: "There's only two British rock 'n' roll songs. One of them is *Shaking All Over* by Johnny Kidd & The Pirates. This is the other one by Vince Taylor & The Playboys..." as the band unleash a great version of *Brand New Cadillac*. Later, during the encore, as Joe introduced *Forbidden City*, "Nine years and four months ago," he is heckled by someone in the audience which clearly annoys him as he angrily raises his voice continuing "AFTER THE BLOODY TIANANMEN SQUARE MASSACRE."

The fan continues to heckle resulting in Joe raising his guitar: "I'll give you this on your bonce if you don't shut up. We're talking about some people who fight for their freedom, right! Don't just doss around like you, YOU CUNT!"

This was greeted with rapturous applause and cheers from the audience.

The following day saw the relatively short flight to Los Angeles and a 5.30 soundcheck. Joe and the boys rocked The Palace on the final night.

Richard Cromelin wrote in the *Los Angeles Times*: "Strummer has earned a rare degree of loyalty and respect from his audience, a fact evident in the attention they paid to unfamiliar songs. Strummer and his young players rewarded that attention with some intense instrumental interplay."

On Thursday 8th an evening flight back to London saw the band arrive at Heathrow at midday on the 9th to be met by a sleeper bus and drive to Glasgow where the following day they made a mid-afternoon appearance at T in The Park.

The band took to the stage to the sound of the Earl King classic *Come on (Let the Good Times Roll)* and a fantastic welcome. After *Rock the Casbah* the band were told they had only five minutes left, to which Joe responded: "We came on late, it wasn't our fault, we were standing there for 20 minutes, so you go back and tell them: 'Why wasn't the stage ready when I was?'"

After the show the band took an overnight drive back to London.

A well-earned break was followed three weeks later with a flight to Japan and a great ten-song performance at the Fuji Rock Fest on 1 August. The show was running late and ZZ Top were upset and trying to get on The Mescaleros' slot.

Scott Shields: "ZZ Top was headlining and they asked us to headline because they were going to miss a flight or something. Joe was just like "Nah, fuck off."

European shows

Thursday 12 August the bus departed West London at just before midnight and via Dover-Calais took the 16-hour journey to Clermont Ferrand for the Free Wheels Festival, where on Friday 13th, following the opening acts of Chris Spedding and The Silencers, the band took to the stage in front of 15,000 and played an hour and a half's set finishing at just before 1.00am.

Scott: "The Free Wheels Festival was terrible – that was where we were advertised as a Clash tribute band. 'A tribute to The Clash: Joe Strummer & The Mescaleros.'

"Joe didn't see it; the tour manager at the time told them to take the posters down. He basically went round telling everyone to get those posters down – 'If Joe sees that he'll fuckin' go nuts' – and he would have. Plus the crowd gave Andy Boo a hard time because he was black. That was really surreal that place."

The following morning Joe and the tour manager Chris Griffiths flew back to London for an appearance on the Billy Bragg radio show. The band drove back arriving in London at 7.00pm.

Wednesday 18th the bus again left West London, complete with a new tour manager Gary Robinson, at around midday for the 25-hour/900 mile trip to Wiesen, Austria, for the "Two Days a Week Festival" appearance on Thursday 19 August where The Offspring were headlining. A tremendous reception was given to the band with the crowd chanting "Joe Strummer, Joe Strummer."

Joe declared, "We're here to rock" as they opened with *London Calling*. Austrian radio recorded the nine-song set.

An overnight journey to Cologne was followed by a day off.

Saturday 21st on the main stage at the Bizarre Festival in front of 20,000, following a set by a group called Bloodhound Gang, Joe & The Mescaleros ripped straight into *London Calling* to start a top-drawer one-hour set, which was filmed and shown on German television.

In an interview with German radio/television Joe stated when asked about The Mescaleros: "I have a big legacy of The Clash to live up to and I don't intend to urinate on a legend. I intend to build forward into the next century."

When asked about his anger being as strong a force as it used to be, he said: "Unfortunately, I'm completely out of control now, because I have nothing to lose and this makes a man very dangerous when he has nothing to lose."

Sunday 22nd saw an early morning flight from Cologne via Frankfurt to Oporto, Portugal, where the band headlined the 15,000-capacity Vilar De Mouros festival at the mountain town of Vila De Parades De Coura near the Spanish Border.

An afternoon flight from Oporto to Heathrow saw the bus collect everyone and start the journey to Holyhead for the connecting ferry to Dun Laoghaire arriving in Dublin in time for breakfast. This concert (likewise Belfast) had originally been arranged for late June. The Olympia Theatre with its 1,600 capacity paid homage to Joe Strummer & The Mescaleros when they took to the stage at dead on 9.00pm on 24 August. Opening with *Forbidden City*, Joe announced to the packed crowd that "some representatives of Mercury Records were in the house" to which the crowd enthusiastically booed.

At the end, despite Joe appearing onstage appealing to the fans, they refused to budge. "OK, we'll have to play another number," and the band played *London Calling* for a second time. Afterwards Joe told the crowd, "Thank you, now will you go home please!"

Scott: "Joe had to go out and say, 'Please go home! We can't play any more.' We were all offstage eating our dinner and Joe came back and said, 'We got to go back on.' Ants had to pull himself out the shower, get his shit together and go back on. The crowd just refused to leave, so we played *London Calling* again."

Gary Robinson: "I had to go to the dressing room and let Joe and the boys know that the crowd were going nowhere and the promoter was panicking. They just didn't want to leave. I went out to the front of house to let the sound engineer know they were coming back on. The curtains were down and then I heard the first few chords of *London Calling* with the curtains coming back up. The crowd went mental. It was just one of them moments."

The *Irish Times* reported: "When Strummer left the stage following an encore of *Bank Robber*, the crowd refused to budge, and cheered loudly for 15 minutes until Strummer was forced to raise the curtain and return to the stage."

Nick Kelly wrote in *The Times*: "The Cockney Rebel and his quintet of Mescaleros treated us to a set of Clash classics as well a preview of his new album... At one stage the triangle-player even mounted one of the amps and implored the faithful to respond... The set was short, sharp and to the point but the crowd simply refused to go home even after the safety curtain had come down and the house lights were switched on, and so Strummer eventually returned for a raucous reprise of *London Calling*."

An overnight journey to Belfast followed the after-show party. The Holiday Inn Express provided day rooms and that evening The Limelight with its 800 capacity saw six exhausted Mescaleros give their all, finishing at just before midnight.

After the show a local reporter joined the band on the bus. He was somewhat the worse for wear drinkwise and Joe kept him talking and drinking on the bus with the curtains drawn till unbeknown to him he was stuck on the ferry to Stranraer. The band said farewell to him in Scotland waiting for the next ferry back to Ireland. The band arrived back in London in the early evening of 26 August.

A week later the band left West London at midday for Munich where they were playing at Kunstpark Ost on 3 September.

The crowd gave the band a hard time and objects were thrown at the stage. The set stopped and several members of Offspring came onstage and told the crowd "If it wasn't for this man, we wouldn't be here today."

Smiley: "It was a horrible gig, really bad vibe, there was a load of troublemakers in the middle. I could see it all from where I was on the kit. They started heckling and Joe was annoyed and said to them, 'Come on then.' It was horrible; more security was brought in afterwards to protect us."

Scott: "I got really fuckin' pissed off getting hit in the head."

Joe had a heated row with one particularly aggressive member of the crowd who was wearing an Anarchy T-shirt. "Anarchy, what the fuck do you know about Anarchy? I bet your mum ironed your Anarchy T-shirt for you. Come on, come on if you want a fuckin' fight."

As Joe jumped down from the stage towards the audience, a rush of security men held both parties apart.

Ants: "When we played Kuntspark in Munich, Joe said, 'I didn't think you meant it literally.'

When Offspring were onstage, after three songs they stopped, brought a sofa onstage and said something like 'We love Joe Strummer and you should love Joe Strummer. We won't play any more songs until you chant We Love Joe Strummer.'

So all the crowd sang, 'We love Joe Strummer.' Joe loved it."

This one-hour gig in Munich as second slot to The Offspring is relatively unknown to many fans.

A 350-mile overnight journey to Italy brought the band to the following day's (4 September) Festa De L'Unita at Parco Nord in a rain-drenched Bologna. The Mescaleros' set was filmed and shown on Italian television. This was followed by a 22-hour coach journey back to London.

UK tour

Mid-October saw the band catch the train from St Pancras to Nottingham for the start of their first big British tour. The crew had met a day earlier at The Depot and travelled up overnight.

The support band Little Mothers opened at Nottingham Rock City with a half-hour slot. One interesting note is that this band included Micky Gallagher's sons Luke and Ben who some 19 years earlier along with their sister Maria had their version of *Career Opportunities* on The Clash's *Sandinista* album. This was a fine example of Joe giving a helping hand to the ones he knew and trusted.

At 9.00pm, Joe & The Mescaleros came onstage to a rapturous response, opened with *Diggin' The New* and played a superb set which included eight new numbers: *Nitcomb, Safe European Home, Nothin' 'bout Nothin', Trash City, Road To Rock 'n' Roll, Pressure Drop* and *Rudie Can't Fail* plus a cover of the Max Romeo & The Upsetters classic *Quarter Pound Of Ishen*.

The noise from the crowd was so intense that Joe shouted, "Can I introduce the band here or what?" and went on, "A very special treat for us, from the Langley Park Massive ... Smiley Culture and that kind of Manc vibe that only Mancs can have ... Mr. Martin Slattery."

An inflatable doll appeared from the audience with Joe making the comment, "No one told me Mick Jones was here." He quickly retracted that statement by declaring, "I take that back; that was a rotten low-down comment."

After-show travel involved the now familiar overnight journey to the next venue and the relatively short journey up the M1 to Leeds.

Tuesday 19 October the band played Leeds Town & Country club and after the show they travelled back to London. Wednesday was a day off. With many of the band being London-based it was a good opportunity to go home for a night.

Thursday 21st the crew had to load in at 7.00am at The Astoria, just before the London morning rush hour. This was the first of two sold-out nights.

The massed choir of the London audience during *Safe European Home* was just one of the many high points of these two great nights. Pablo recalls, "The first night was blistering."

David Cheal reported in the *Daily Telegraph*: "The former Clash frontman and his five-piece band, The Mescaleros, opened with *Diggin' The New*, one of the best tracks from Strummer's engaging *Rock Art And The X-Ray Style* album."

The second night saw a change of support band with Medal taking the support slot for one night only.

Saturday 23rd the band travelled by train to Norwich, to play Norwich UEA ... Johnny Green and his son attended.

Andy Boo: "I was about to be sacked, but Johnny Green had mentioned to Joe how much he thought I was old school, roadie-wise, so my job was safe ... for a week or two!"

Afterwards involved travelling overnight to Cardiff. Sunday was a day off.

Monday 25 October, the band entered the second week of the British tour by playing at Cardiff University.

They rolled into Wolverhampton on the morning of 26th with the Civic Hall in North Street being the largest venue of the tour.

Wednesday 27th ... day off in Manchester

Thursday 28th, Manchester Academy; after-show sleeper bus to Glasgow.

The final night of the tour was 29 October ... Joe Strummer & The Mescaleros and the sell-out 1,900 fans rocked Barrowlands.

The band had been joined on the bus by a ten-man Manchester crew and as they arrived in Glasgow the bus driver threw everyone off the bus and threatened to call the police as he had been threatened and the party had been a somewhat wild one.

Scott recalls the evening: "Joe went absolutely mental, I've never seen him so angry and he tried to pull the bus's window wipers off. We ended up staying at the Glasgow Hilton – there was like a policeman's convention there and we ended up sitting in a circle in the middle of them deliberately smoking weed. For some reason we got away with it."

Smiley: "I was in my bunk and the first thing I knew was we were all ordered off the bus. Joe did a one-man demonstration around the bus. It was a nasty vibe; they scared me. Gary Robinson was threatened. Some of them were OK. Tommy, Dermot were fine, but there was some nasty moments."

Pablo puts a slightly different light on it: "The musician side was one thing but these people (the Manchester crew) that Joe attracted were totally different; these were some serious bad guys."

Ant adds: "I remember Glasgow. Wags, Cresser, and Winker all came up with us to Glasgow. The driver thought we were all animals. After that all the bus companies banned us."

Gary Robinson: "Shit, there must have been 40 people on that bus going up to Glasgow – an array of colourful characters. Oh man, Glasgow. I got off the coach that morning to find the driver pulling out the landline and saying he was going home. It was either that or call the police to come and search the bus. With that in mind, I had to get everyone up, including Joe, at 7.30am to get them off the bus as the driver had had enough. Let's just say myself and Joe had an interesting, and somewhat loud, conversation that morning which resulted in Ants intervening. Colin McWilliams, the promoter from DF Concerts, found all of this highly amusing. A few days later someone came up to me and said, 'I heard about you in Glasgow and Shaun Ryder pulling a gun on the bus driver.' It's amazing how a story can get so diluted."

The band travelled overnight back to London by sleeper train.

America and Canada tour

After just over 24 hours' rest, the band departed for Seattle on Sunday afternoon from Heathrow. The following day, Monday 1 November, Joe Strummer & The Mescaleros started the 18-date America and Canada tour at the Showbox on First Avenue, Seattle. The bigger-capacity Moore theatre was the original venue. One Man Army occupied the support role and at 9.15pm the band kicked off the tour with *Quarter Pound of Ishen*.

Jackie McCarthy wrote in the *Seattle Weekly*: "When Joe Strummer brought his latest band, The Mescaleros, to Seattle, he was careful to warn the hardcore types in the audience before launching into any 'mushy' songs from his new record, *Rock Art And The X-Ray Style*. The former Clash frontman needn't have worried…"

Terry Wood reported in *The Seattle Times*: "The new-song highlight of the evening was *X-Ray Style*, a percussion-driven audio odyssey during which

Strummer evokes images of tenderness atop a mesmerizing chorus of gently chiming guitars."

Overnight travel to Portland, OR, for the second date at Roseland Theatre.

Willamette Week's music editor Zach Dundas had written in frightening terms:

"Heckled by some joker up front, he dropped his guitar and dived into the crowd looking for action. He stalked his domain like a meat-starved panther, spitting the lyrics of his surprisingly good new songs with the same venom he lent to the liberal dose of Clash classics."

2 November also saw the release of the debut Album *Rock Art And The X-Ray Style* to some quite glorious acclaim.

www.musicinsight.com: "*Rock Art And The X-Ray Style*. Put briefly, this album is *Sandinista*'s worthy successor."

Earlier in the afternoon Joe had done an instore five-song acoustic set at Music Millennium on NW 23rd Street with backing vocals by an unknown female and a drummer called Mathew from local band Roz. Joe had offered to put all in attendance on the guestlist for the evening's show as a point of disapproval at the $21.50 ticket charge at Roseland.

The 11-hour overnight journey to San Francisco was followed by a day off and time to relax at the Phoenix Hotel on Eddy Street.

Thursday 4 November saw a double support act with One Man Army and the Pietasters at The Fillmore.

Neva Chonin would later in an article in the *San Francisco Chronicle* describe The Mescaleros as:

"His weapons of choice: three-chord garage guitar, a heavy reggae backbeat and panoply of Caribbean percussion."

The sleeper bus continued its journey down the west coast overnight to Anaheim Sun Theatre ... 5 November, better known as "The Chicken in a basket gig." The Pietasters had become the regular support band.

Scott: "Anaheim was a weird one, it was all tables. It was 'chicken in a basket.'

The Pietasters who were supporting us were good guys – they were funny."

Ben Wener reported in the *Orange County Register*: "He can still remind why America was so taken with the dance politics of *Rock the Casbah*. And with his five limber Mescaleros, he can blast out *Tommy Gun* and *Safe European Home* like it's 1978."

House of Blues, Sunset Blvd., West Hollywood, Saturday 6th was followed by an overnight six-hour journey to Las Vegas, NV, where Joe played for the first time in this city in the desert at The Joint, Hard Rock Hotel. It wasn't a full house. Nevertheless Joe was on top form. One particular fan who climbed on to the stage during *Tommy Gun* and was a little heavy-handed in his excitement somewhat bore the brunt of Joe's displeasure at the end of the song:

"I'd just like to say I don't give a shit who jumps on the stage, but that guy knew there was still a verse more to sing; he knew, he ain't no fuckin' moron, that you don't shove someone in the back, so their teeth go into the microphone. That's why I turned round and tried to chin the cunt! Do what you like but don't fuck with me here."

Also during *Rudie Can't Fail* Joe had offered the band words of encouragement at the chorus: "Sing you bastards, sing."

Pablo: "Andy Boo had got sacked after the British tour; this other guy came on board and he was actually quite a nice guy, but fuckin' catching one of the world's most famous guitars coming at you at 100 miles an hour, struggling to pull it out of the air, the neck flying around his neck. This is really only a job for one man. Andy and Joe were really knuckle-down mates, so Andy had been flown out to rejoin the band in time for the Las Vegas gig."

After-show saw a 15-hour drive to Denver and Monday 8th was a day off.

Tuesday 9th Joe & The Mescaleros took to the Ogden Theatre stage at 10.00pm.

The crew travelled overnight, whilst the band had an extra night in Denver, catching an afternoon flight to Minneapolis.

The following morning the crew arrived in town and went straight into loading the equipment into The Quest on Minneapolis's North 5th Street. An all-ages show meant the band coming on at the earlier time of 8.00pm with a 9.30pm curfew.

Friday 12 November saw the band arrive in Columbia, Missouri after a 12-hour overnight journey.

Joe did an interview with KBXR 102.3FM DJ Simon Rose: "I picked Joe up at the venue (The Blue Note). When I got there he was waiting by the bus, signing autographs, very relaxed. We headed over to the radio station, only about a five-minute ride. He leant out of the window the whole way remarking on the great weather. When he got there he was great. Relaxed, affable, we had a great 20-minute or so interview. He had lots of time after for pictures with me and my colleague, Lana. He did voicers for the station, signed our sign etc. I took him back to the venue after. He was telling me that there were some arguments going on with the band and the crew but he enjoyed it as he said they always played better when there was a bit of tension. He seemed to be taking a bit of pleasure in the whole minor conflict!"

In the interview Joe starts off by talking about his dislike for fast food, the origin of the album title *Rock Art And The X-Ray Style* and the band/crew not getting on.

Simon Rose: "Interesting story about where the title *Rock Art And The X-Ray Style* comes from." Joe: "Yeah, I found it in a archaeology book. What it was referring to was cave painting and then a new phase of cave painting, which is called X-Ray Style because they drew the bones so you could see the bones through the animal shapes. So I just grabbed it and thought I'm having that. It made it all real for me actually once I had a title."

SR: "Are you the kinda songwriter, Joe, that comes up sometimes with the title first and then the lyrics come together?"

Joe: "I'm a sort of cigarette packet, napkin man, everything scrunched up. I've probably dropped more lyrics than I've saved. In fact I hate that when you get a great idea for a lyric and the bus goes round a corner or somebody falls over and you can't remember what it was seconds later. I reckon, if you have the idea just push people out of the way, throw yourself on the floor and write it down, because it only makes sense in the moment, and if you don't make a fuller note of it you can look at it the next day because lyrics can be a bit weird. They can be nonsense and when they're nonsense sometimes they can be great. I like it because it doesn't have any rules this racket. You can't get your head round any of it."

SR: "Of course the tour is in full swing, Joe Strummer with The Mescaleros ... are you enjoying being back on the road again, enjoying the live music vibe and playing with these guys?"

Joe: "I tell you what, one thing I forgot from laying out of the road for a while was that you can never tell what is going to happen next on the road. You think just as everything's cushty mushty, blam you know. I'm more nervous when things are cushty mushty than when they're all at war, because I guarantee we've had a bus impounded, we've had a roadie deported, everything that possibly could go wrong has gone wrong, but we're still here rockin'. At least today there's a big row going on so I'm kinda more relaxed. When there's a row we can see what we're doing. If things are going too cushty mushty the warning bells go off."

SR: "A lot of bands say if there weren't rows and arguments about it they wouldn't have that force that makes the band what they are."

Joe: "True, but we don't row so much – it's our roadcrew that row."

SR: "They all seemed harmonious when I was over there!"

Joe: "It was an act."

SR: "It must be the nice weather or something like that."

Joe: "Yeah, I think it was the nice weather."

Courtesy of KBXR 102.3FM Columbia, Missouri.

"Joe invited us to come backstage after the show. A lot of artists say this in my experience, but don't mean it. Joe did and after a great show he welcomed me and my friends back to meet the band to have a few beers etc. Great! He then announced he was off to a bar here called East Side Tavern, this was at about 1am. We bid him farewell, but he bartended and stayed at this bar until about 4am as I understand! He truly gave all who saw him and met him a day to remember here in Columbia, Missouri."

Southern Culture at The Blue Note took the support slot. Only about half the tickets available were sold for this show,

Richard King, owner of The Blue Note, recalls: "I can tell you he was a great person to work with. I was told before they arrived that Joe was not very friendly but that was so untrue. He signed autographs for all who asked. Needless to say the show was just great. I thought it to be very sad that people were not hanging from the rafters for this show but it was still cool. It was a great honour to have Joe perform in my club."

Afterwards the band headed north-west to the Windy City and a date at the Metro on North Clark Street. Pietasters were back on the support list.

Jill LoPresti reported in the *Columbia College Chronicle*: "The legendary Joe Strummer and his newly formed Mescaleros lived up to expectations Saturday night at the Metro."

Sunday 14th was a day off in Columbus, OH.

The band began their third week on tour with a date at the 1,400-capacity Newport Music Hall and the inevitable overnight journey followed to Cincinnati, OH, for a date at Bogarts.

The 21-song set was reported on by Chris Varias in the *Cincinnati Enquirer*: "The Mescaleros' new music might not be as strong as The Clash's classics, but the band did a great job of covering said classics."

Next stop Detroit, arriving on the morning of Wednesday 17 November. The band booked into the Atheneum Hotel and had the day off to catch up on some sleep.

Thursday 18th, the crew started loading in at midday and the band had the bonus of a late checkout from the hotel with a 5.00pm soundcheck at St Andrew's Hall.

19 November, The Odeon, Cleveland was the next stop.

With surprise at a full house, Joe announced, "The promoter has already hung himself in the car park" and dedicated *Diggin' The New* to him.

Bank Robber was nearly ten minutes long with Joe introducing the band halfway through. This was the band's longest set to date. The concert also saw *Shouting Street* have a rare play.

Afterwards a 300-mile journey and a first appearance for the band in Canada.

Kieran Grant in the *Toronto Sun*: "Strummer credits his band – guitarist and producer Antony Genn, former Black Grape keyboardist Martin Slattery, bassist Scott Shields, drummer Smiley and percussionist Pablo Cook – with much of the success. 'These guys are a different generation', he says. 'They're all barmy. But then, they can't get near me on that one.'"

The original venue had been The Guvernment but it was switched to the larger venue Warehouse as the show was a complete sell-out. Joe started the evening off by announcing to the audience, "These are The Mescaleros" before going straight into *Diggin' The New*.

Jennie Punter reported in the following Monday's *Toronto Star*: "No one could doubt the frontman's heart and sincere desire to entertain. Strummer was in fine form... The Mescaleros' rear flank was definitely exciting to watch, as drummer Smiley and percussionist Pablo Cook gave a lively rhythmic kick to numbers."

The journey turned south and an overnight 12-hour haul back across the border to Boston. The band and crew endured a six-hour delay on the American border as a small amount of resin had been found on the tour bus.

Pablo: "We all had to get off the bus and stand in no man's land for nearly six hours because they had found a small amount of weed or something. They took the bus to bits, literally ripped it to bits. I had already been through this with Elastica previously. It's a nightmare but people walk through there with 12-bore shotguns; it's like well, that's cool, but you get a rock 'n' roll tour bus in there? Any band travelling across the Canada/USA border always throws everything out of the window about ten miles before the border! Guess someone forgot! I think one of the roadcrew was fined $20.00."

Sunday 21st was a day off and a stay at the Royal Sonesta hotel.

Monday 22nd ... fourth week of the tour and a sell-out 1,460 at The Roxy. The full house went crazy when The Mescaleros played *White Riot* for the first time as the finishing number. The stage riots resulted in Joe later telling the band, "Tonight was the closest thing to 1977 I have done."

Smiley later admitted, "I shit myself."

Antony Genn states: "The American Tour was pretty mental 'cause Cerys came out. There was a fuckin' lot of drug abuse going on there. At that point I was seriously into the twilight zone. But we did some great gigs; we did the Fillmore, and the amazing Boston Gig. It was like '77, no barrier. At one point I got hit by two pints thrown from the crowd within a split second of each other. It was quite incredible, pure rock 'n' roll. It was the first night we did *White Riot*."

Scott recalls: "Boston, The Roxy was nuts, I was fighting people off the stage. I felt a bit scared at that one; I felt it was a bit out of control. It was just too many people on the stage. They were all grabbing at Joe. I felt a bit pissed off that all these people were on the stage and not watching the music. On reflection, it was a punk moment but at the time I was pissed off. People were bumping you out of the way and grabbing your guitar."

Martin remembers vividly: "Boston was mental, it was a proper pogo night that. It was kinda like that one at 100 Club where you were stood on geezers' heads basically as they passed out on your pedals. Geezers everywhere reliving their youth."

Sarah Rodman reported in the *Boston Herald*: "Joe Strummer's feisty set Monday night at the Roxy was as good as it could possibly get... Touring behind his first album in a decade, Strummer and the hot band of young guns he calls The Mescaleros blazed through a 100+ minute set."

Tuesday 23 November Joe & The Mescaleros played the Roseland Ballroom on New York's West 52nd Street. For the second night running the band played a breathtaking set, but Joe was having some technical problems and kicked his monitor into the gap between the stage and the crowd barrier.

The security was being heavy-handed with the fans and Joe shouted out,

"Oi, Oi, fuck this. You're too fuckin' keen mate." He also encouraged the HBO cable television cameraman filming the concert to witness the security's handling of crowd-surfing fans by telling him, "Film that, you cunt!" The only omission from previous sets was *Nothin' bout Nothin'*.

Interestingly, two years on Dave Simpson would reflect in *The Guardian*: "His awesome comeback shows two years ago were packed with political ragings and dynamite humour."

A short overnight journey to Philadelphia and the smaller venue, Theatre of Living Arts, saw the band bring the tour to a close on Wednesday 24 November at approximately 11.45pm with *White Riot*.

The overnight journey took them back to New York for an appearance the following day on the Conan O'Brien show, where they played *Tony Adams* and *London Calling*. On 25 November the band and crew flew back to London on an evening flight from JFK.

A planned appearance by the band on Chris Evans's show TFI in London that Friday evening never materialised and a few days' well-earned rest was had.

European tour

The three-date European Tour started on 2 December in Spain. The Barcelona show was originally booked at Zeleste, but there had been a last-minute switch to the smaller Bikini Club, because of slow ticket sales, and the promoter had "lost his bottle". Joe Strummer always had been (and still was with The Mescaleros) "a walk up artist" ticketwise, and the band took to the stage to a sell-out audience. The highlight was a nine-minute version of *Straight To Hell*.

After a day spent travelling the band played Milan's Rollingstone on 4 December.

With two days off, they proceeded to Paris.

Monday 7 December 1999 was one of those evenings that go down in a band's history as very special indeed. Hellboys had opened and Joe and the 1,400 sell-out crowd at Elysée-Montmartre that evening witnessed a performance that Joe Strummer & The Mescaleros would never surpass in their three and a half years. Twenty six songs, including an eight-song four encores, *White Riot* twice... it was only sheer exhaustion that ended the night.

Scott: "It felt great coming off at the end of the Paris show in December. The crowd weren't going mad throughout the whole show but at the end we'd got them. It was the best ever Mescaleros show."

Gary Robinson: "That show was the turning point for The Mescaleros in a very positive way. The whole night was just electric."

In the dressing room afterwards, Joe and the band were totally emotionally drained and exhausted – a culmination of having played 57 concerts in 18 countries in six months and a final night when six great men had given their all. On that night Paris rocked.

Tour manager Gary Robinson: "If you've toured with Joe and the associated entourage you go to hell and back fuckin' ten times over. You find yourself along the way, passing yourself on the way back."

2000

Japanese tour and Big Day Out

The band arrived in Japan on the evening of 15 January. The following day saw a mid-afternoon soundcheck. Knuckles were the support band at Zepp Osaka and at 8.00 The Mescaleros took to the stage to a tremendous reception from the sell-out 2,000 crowd, opening with *Diggin' The New*.

Monday 16th saw the band travel by Bullet Train for the two-and-a-half hour journey to Tokyo and the first of two sell-out nights at Akasaka Blitz.

This show marked the first airing of *Police on My Back*, which the band had only played for the first time some three hours earlier at the soundcheck.

Antony Genn: "The first night we did *Police on My Back* in Japan, Joe had been playing it on his ghetto blaster in the van on the way there."

The last night of this three-date Japanese tour saw the band take to the stage late as a result of an oversight of there not being a support band. They opened with *Ishen* and the 1,900 fans were treated to a great 20-song set.

On the bootleg of this show can be heard the closing track on the sound system, a great cover of the Elvis Presley classic *Always on My Mind* which was sung by backline tech Des "Evlis" Hill.

The band left Tokyo late in the evening of the 19th and arrived in Auckland at midday on the 20th.

Scott Shields: "We did Japan then went on to the Big Day Out. That was great apart from I got busted for drugs and strip-searched on the way into New Zealand. One of The Pietasters had put a hash cookie in my bag and it had all crumbled up but I had scooped it out. So on the way in to New Zealand the customs dogs were sniffing all over my bag.

At the end of it one of the custom guys went, 'You'd be crazy to bring weed in here mate; we've got great stuff.' They let me go on my way."

Friday 21 January saw the start of Big Day Out 2000 at the Ericsson Stadium, Auckland.

There had been intense interest in Joe Strummer returning to New Zealand for the first time in 18 years in the weeks leading up. The *New Zealand Herald* had carried an interview with Joe.

The event was a total sell-out and earlier in the day fights had started outside two record shops selling the last 2,000 tickets when it was realised that several hundred had missed out.

The band came on at 10.15 pm headlining the Green Stage with an hour-long set and kicked straight into *London Calling*.

A few days later, the Sydney-based *Daily Telegraph* reported how their correspondent had been backstage after the Ericsson Stadium and had been given an exclusive by Joe about The Clash reforming ... in 2020!

The following morning saw an early flight to Brisbane and arrival on the Gold Coast.

Australia like New Zealand had waited with trepidation for Joe's return. Several newspapers had carried features and interviews.

The much-respected *Australian* magazine's Iain Shedden had commented in his article:

"With his new band travelling the world and favourable album reviews, it seems the vibe is still very much with him."

23 January, at Parklands, Southport on The Gold Coast Leg, the band had an earlier stage time of 6.15pm.

Noel Mengel reported on The Mescaleros' performance at Parklands in the *Courier Mail*:

"In the hands of The Mescaleros and motorised by Joe's electricity, the old Clash material still obliterates everything in its path." He added at the end of his report: "I remembered that there is a God, and his name is Joe Strummer."

Monday 24th the band took a midday flight from Coolangatta to Sydney, booking into the Sebel of Sydney Hotel, and that evening several Mescaleros went to The Metro to see the Foo Fighters gig.

The following evening the band returned to The Metro, where a full house waited for Joe's return to Sydney after nearly 18 years. The wait had been worth it, as a great hour-and-a-half's set by The Mescaleros followed. *Sandpaper Blues* and *Willesden To Cricklewood* were given their first live airing. Amongst the audience that night were the Foo Fighters and the Red Hot Chilli Peppers.

Scott: "It was definitely a holiday being in Australia, everybody hanging out and partying together. We were hanging out with Primal Scream and The Foo Fighters."

Several local newspapers had run a story complete with photo of Joe out buying the groceries in Sydney.

Wednesday 26th saw the band play their shortest set on the Big Day Out. A technical problem with the sound system led to the band coming on some 25 minutes later than scheduled. The 45-minute set kicked off with *Diggin' The New* in the pouring rain, at Sydney's Showground. Earlier in the week mounted police had been summoned to control thousands queuing for the Showground's remaining tickets.

The 27th was a day off and on the 28th they took a midday flight to Melbourne.

Saturday 29th, with Luxedo as support band, Joe & The Mescaleros took to the stage at just before midnight at The Corner Hotel, Richmond, before another sell-out crowd.

Sunday 30th saw The Mescaleros return to a one-hour set at RAS Showground in Melbourne.

The next three days were rest days in Melbourne and on Thursday 3 February the band took the relatively short flight to Adelaide.

Friday 4 February. This being the smallest of the Big Day Out events, Joe was able to spend 30 minutes signing autographs for fans in a signing tent. The band came on at 7.00pm at the RA & HS Showgrounds in Wayville.

They flew to the last leg of the Big Day Out on Saturday afternoon and played perhaps their best set on Sunday 6th at Bassendean Oval, Perth.

Chris Shiflett of The Foo Fighters describes the tour and meeting Joe: "Ahhhhhh, Big Day Out 2000! Now that was a good time. Those were the first and last times I ever got to meet Joe Strummer. Of course, I wound up coming off like a nervous super-fan every time I talked to him, but I managed to have a couple nice chats with him anyway.

When we were in Perth, I even wound up switching hotel rooms with him cuz my room was the only one that had open windows and I guess Joe didn't like air conditioning."

Articles even appearing in the *Northern Territory News* sum up the importance of Joe Strummer and the Big Day Out in Australia. The band arrived back at Heathrow in the early hours of Tuesday 8th.

Seven weeks later they flew out to New York for a one-off gig at Bowery Ballroom, where, along with Run DMC and Long Beach Dub Allstars, they played live to an invited audience from the music, film and entertainment world to celebrate *Spin* magazine's 15th anniversary on 31 March.

Antony Genn recalls: "At the Bowery gig, I missed my flight, had to get another flight. I brought Cerys with me. I missed the soundcheck, turned up late. I was out of control at that point."

A few days later Joe and Pablo played three acoustic numbers: *Island Hopping/Junco Partner/London's Burning* at the Poetry Olympics at the Royal Festival Hall on the South Bank, London.

Pablo recalls "I had just come off another tour. I basically turned up out of my fuckin' mind.

I had settled down on my couch ready for a night in and Laura just went 'Aren't you supposed to be doing something?' I went 'No, definitely not!' Then the phone went, it was Joe, 'Pabs, what time are you going to get here?' Apparently I had agreed to do the show months before."

May 2000

Sunday 30 April meant a 9.00pm departure, complete with new tour manager Neil Mather, from The Depot and an overnight journey to Dublin via Holyhead and a return to the Olympia Theatre.

Nearly eight months since The Mescaleros last rocked the Emerald Isle; support band this time was Neon. The capacity was down to 1,200 and yet again a full house awaited. The setlist had four new songs including three great covers of The McCoys' 1965 hit *Hang on Sloopy* (the one and only time the band performed this particular cover) and *The Harder They Come*, the Jimmy Cliff hit from the 1973 film of the same name, plus *Police on my Back* and a rare outing of *Sandpaper Blues* (carried on from outings on the Big Day Out). Throughout the day Joe did various interviews with *Planet Rock Profile* plus various Irish newspapers and radio stations.

Heineken Green Energy Documentary videoed the soundcheck.

An early-morning ferry back to Holyhead and then on to the Leadmill, Sheffield. Ten Benson join for the rest of the tour as support. Because of a 10.15 curfew, due to the disco that always follows at the Leadmill, the band are onstage at 8.30, opening with *London Calling*.

Reported in the *NME* the following week: "What carried him through the darkest hours and propelled him to such heights of brilliance this evening was something very simple. A writer who uses his own, humbling experiences to communicate with his audience."

Wednesday 3 May, Newcastle University, is followed by a day off in Liverpool.

Friday 5 May, Royal Court, Liverpool: during the encore the band play *Liverpool's Burnin'* with an after-show overnight drive to London.

Saturday 6 May at Brixton Academy: With additional support band LSK, a full house – 4,300 await Joe Strummer & The Mescaleros... Joe takes to the stage and announces to the crowd "Now let's swing it tonight" and a blistering version of *London Calling* follows. A great night finishes with *London's Burning* and *White Riot*. *Safe European Home* has its last Mescaleros' playing.

Smiley: "This was The Mescaleros at their peak. For once I was really nervous before the gig, but when we kicked off with *London Calling*, it was great. We could never equal that night – we were awesome."

Michael Bonner in *Uncut* couldn't have put it better when he said "The Mescaleros are playing like they've got a gun to their collective heads – guitars like artillery fire, drums like a creeping barrage: this is combat rock. A blistering assault of musical napalm levelling everything in its path."

8 and 9 May saw the band at Shepherd's Bush studios for the *Later with Jools Holland* show, performing, *Louie, Louie, London Calling, Tony Adams, X-Ray Style* and a unique version of *I Fought the Law* together with Jools Holland, Tracy Chapman and band plus Angie Stone.

Pablo recalls: "During the day we're soundchecking. It's a family situation, playing soul and funk, it's horses for courses etc. One particular band had a bass player with a difference. Now, the cardinal sin is when playing bass you only have four strings; any more than that you get targeted. This guy had an eight-string bass with lights on it; whenever you touched the fret the light comes on, so it gives you a full star-spangled Blackpool situation. Now if you're like an older rocker like us, you really want to take the piss out of it.

"But Joe was saying to us, 'Listen man, don't say a word, don't say a word, don't talk to him.' We were all gagging to take the piss, but we left it and the band had been really well behaved, 'cause Joe had kept us all calm.

"We did the gig, it was quite a good night. I remember us being on the ball that night, but Joe had certainly kept us from going anywhere near this geezer or making any type of remarks. As we left the studio – and I've been to the studios on several occasions ... cars, limousines etc are all waiting to take everyone home – but in true Strummer style there was never a car and you have to get a cab, which is really quite nice, because it's reality. So we were all on the street waiting to hail a cab and this bass player happened to turn up and he had his bass strapped across his back and we were all standing on the street a little bit pissed, when Joe nailed it. He walked up to the guy and just went 'nice bass'.

"He had sat on it for six hours. We had said, 'Ok, you're the boss, we won't take the piss.' Joe just dropped it."

The planned release of the single *Tony Adams* had been originally pencilled in for 8 May, was put back to 22 May and then cancelled. The promo plug read: *"Tony Adams*, one of the stand-out tracks from his recent album *Rock Art And The X-Ray Style*. Strummer has been gigging hard with his band of Mescaleros."

On 29 June the band flew out to Venice to play at the Beach Bum Festival in Jesolo the following evening (30th). For the first and only time, The Mescaleros were a five-piece band, with Antony Genn being a last-minute withdrawal.

Antony puts the record straight: "I didn't go to Jesolo, drugs, drugs. Basically I just phoned up the tour manager Neil Mather and said I couldn't go because me and Cerys had degenerated into total Sid and Nancyism. I think we went away somewhere, living in the vain hope of getting off drugs."

Joe announced after the first song: "Tonight 'cause it's late and it's cold, we're only gonna play favourites, OK! All of these songs are my favourites."

Despite numerous technical difficulties the band completed a great 13-song set with only one Mescaleros number (*X-Ray Style*) played. On the last number, *Police On My Back*, The Mescaleros were joined onstage by Yugoslavian band Emir Kusturica & The No Smoking Orchestra.

After a long break, the band returned to The Depot for rehearsals on 16 August and a sell-out warm-up gig on 17 August at The Charlotte, Leicester.

Antony: "When we did the gig in Leicester, by the time we went onstage I had drunk 12 pints of cider and had ten valium. What the fuck I was playing on there I had no idea.

When we came off, Martin Slattery said to me something along the lines of 'You're a fuckin' disgrace.' Which for Martin to say something like that is quite a big deal, because he's not the kinda of guy who says stuff like that. But, he was right I was a disgrace."

Afterwards there was a two-hour drive on the bus to Sutton Coldfield. With Friday 18th a day off, the band departed at midday Saturday to Weston Park, for V2000. They played a 50-minute set.

Afterwards the usual overnight journey and sleeping on the bus to Hylands Park.

On Sunday 20 August, Chelmsford V2000, Joe Strummer & The Mescaleros took to the stage at 6.40pm and the next 50 minutes saw the lastever appearance of Antony Genn in The Mescaleros.

Antony describes coming to the end: "Joe called me up one day. It was a sunny morning. We probably hadn't really had a proper conversation for a long time. Now my behaviour was undermining the stability of the band. He said, 'I think it's about time we parted company.'

I genuinely thought he was saying that the band should split up, for some delusional reason.

I then realised what he was saying. So I said, 'OK! But I'd like to do these V2000 gigs.'"

Antony's importance in The Mescaleros can never be spoken of highly enough, Ant was the main force behind Joe's return. Ant was the one who had got Joe to put a guitar round his neck again. He produced the first album and co-wrote with Joe beautiful ballads such as *Nitcomb* and *The Road to Rock 'n' Roll* as well as *Tony Adams*, *Techno D-Day* and perhaps their finest, *Willesden To Cricklewood*.

Antony Genn's departure would also see The Mescaleros change direction musically.

In early October Joe and Pabs were playing at The Astoria at a Poetry Olympics bash.

It was at this gig that Joe was again reunited with his long time friend Tymon Dogg.

Tymon: "I met Joe and Pabs at The Poetry Olympics at The Astoria in October 2000.

I just bought a ticket and went as a punter. I met up with Joe and said 'hi' and he said 'where's your instrument? Do you mind playing with us tonight?'

I said I didn't mind because I owed him a gig anyway. We went on stage did 4 or five numbers; *Silver and Gold* was one.

A couple of days later Joe called me and said 'do you fancy coming down to the studios?' So I went down and it was just Joe and Pablo there. They were working on *Gamma Ray*. We were knocking out basically from scratch a tune a day. I was sleeping on the couch at The Battery. I wasn't even in the band; I just popped into the studio, five days later or 5 tracks later I left."

On 27 October a semi-secret gig at the famous 100 Club in London saw Joe & The Mescaleros warm up for the forthcoming British tour supporting The Who. It also enabled *Q* magazine to film the gig for partial showing a few days later when Joe received its "Inspiration" award at the Park Lane Hotel (several songs later appeared on a Channel 4 documentary).

The set saw a vast change, with new songs *Minstrel Boy*, *Bhindi Bhagee*, *Bummed Out City*, *Gamma Ray* and *Before I Grow Too Old* being the opening numbers. This was the last concert where the band played *London Calling*.

Joe's long-time friend Tymon Dogg made his debut with The Mescaleros and Jimmy Hogarth made the first of three appearances on bass, covering for Scott Shields who was absent through nervous exhaustion.

Jimmy Hogarth: "It was a very brief encounter with Joe really. Joe really wanted me to carry on doing it. When I told him I had other things to do, it didn't go down too well. I told Joe right at the beginning – in the rehearsals I said I could only do a certain amount of time as I had writing sessions coming into the studio and I had to carry on with it. I think Joe respected what I was doing and all that, but Joe's quite hardcore about things like that and he called me 'a quitting cunt' at one point, which is very Joe. Martin said it's a sign that he liked me but I'm not too sure myself."

Scott's illness had been passed over as nervous exhaustion but was in fact early signs of multiple sclerosis.

Scott Shields: "I was getting a kinda electric shock feeling running up and down my spine every time I moved my head. That just wouldn't go away and that was what eventually led them to think, right, we've tried all these things, if this isn't working then it must be something else. I went on making the record before I knew anything about it. I had pulled myself together a bit. Eventually I got to see a neurologist and he told me it was MS that I had."

The Who tour started earlier than originally planned at Birmingham NEC (as an extra date to the already sold-out 8 November) on 30 October with a ten-song set including the same five new songs first played at the 100 Club plus *The Harder They Come*, *Brand New Cadillac*, *Rock The Casbah*, *I Fought The Law* and a folk version of *White Riot*, entitled *Folk Riot*. *Gamma Ray* also saw Smiley playing guitar.

The tour moved on to Manchester. John Blackburn had joined The Mescaleros, as Scott was still unwell.

John Blackburn: "I got a phone call from Martin's wife, Kirsty, asking me if I could play bass with Joe Strummer & The Mescaleros on The Who tour. I met up with the band the following day at The Depot. I didn't know any Clash songs as such and whilst travelling across London on the train I had my walkman on listening to a Clash CD.

"At the Depot, I rehearsed with The Mescaleros for a few hours and then it was off to Manchester. We did the soundcheck and I felt fairly confident that in such a short space of time I had learnt the set that was listed. The first night had been fine. The following night at Glasgow, we were due to go onstage when Joe said, 'Let's do *White Man In Hammersmith Palais* tonight!' I hadn't rehearsed that one! Joe was great; he drew me a diagram of the notes/bars with a blue highlighter pen, which would be placed by my monitor. When I looked I thought it had been placed back to front and as I reached down to turn it over with *White Man* due to be the next song, the purple lighting had made Joe's diagram invisible.

I immediately went over and stood next to Martin on the keyboards and watched his left hand playing for the notes."

Next, two nights in Glasgow (the setlist saw a slight change with *London's Burning* and *White Man In Hammersmith Palais* replacing *Bummed Out City* and *Before I Grow Too Old*), followed by Newcastle, back to the NEC, Sheffield, London Docklands and finally two nights at Wembley Arena.

Paul Sexton wrote in a review in *The Times*: "Those who arrived on time at London Arena on Monday witnessed one of the most storming warm-ups of the year. Spurred on by his youthful band The Mescaleros, Strummer was an imposing example of how a new wave figurehead need not become a chat-show cartoon, excelling both on contemporary material such as *Gamma Ray* and *Bhindi Bhagee* and decorated warhorses like *Rock the Casbah* and *I Fought the Law*."

John Blackburn has particularly fond memories of 15 November at Wembley Arena, "My dad was in the audience and it was such a great feeling that I was playing with Joe Strummer, supporting The Who. It was a kinda thanks to my dad for all those years he had backed my love and dreams to be a musician. Afterwards, backstage Joe signed a setlist for my dad:

To Big John. The boy done good ... Love Joe."

15 November was John's last appearance with The Mescaleros, as the following day he had a flight booked to California to marry his fiancée Virginia.

John recalls: "I had booked the flight before I had joined up with The Mescaleros and I couldn't change the flight. We had arranged for Virginia to fly over to see the Wembley Arena gig. Of course now it's one of those things that I often reflect on, I would have loved to have played that last show, spent another 24 hours with Joe!

"Joe said simply, 'If you've got to go, you've got to go, don't worry about it. We'll be alright.' As soon as they took me on I went straight up to the tour manager and told him. No one was really sure how long Scott would be absent for. Then it became evident he'd be out for a bit. Before that it had been pretty much gig by gig."

The following night, Jimmy Hogarth replaced Scott on bass. During the set the band were joined onstage by Keith Allen's daughter Lilly during *White Man In Hammersmith Palais*.

16 November was indeed a sad date; it was Smiley's last performance on the drum kit for The Mescaleros. Never again would the crowd hear Joe's cries of "Smiley" before those magnificent drum rolls at the start of *Tommy Gun* and those majestic six crashes of the drum as Joe sang "Robbin' people with a six-gun" to the Sonny Curtis classic.

Smiley: "If it was about me as a person I could take it, because everyone is not always someone's cup of tea but when it comes to drumming I knew I had played drums with The Mescaleros the best I could have done. So the time had come!"

In hindsight this was also Andy Boo's final concert with Joe & The Mescaleros. Andy was Joe's guitar tec, close friend and Mescalero: "I'd still walk that extra mile for all of them. I wouldn't change any of it. Though I might have got his guitar 30 seconds earlier at Wembley!"

2001

Over the next six months the band completed the new album *Global A Go-Go*. Roger Daltrey sang on the title track.

Scott recalls: "I can remember Roger coming in and not really knowing what he was coming in for. He just came into this crazy environment. I think he thought he was going to co-write a song with Joe, but Joe had his own idea about what he wanted to do. It was quite hard for me because I was sort of coaching Roger Daltrey on what to sing. I was singing to him through the glass. I remember him getting quite angry with me and telling me, 'Yeah, yeah, yeah, fine OK!!'" Scott adds: "Not that I could sing it as good as him, but here was I, this young producer, telling the great Roger Daltrey what to do! But in the end it all worked out pretty good."

A one-off gig at Ole Blues – Bergen Music Fest, Norway, in April was planned, but the band pulled out.

Martin recalls the time spent in the studio: "Joe would come into the studios and full of praise for what we were doing so obviously that spurs you on. It was highly drug fuelled and booz- fuelled (apart from Flacky). A fair amount of schnifter. Pablo loves all that kinda shit."

The *Johnny Appleseed* video was shot on the roof of Townhouse Studios and the surrounding area in Goldhawk Road, West London. Martin and Scott were at the studios working on Paul Heaton's album.

Scott: "Joe just turned up and said, 'Can I grab you for 20 minutes to make a video?'"

Richard Flack: "I was pressganged (by the ever-persuasive Joe) into shaking a banana and generally dancing around like a loon, or rather doing an impersonation of someone dancing around like a loon."

The release of the *Global A Go-Go* album and new single *Johnny Appleseed* was promoted by instore performances with two British and five North American appearances.

Stephen Dowling wrote in *The Independent*: "Two years ago, the prospect of Joe Strummer taking the stage and snarling his way through *White Man In Hammersmith Palais*, let alone making records again, was the stuff of fantasy. But 18 months later Strummer returned with a new band, The Mescaleros, and a new album, *Rock Art And The X-Ray Style*. As the dust was settling from his first gigs in over a decade, Strummer and team were wrestling with album number two."

At the HMV shop in London's Oxford Street on 16 July, there appeared a new Mescaleros line-up with Luke Bullen on drums and Simon Stafford on bass. Pablo Cook was absent as he was touring with Moby. The setlist was completely from the new album; this stayed the same for the North American in-stores, except that *The Harder They Come* was later brought back as a finishing number.

The roadcrew had completely changed. Simon Foster was the new tour manager. The only original crew member was "The Lobster" Justin Grealy on the monitors, though he too was soon to leave.

Simon Foster: "I think Joe just wanted some new faces around. My connection with Joe had come through Simon Moran."

A planned instore in Manchester had been cancelled and the following day the band played instead at Virgin Mega store in Leeds.

The second album *Global A Go-Go* was released on 24 July to very good reviews.

Jonathan Takiff in the *Philadelphia Daily News* had given it *"Pick of the week"*

Marty Behm in the *Illinois Entertainer* described the new album thus: "*Global A Go-Go* is Strummer's most earnest love letter to world music to date."

Dan Cairns, *Sunday Times*, wrote: "Best by far... *Johnny Appleseed*, where Strummer shows he can still marry perfect chord with spine-tingling sentiment."

Spyder Darling, review on nyrock.com: "Thoughtfully penned, pleasantly performed, and produced with panache." He finished by adding: "However, I should issue a word of warning: Those looking for a punk-rock riot of their own won't find it here. *Global A Go-Go* is a whole new experience."

Monday 23 July, the band took an early morning flight to New York and booked into the Gramercy Park Hotel. Joe also appeared on several radio stations.

The following day the band spent the afternoon rehearsing and being filmed for the Conan O'Brien show and straight afterwards went to Virgin Records, Times Square, for a nine-song instore gig.

The band flew from La Guardia late afternoon on the 25th for the next stop on this short tour, Toronto, where that evening, they played another nine-song set at HMV.

With Joe due to do several radio/press interviews, the band and the crew took a late-evening flight to Chicago on 26th.

The instore was at Tower Records; this was on a very tight schedule, with the band due on at 6.00pm and then having to catch a 22.00 flight to San Francisco.

Saturday 28th, Amoeba Records at 2.00pm in-store was followed by a stay in San Francisco and the following day a midday flight to Los Angeles and a seven-night stay at The Standard Hotel on Sunset Boulevard.

After a couple of days' well-earned rest, Joe & The Mescaleros resumed their instore tour with an appearance at Tower Records on the evening of Wednesday 1 August.

Thursday 2nd saw the band play at the 250-capacity Viper Room. This concert marked the band's first airing of *Blitzkrieg Bop*.

Simon Foster: "I remember a couple of the Chilli Peppers came down with one of the Ramones when we played at the Viper Rooms. Joe had lived in LA – this was a place where he had gained living legend status. It was wonderful to see."

Two days later (4th) Joe Strummer & The Mescaleros were special guests to Brian Setzer at he Greek Theatre. This was Pablo's only appearance on this whirlwind tour and sadly his last as a Mescalero.

Pabs: "They had flown me over to LA. I had that plastic fuckin' surgeon, pissing around with my eye. I turned up at the gig; it was lovely to see the people. I knew there was something up anyway. Joe was pissed that I had left. But he knew I was a fuckin' prostitute anyway; he didn't mind that side of it, he knew that I have to supply my family, fair enough.

But when I turned up there and it was all that acoustic stuff, I thought what is going on here?"

Never again would we see Pablo on top of speakers, going like a wild man to *I Fought the Law*. Gone was the man who co-wrote with Joe and Richard Norris perhaps the greatest of Mescaleros songs, *Yalla, Yalla*. Never again would Joe announce "From the wrong side of Camden Town, Mr Pablo Cook."

The next day the band took an evening flight from Los Angeles International and arrived at Heathrow at lunchtime the following day.

An appearance by Joe and the band at the Tibetan Freedom Concert due to have been held at London's Brockwell Park on 15 September was dashed when the concert was cancelled due to logistical issues and scheduling complications.

20 September saw Antony Genn, Pablo Cook, Martin Slattery and Simon Stafford, together with Becky Byrne, form the mainstay of Help! at their debut gig at the Water Rats in London. Jarvis Cocker was DJ.

Four days later the soundtrack to the film *Mike Bassett: England Manager* was released by Telstar. This album features two tracks by Help!: *I'm in Trouble* and *The Serious Business of Football*.

Antony Genn co-wrote with Robbie Williams the beautiful tune *Summertime* and has a brief part in the film.

With the tragic and devastating events of 11 September, the planned 18-date America and Canada tour, which was less than a month away, was thought to be in doubt to say the least.

Simon Foster recalls: "It was only in doubt because nobody knew how to react to it. All the American bands cancelled everything in Europe straight away; nobody was flying as far as they were concerned. It was a time when no one knew how to react really. The whole world had turned upside down,

4,000 people dead. Would it be seen as disrespecting these people by playing music? It was only music at the end of the day. The band just waited and waited, really, to see what was going to happen. There was never a point when somebody said it's not going to happen. I was still making all the plans."

However, the tour went ahead and this decision is best explained in an interview that Joe did with Kristine McKenna of the *LA Weekly*: "We considered cancelling our US tour, because we wanted to do the respectful thing, but after a few days I called my friends in New York and got information about what's going on there, and the feeling was, yeah, come on. I love New York."

After several days at The Depot rehearsing, The Mescaleros left for America on 3 October and upon arriving went straight into the studios for the *David Letterman Show* and played one number: *Johnny Appleseed*.

Tymon: "We only did the Letterman show because some other band had pulled out.

We went because you can't back down when the going gets tough. You might as well stop your life right now, if you're scared to go somewhere."

04/10/01, Washington, 9:30 Club: Following support band The Players The Mescaleros opened the 20-song set with *Cool 'n' Out*.

The setlist was completely overhauled: *Rock The Casbah*, the song Joe had for the previous two years always dedicated to Topper Headon, *Brand New Cadillac* and *London Calling* were dropped from the set (all three would not be played live again!) Other "crowd favourites" dropped from the set were *White Man In Hammersmith Palais* and *White Riot*, though both would return to the set in 2002. *Armagideon Time* and The Specials/Dandy Thompson classic *A Message To You Rudy* were added.

In the first two shows *Island Hopping* was given a rare outing.

Luke Bullen: "Washington was the first time I had walked on and everyone there went mental. That will forever stay in my memory. That kind of response was pretty phenomenal."

Richard Lieby wrote the following day in the *Washington Post*: "Joe Strummer and his deliciously versatile band, The Mescaleros, know how to push all the right buttons on the world beat blender, and they whipped the 9:30 club into a fine frenzy Thursday night.

The singer's mania was well stoked by fiddler Tymon Dogg, a longtime Strummer mentor and who cavorted all night like a daft genius, clutching the bow pirate-like between his teeth."

The band travelled the 140 miles to Philadelphia overnight by bus. A sell-out crowd at the Theatre of Living Arts saw The Mescaleros' first cover of *Police and Thieves*.

After the show, a short overnight journey to Atlantic City and an appearance at the Trump Marina's Hotel – the 550-capacity The Shell in the hotel's entertainment building.

John Curran wrote a glowing review in the *Press of Atlantic City*:

"Joe Strummer delivered a knockout one hour and 50-minute set that was every bit as punky, political and passionate as his old band's concerts were 20 years ago. And that's saying something. Strummer and his five-man band, The Mescaleros, played a lively mix of new material, lesser known Clash greats and reggae standards..."

Playing the somewhat strange venue in Atlantic City is perhaps best explained by tour manager Simon Foster: "We played Trump's Casino at the Marina in Atlantic City for the money. It was enough to keep us on the road for another week. It would otherwise havef been a day off if that lump sum hadn't have come in. It paid for the bus etc, so that's why we did it. Purely financial."

Sunday 7th was a rest day in Hartford, CT, and the following night the band played to a sell-out crowd at the Webster Theatre.

India Blue wrote in the *Hartford Advocate*:

"Joe Strummer show was one of the best shows I've seen this year. If you weren't at the Webster that night you missed a great one."

In the *Hartford Courant* Roger Catlin noted:

"*Armagideon Time*, which seemed to be amended, on the second night of US bombing, with a lyric that said, 'A lot of people will get their justice tonight'... Strummer's fine new band. The quintet of versatile multi-instrumentalists."

A review by Sean Spillane in the *Connecticut Post* carried the headline: "Strummer rocks the Webster."

Greg Brown in the *Journal Inquirer* a few days later stated: "The guttural guitars that are Strummer's trademark were accompanied by sax, trombone, keyboards and fiddle, as well as a brilliant drummer."

Afterwards saw a relatively short 130-mile overnight drive to New York for two nights at Irving Plaza on the 9th and 10th. Both shows were sell-outs and also saw the first live performance of *Minstrel Boy*.

A review by Jon Pareles in the *New York Times* carried the headline: "Rowdiness Reflects A Time Foreseen" in relation to Joe ignoring requests to sing *Rock the Casbah*.

Otto Luck in *NYROCK* stated: "Within moments of the opening number, Strummer, with his infectious presence and trademark pained baritone, had me remembering what is good about the music business – and, yes, sometimes it does take a reminder or two."

John D. Luerssen on *Billboard.com LiveReviews* stated: "Opening with a somber, fiddle-fed instrumental that Strummer dedicated to 'all our friends in New York,' he made no mention of the terrorist attacks that devastated the city exactly four weeks earlier."

Fozzie remembers: "The reception was incredible, especially in New York, because a lot of bands had cancelled going there. It was very special at that time; the backdrop was a huge American flag which a friend of Joe's had given him. It was very moving definitely."

The band departed New York the following evening and headed overnight to Boston.

On Friday 12 October an extremely enthusiastic audience awaited at the Palladium, with numerous stage invasions especially when The Mescaleros played Clash numbers.

The following day's *Worcester Telegram & Gazette* carried the headline "Strummer masterful at Palladium."

Although the crowd went wild when Clash songs were played, Scott McLennan wrote in the same article: "The heart of the concert was found in Strummer's latest work. The cries for justice in *Shaktar Donetsk* and palpable heartbreak of *Bummed Out City* made fresh emotional connections between Strummer and his listeners. The boisterous *Johnny Appleseed* showed Strummer can still knock off a righteous anthem with the best of them."

With the band coming offstage at gone midnight, they took the 300-odd-mile journey across the border to Montreal and a Saturday night gig at Le Spectrum de Montreal.

Fozzie: "I do remember Dick Rude got turned away at the border going into Canada, I think it was because he had some conviction for something; he never said what it was for.

We drove off on the bus and he was just stood there. The last we saw of him was him walking back to America; it was a long walk as well. We caught up with him a few days later in Los Angeles. There was nothing we could do about it; we had to go. We had a show to do."

The following evening saw a second Canadian concert, this time in Toronto at the Guvernment.

A few days later the *Toronto Sun* carried the headline: "Toronto's clash with Strummer."

Overnight journey followed to Chicago and the evening of Monday 15th saw the band take to the stage earlier than usual due to a 10.00pm curfew at The Metro. Amongst the 22-song set was a now rare playing of *Trash City*.

In the lead-up to the Metro gig, J.R. Jones wrote an article in the *Chicago Reader*: "Strummer, former front man for the legendary punk band The Clash, pulled off one of the most unexpected – and welcome – rock comebacks in recent memory, assembling a band of young guns, recording the excellent *Rock Art And The X-Ray Style*."

The band took an early morning flight to Seattle, having to hand-carry their guitars. Tuesday was a rest day and the first of a couple of nights at the Westin Hotel, by now a rare treat.

Wednesday 17th The Mescaleros played at the Groundworks show. This was a concert bands did for free and in later interviews Joe regretted putting The Mescaleros through the extra hassle,

In a later interview with *www.strummersite.com* Joe admitted:

"There was pressure on that tour because I booked us into that charity show in Seattle [Groundworks benefit concert], which should have been a day off, just when we needed one. But we had to work thousands of miles away. That nearly killed everyone. Well I hope we did something for the cause."

Luke recalls his own exhaustion: "Seattle nearly broke me; that's the only time I thought this has beaten me. I got sick, flu or something, and had very little sleep. Basically it was get on a plane, check in, soundcheck, do the gig, another couple of hours' sleep, get on another plane etc. I felt absolutely awful. I remember getting to the hotel in Seattle and I just thought I'm getting into my bed. Just let me get over this. Joe knew we were all shattered at that point. Everyone was exhausted – crew, band, the lot but we did a great show."

Simon Foster: "The Groundwork show was held in a museum, provided by Bill Gates' ex partner who was one of the founder members of Microsoft. This museum also has the largest collection of Jimi Hendrix memorabilia in the world. It was designed by the architect who designed the stadium in Barcelona, I believe. An amazing building, very organic.

"It was strange setting, howeve, for Joe, a very sterile environment in a hall, in a museum. It was a very weird show. We also had problems with the technology on that show. Some of the drum sequences were not working properly. We had some of the Pearl Jam guys come along to check Joe out. Tresa, Joe's publicist, worked with them too."

Patrick McDonald in the *Seattle Times* stated: "The five-member Mescaleros is a talented outfit..." he added with obvious lack of taste (personal opinion) "but they're at the service of mediocre songs."

The following morning they took a very early morning flight to Phoenix via Los Angeles. Before the show Joe and the band did an instore signing at Zia Record Exchange on West University Drive and that evening played at Cajun House, Scottsdale, AZ.

Cajun House manager Orion Eckstrom: "I do want to say that he was one of the nicest guys that have come through here. At the end of his show he sat out in the parking lot next to his bus and was just talking with the people who came to the show. To me that says it all."

Fozzie states: "Scottsdale, Arizona is as far from civilisation as you can get really."

After-show it was an overnight 375-mile journey to Orange County.

Friday 19th: The Mescaleros came onstage at 10.00pm at the House Of Blues in Anaheim, which included John Doe opening.

Shawn Price stated in the *Orange County Register*:

"Strummer's solid new band, The Mescaleros, scorched through a 100-minute set that focused first on the songs from his great new album, *Global A Go-Go*, while the second half slipped into a rocket ride through the past."

Afterwards they took the overnight 400-odd-mile journey to San Francisco and perhaps one of the band's favourite venues, The Fillmore. The tour bus pulled out from San Francisco at 2.00am and returned south to Los Angeles.

Sunday 21st was a rest day and the band checked into the Grafton Hotel for a seven-night stay.

Monday 22nd, after a mid-afternoon soundcheck, the band undertook at 9.15pm the first of four sell-out nights on Santa Monica Boulevard at the Troubadour opening with *Minstrel Boy*.

Fozzie recalls: "When we played at the Troubadour, we recorded one night, so somewhere there's some live recording of one night. We got in multi-track tapes. I guess SJM have got it somewhere."

In the *Daily Variety* dated 25 October Phil Gallo reported: "Arguably the most important member of the most important band since the Beatles, Joe Strummer picked a fight with a rowdy patron in a packed sweaty Troubadour, right there onstage."

John Lappen reported in the *Hollywood Reporter*: "It's obvious that Los Angeles missed him as this first night of a four-gig, nearly weeklong stand at the famed Troubadour was packed to the rafters with howling fans." John Lappen described the band as a "swaggering four-piece bunch of London-based yahoos."

Sunday 28th the band left LA on a midday flight to Tokyo which arrived early evening on the 29th, followed by a further two-hour flight to Fukuoka. The following night The Mescaleros appeared at Drum Lagos.

This was followed the next day by a return flight to Tokyo and the first of a three-night stay.

1 November saw Joe Strummer & The Mescaleros open with *Minstrel Boy* at Shibuya Club Quattro.

The next evening they again played Tokyo, this time at the much larger Akasaka Blitz. The band did a soundcheck and then appeared at HMV, Tokyo for a signing session before returning to the venue.

Saturday 3rd was a rest day and also a travelling day with a short flight to Nagoya. On Sunday 4th, the venue was the 500-capacity Nagoya Club Quattro.

With the band now entering their second month of touring, the final date in the USA-Japan 2001 tour was On Air Osaka and the tour was completed by a five-song encore of *Bankrobber*, *Yalla Yalla*, *A Message To You Rudy*, *London's Burning* and *Blitzkrieg Bop*.

The band arrived back at Heathrow mid-afternoon on the 6th.

After a few days' well deserved rest, they flew out to Gran Canaria for the Womad Festival on the 11th.

On a windswept evening the band headlined the final day of the festival, opening with *Minstrel Boy*.

In an interview with *BBC News Online*'s Martin Vennard a couple of days after the Womad Festival Joe gave a very honest point of view about the recent worldwide terrorist attacks. "I think you have to grow up and realise that we're facing religious fanatics who would kill everyone in the world who doesn't do what they say. The more time you give them the more bombs they'll get. Bin Laden is going to try and kill more people."

When questioned about The Clash reforming, Joe replied, "Haven't you heard? Mick Jones has entered a monastery."

Regarding The Mescaleros' future, he said: "We'd like to be known as one of the good groups from London... I haven't even started yet."

A day earlier on *BBC News Online* Martin Vennard had reported

"The folk-like instrumental that opened the concert, and closes their album *Global A Go-Go*, was no indication of the rocking and reggae to come. The three guitars, bass, drums, violin and keyboards soon had Santa Catalina Park pogoing to sounds of the 70s and 80s as well as their latest offerings."

The band spent a couple of days in the studios recording *Minstrel Boy* for the forthcoming film *Black Hawk Down*.

Simon Foster: "There were two versions of *Minstrel Boy* one for the film and one for a commercial for a telecommunications company in America. They reworked it though, because the film company owned this version, so they weren't allowed to use that version.

So they reworked it slightly, then sold it on again."

The band had a warm-up show at Concorde 2, Brighton, on 15 November, supported by Wreckless Eric. During *I Fought The Law* Joe & The Mescaleros were joined onstage (somewhat uninvited) by Gene October, lead singer of 70s punk group Chelsea. (He appeared to enjoy himself.) Sometime later, Scott dryly commented: "Aye, he was rubbish."

Friday 16th was a day off and the bus departed Battery Studios at 10.00pm for the overnight trip to Manchester. The opening date of the British tour was a sell-out at Academy, Manchester on Saturday 17 November.

The set was to remain the same throughout the tour. The band had obviously found what they thought was the correct listing and stuck rigorously to it. Support act was John Cooper Clarke.

Sunday 18 November saw the roadcrew load in at 7.00am as Sunday is market day at Glasgow, Barrowlands. Joe & The Mescaleros came onstage at 9.00 and performed a great two-hour show. Afterwards it was overnight by bus to Birmingham. Monday was a day off and the band stayed at the Post House Hotel.

Tuesday 20/11/01: Birmingham Academy saw the band soundcheck at 4.00pm. The support had a half-hour slot at 8.00 and the band came onstage at 9.00. Joe told a persistent heckler: "If I had a huge great gobstopper, I shove it in your gob."

After-show was an overnight journey and an early morning ferry to Ireland. This was the band's third appearance at Dublin's Olympia Theatre. On the 21st another sell-out crowd greeted Joe & The Mescaleros.

Mick Heaney had written in *The Times*: "Old punks don't die, they just carry on playing in bar bands. Now in his 50th year, Joe Strummer, has moved on from the mouthy radical chic of The Clash, the seminal punk outfit he fronted for nine years. These days he plumps for a good-time fusion of world music with his new group The Mescaleros. His latest album, *Global A*

Go-Go, is a slightly stodgy melting pot of Tex-Mex, reggae, rock and ethnic folk."

Following the journey back to England the band had a day off on the Thursday.

Soundcheck was 4.00pm and the band came on at 9.00 for the first time playing at Colston Hall, Bristol on Friday 23 November.

Saturday 24 November: London, Brixton Academy. Over 4,000 fans turned up to see Joe Strummer & The Mescaleros. This date was the highlight of the tour. The band absolutely blitzed through the numbers.

Nigel Williamson had written in *The Times* that morning:

"The former Clash man Strummer returned to the fray two years ago with a new band, The Mescaleros. Since then they have made two albums, the most recent of which, *Global A Go- Go*, found Strummer experimenting with world music rhythms from South America, the Caribbean and the Celtic fringe. This date should see a few new songs alongside splashes of world beat and plenty of old Clash favourites."

David Sinclair wrote in *The Times* three days later: "His current five-piece band, The Mescaleros, are a lean and versatile bunch. Everybody seemed to play at least three instruments: as well as the usual mix of guitars, keyboards and drums, there were numbers featuring saxophone, flute, trombone, violin and mandolin in various combinations. Strummer, trim and dapper in a dark suit, was a restless stage presence, dragging the microphone stand around like a wandering spirit during the poignant tale of *Shaktar Donetsk* and swaying like an old-time crooner to the delicate Latino rhythm of *Mondo Bongo*. A sensational version of the Bobby Fuller hit *I Fought the Law* turned the response from respectful to rapturous."

On Sunday the band travelled by Eurostar to Paris, booked into the Libertel Le Moulin Hotel and enjoyed a day off in Paris.

26/11/01 Paris: Elysée-Montmartre. Due to the strict 10.30 curfew the band took to the stage at 8.20pm following the now regular Parisian support band The Hellboys.

Simon Stafford: "Our European tour we only played France and Greece. I think the idea was to do a few other places but for one reason or another it all didn't get arranged."

Tuesday 27th was travel day: flights to Thessaloniki, Greece. The following day was a day off.

Luke fondly remembers: "The time in Greece was mental. Because we knew it was the end of the tour, after the Thessaloniki gig, the penultimate gig, we couldn't wait for the last night and we went out and got absolutely trashed. It was a proper rock 'n' roll night out. I remember at 6.00 in the morning, the hotel fire extinguishers were going off, luggage getting emptied into baths, it was just chaos. Everyone falling about.

"We had to get up at 8.00 in the morning to get the flight to Athens. It was like some nights when you get absolutely hammered, you wake up and think you've got away with it, but really you're still drunk. Slowly everyone's starting to go 'Ohhhh God'.

"We felt absolutely awful. When we got to the hotel in Athens I didn't know whether to see it out or go to bed. I felt like death. We did the soundcheck, went back to the hotel, got another hour's kip, got to the dressing room, and I'm still feeling absolutely rough.

"Ten minutes before we went on the hangover just went and we played a blinder. It was one of the best gigs we did. Before the show everyone was just holding their heads and thinking 'How are we going to get through this', but we just rose to the occasion"

This was the first time the band had played in Greece.

29/11/01: Thessaloniki at Ydrogeios Club, located in the industrial west of the city.

The following morning the band flew to Athens for their second Greek date at Sporting Arena, Athens, on Friday 30 November. The band returned to London on 1 December

Straight after, Martin, Scott, Joe and Richard Flack flew direct to Los Angeles to finish off work on *Minstrel Boy* at the Hans Zimmer studios.

Richard Flack: "This was maybe Joe's greatest test as a singer. The melody of *Minstrel Boy* is very dynamic and the key the track was recorded in was very high, probably too high for Joe's range. We didn't have time to re-record it so Joe sang on it as it was. He found it very difficult, but didn't give up. It took us nearly two days of doing vocals for Joe to finally nail it. I'm not sure Joe's voice had been up there before and, if it had, not since he was a lot younger!"

2002

In January, a proposed tour in April to South America (Brazil and Argentina) was cancelled. This was most probably due to the fact that Argentina was in economic crisis. Simon Foster best sums this up: "All the offers from South America were worthless, so we didn't go."

The band's version of *Minstrel Boy* (with Joe on vocals) was on the Ridley Scott film *Black Hawk Down* based on the true story of US involvement in Somalia in 1993. The band attended the film's UK premier on Thursday 17 January at the Odeon, Leicester Square, in London.

The first week in April and "Five Night Stand" was the headline for this short tour to New York. Promoter Sam Kinken had been asked to arrange a venue that the band hadn't played before and had found St. Ann's Warehouse in Brooklyn. Joining up for the first time with Joe & The Mescaleros was Barry Myers, better known as DJ Scratchy, who together with Don Letts had been a resident DJ at The Roxy in 1977. The opening night, with The Realistics supporting, saw the set open with *Yalla Yalla*. Back on the setlist was *White Man In Hammersmith Palais. Get Down Moses* had its debut playing.

Joe announced to the crowd: "This is special tonight ... was actually recorded in this city 22 years ago to this very night." Tymon added: "I haven't sung this for a while," and went into the now legendary Sandinista album song *Lose This Skin*. Despite strings snapping on his violin, Tymon delivered a cracking piece of history. Afterwards he thanked "Joe and Mick for putting it on the record."

Tymon Dogg: "I never wanted to hoist my own strengths at all. Joe said 'it's the anniversary of *Lose This Skin* and I said 'if we're going to do it lets just do it.' Joe wanted to do it. The only lad that was interested in doing it was Martin; the other lads weren't interested in doing it at all.

Anyway I just put it to them and said 'look, I don't care who does it, I'm going to do a solo,' Joe said, 'I'm going to do it.' Martin said 'I'm doing it."

The band played a great cover of the Lou Reed classic, *Walk on the Wild Side*. Introduced by Joe as "tonight's blue plate special". He added: "I hope Lou is over in Manhattan and can't hear this!" A great opening night finished with *Blitzkrieg Bop* and *White Riot*.

Luke Bullen: "The five nights in Brooklyn were a phenomenal experience. We soundchecked for the first couple of days and after that all we did was turn up and play. There was usually a car to take us to the gig but New York's traffic is like London's, a nightmare. So after the first night, I just took the subway down to the Manhattan Bridge and walked across the bridge to get to the gig. It is an incredible view from Brooklyn Bridge especially at night."

Over the following four nights – 2nd, 4th, 5th and 6th, including different support bands every night, Nada Surf, Radio 4, Dirty Mary and Stellastar – The Mescaleros broke with recent tradition, varying the set every night and played the remaining nights to sell-out crowds. The band finished the final night to rapturous applause with *Junco Partner*.

During their stay in New York they went to Electric Lady studios to record a version of *Minstrel Boy* for a TV ad for MCI (the phone people).

Further plans were afoot to repeat the visit to New York. Fozzie later stated: "Simon Moran and Joe wanted somewhere different. The next venue, which Sam was planning, was that we were going to go back and play the Harlem Apollo for a possible two nights with Lee 'Scratch' Perry opening the show. Now that would have been a show to see. That was the next planned New York shows."

On Saturday 8 June, Joe Strummer & The Mescaleros were second on the bill (The Pogues headlined) at the Fleadh, Finsbury Park. The 13-song set included a first-ever playing of *Guitar Slinger Man*.

Steven Dalton wrote in *The Times*:"Joe Strummer and his Mescaleros whipped up the crowd with a set heavy on reggae covers and old Clash favourites, which was a solid enough effort but hardly riveting."

Elslatto: "The Fleadh was probably one of the worst shows we had done – it was shit."

Scott: "The Fleadh was terrible; it was a really rough show. Don't think we did enough rehearsals."

On 28 June the band were supposedly due to appear at Glastonbury on the Jazz World Stage but this never occurred. Simon Foster explains why: "We never played Glastonbury because Joe wanted to go and hang out. He thought he'd have a better time doing that than going and playing."

A proposed gig in Mexico City on 2 July at Salon 21 had been cancelled. Fozzie again: "The original Mexican offer got withdrawn. Like most of South America, the economy had gone, there was no money, so it never happened."

The band flew from Gatwick to Las Vegas on Wednesday 3 July and on Thursday 4 July played at House of Blues, supported by local band Flogging Molly. Simon Foster explains how it was sometimes hard for bands to support Joe Strummer & The Mescaleros

"Flogging Molly were an American band with an Irish guy singing and a female fiddle player. They were really good. They came through the agent or local promoter. If you don't specify somebody, they'll just sort it out for you and put 'em on. It's expensive for a support band to be on the road. At least the headline bands get a decent fee whereas the support band pick up $200 or $100. They can't survive on $100 a night.

"I don't know whether it does their careers any good long-term supporting Joe. Anyone who knows Joe's live show generally will be a middle-aged male who stays in the local pub until about five minutes before Joe & The Mescaleros took to the stage. Then make a dash for the venue filling the empty hall to the brim – got to feel sorry for the supports but I guess it raises their profile locally if nothing else."

They travelled by bus overnight to San Francisco and on the 5th played the first of three Hootenanny shows at Shoreline Amphitheatre, Mountain View. The Mescaleros came on at 5.30 and opened their 11-song, one-hour set with *Shaktar Donetsk*. The other two dates were on the 6th and 7th at Hidden Valley where the band experienced trouble with the sound, especially Joe's microphone, and Embarcadero Park in San Diego.

In the *Press Enterprise* Cathy Maestri wrote: "Joe Strummer – was the center of curiosity and, it turned out, star of the show on Saturday ... with exquisite instrumentation from his band, The Mescaleros."

Simon Foster: "When we did the Hootenanny it was the first year they tried to split it into three festivals, whereas before it had just been LA-based. All it ended up doing was diluting the audience and spreading it over three nights, with no more tickets sold and a lot of extra expense."

The band arrived back in England on the morning of the 9th. With a few days' rest, next was Shepherd's Bush Empire on Thursday 11th. A nearly full house gave Joe & The Mescaleros a truly great London welcome. Amongst the night's set was a return for *X-Ray Style* and an extremely rare live playing of *Willesden To Cricklewood*.

The *Mail on Sunday* had the headline "A long hot Strummer" heading its review of the show.

The by now familiar overnight journey and sleep on the tour bus continued as they travelled to Manchester. This was the third day of a four-day event at the Move Festival at Old Trafford cricket ground. The band came onstage at 6.00 and the set included a superb airing of *Get Down Moses*.

Saturday 13 July, the band returned after three years to T In The Park at Balado and played what was reported to be their finest concert of the year so far.

22 July saw Martin, Scott, Luke and Simon together with Paul Heaton start a five-date British tour to promote the release of the album *Fat Chance* which featured six songs co-written by Heaton/Shields/Slattery and co-produced by Shields/Slattery. Also featured on the album were Pablo Cook, Ged Lynch and Richard Flack.

Fozzie: "Touring with Paul Heaton was fun. We took the same crew guys as well – Mike, Tim and Chumpy. I still see a lot of Paul, socially and in my tour manager's capacity with The Beautiful South."

A planned trip to the Paleo Festival, Switzerland, as headlining act, had been cancelled. The reason given by Simon Foster was, "Paleo was most probably cancelled because Joe didn't have a band as The Mescaleros were committed elsewhere."

So Cambridge Folk Festival on 3 August was the band's next concert. Joe and the band had spent the previous night on the tour bus at the festival, with part of the band arriving on the day. Headlining on the Saturday night, the highlight wasg the first-time live playing of The Stooges' classic *1969*. Despite a very mixed crowd musically, the band were given a great reception

David Sinclair wrote in The Times: "On Saturday night, the damp and tousled survivors of a torrential downpour were treated to a lively set onstage 1 by Strummer and his group The Mescaleros. More folk hero than folk-singer, Strummer maintained something of the old swagger, as he bowled through Clash favourites like *London's Burning* and *I Fought The Law*, along with more self-consciously "multicultural" offerings from his recent album *Global A Go-Go*."

Late September brought the first of three dates in Japan
28/09/02 Fukuoka Zepp included the first live performance of *Coma Girl*. *Guitar Slinger Man* was given its first play since the Fleadh. *Pressure Drop* was removed from the setlist.
29/09/02 Asagiri Jam Festival. Fozzie fondly recalls Joe referred to this as "The old-timers' festival."
01/10/02 Liquid Room, Tokyo. Martin recalls: "When we played Tokyo Joe came in with this riff before the gig; he had written this song about Harajuku. When we jammed it on the gig it was like fuckin' amazing."

Whilst in Japan the band had notification of the FBU's request. Simon Foster: "The Acton date was added into the plan that had already been made.

Anything that used to come through me for Joe, I would print off there and then and hand it to him. He was not interested in looking at the computer screen and reading it off the computer, he wanted something in his hands that he could read. He always said yay or nay straight away, he didn't like to mull over things."

Bringing It All Back Home tour

Following three days' rehearsals at The Depot, on 10 November The Mescaleros undertook a pre-tour gig at the Royal Opera House, in aid of the Diane Fossey gorilla fund. Despite having sound problems, they played a six-song 20-minute set: *Shaktar Donetsk, Bhindi Bhagee, Rudie Can't Fail, Get Down Moses, Johnny Appleseed* and finished with *White Riot*. They became the first rock band ever to play at the world-famous St. Martin's Lane venue.

Simon Foster remarks: "Playing at the Royal Opera House was a fairly strange night – you had Bryan Adams and an orchestra, Joe Strummer and, er, a lot of posh knobs really. The sad thing about it is, if I remember rightly, they actually lost money because they spent so much on this grand production and hiring the Royal Opera House is not cheap. When all the dust had settled and everything had been counted, the outgoings were more than the incomings. Afterwards they held a charity auction; it was all very grand. It would have raised awareness, but financially I think it lost money."

The tour bus departed at 1.00am on the overnight journey to Edinburgh and the first date of the "Bringing It All Back Home" tour.

The setlist had been altered. Fozzie explains why: "The thing Joe hated most of all (well, once he had taken to the stage at least) was people shouting the next song. It was really a case of 'I want to look down and see for myself, I don't want you telling me what it is.'

That's really why *White Riot* was called 'You Know what' on the setlist."

Monday 11th saw the opening date of the tour at the 600-capacity Liquid Room in Edinburgh. Following support band The Basement, Joe Strummer & The Mescaleros received a fantastic welcome from the sell-out crowd and opened with *Shaktar Donetsk*.

"Smokin' Joe has a white riot in Capital" was the headline in the following day's *Edinburgh Evening News*.

Next stop on the tour was Newcastle at Northumbria University where a sell-out crowd gave the band a fantastic Geordie welcome, even to the extent of singing, "There is only one Joe Strummer, One Joe Strummer."

On Wednesday 13 November it was the turn of Blackpool's Winter Gardens to play host to the tour. Afterwards it was overnight to London and a day off.

Fozzie remembers Blackpool: "I remember Bez, Dermot and all the Manchester Posse turning up at Blackpool and coming and drinking all the rider. Joe loved having them around but boy could they drink."

15 November 2002 London, Acton Town Hall. With London television cameras outside, a near-full house inside, the evening was going to be special. The evening kicked off with support from the firefighters' very own Velvet Sisters and No Bitchin'.

Joe & The Mescaleros took to the stage and opened with *Shaktar Donetsk*. Joe dedicated *White Man In Hammersmith Palais* to Mick Jones and his newly born daughter Stella.

At the beginning of *Police and Thieves* Joe dedicated it to "Those other two cunts in The Clash … that's affectionate of course … namely Paul Simonon and Nicky 'Topper' Headon."

An awesome version of *Police and Thieves* followed.

Joe was joined onstage halfway through by a fan playing air guitar. As security came onstage to pull him off, Joe put his hand out signalling to let him stay. Come the end of the song that fan was the happiest man in the world.

Towards the end of the set, *I Fought The Law* was halted after ten seconds as Joe decided he wanted to play *Coma Girl*. As the band came back onstage for the encore Joe was presented with a bronze firefighter statue by Andy Gilchrist.

Two minutes into the encore and *Bank Robber*, a now-legendary event: Mick Jones joining Joe onstage for the first time in nearly 20 years followed as they played an extended nine-minute version. Joe shouted out "In the key of A" as all seven went into a blistering *White Riot* and it couldn't have been any other song than *London's Burning* to finish with.

Luke Bullen: "I remember looking at Joe when Mick came up and Joe's face said it all. It was a very youthful smile. He looked genuinely pleased to see him. Afterwards in the dressing room Joe said in dry humour, referring to Mick: 'Bloody cheek, coming on our stage at my gig.'"

Scott: "Acton was just another gig to me. The fact that it was just around the corner didn't really help. It's funny when you go home after soundcheck, have your dinner and when you turn up for the show you're not intact. Then just drive down at show time. It just didn't feel like you were on tour."

That three-song reunion created a lot of interest in the music media on both sides of the Atlantic.

NME carried the headline: "Clash Back!"

Punknews.org stated: "The webmaster of Strummer's official website spoke to Joe and Mick afterwards. They said that the reunion had not been planned and Jones was at the show simply as a guest. Mick said the moment just felt right."

December's edition of *Mojo* carried the headlines "BackClash" and a quote from www.strummersite.com stating: "Speaking to Joe and Mick afterwards, they assured me that the reunion had not been planned at all."

The firefighters unfortunately lost their deposit on the hiring of the venue, as the show had overrun and it wasn't until 3.00am that they had cleared the last of their equipment out.

Tour manager Simon Foster recalls: "I guess all the people that should have been working were pissed up, that's why they lost their deposit. The firemen were supposed to be helping with all the sound and lighting gear. I was getting quite cross because we were having to go overnight to Wales and they weren't helping us.

I fell out with them as we were leaving. They should have been loading the gear. We did our bit. They got caught up in the evening really. At the end of the day they should have been professional and they weren't really."

The tour bus departed on the Saturday morning as the tour continued, next stop Wales and in particular TJ's in Newport. This venue, like many, had a curfew time and limited the number of songs that could be played in a set.

It had been over three years since The Mescaleros had played in this part of Great Britain, which always held a lot of happy memories for Joe.

Sunday 17th, Bridgwater: The Palace. Another benefit gig, this one supporting the Machine Room initiative at Bridgwater College. (The Bridgwater benefit is still going. Badly Drawn Boy played it in 2004).

After a day off the band resumed the tour at Portsmouth, Wedgewood Rooms, on the 19th. The Raveonettes started the first of a three-date support. *Dakar Meantime* was given its first outing, replacing *I Fought The Law* on the setlist.

The following evening further along the south coast the band played Hastings, the Pier. A rather disappointing turnout on a cold and blustery evening saw them play one of their shortest-ever live setlists of only 16 songs.

Simon Foster: "Hastings was definitely picked for Tymon, the rest were out-of-the-way places off the beaten track. Places we hadn't been before. Hastings was a particularly sad night – it was an abysmal turn out. Tymon had convinced everyone that there was enough of a local scene down there that it would be worth doing! He was wrong!"

21/11/02 Sheffield: the Leadmill. Another full house was there to greet the band. Simon Stafford: "Sheffield was the best gig of the tour. It was like the first proper gig. I felt we delivered then."

The final leg of the tour was on a Friday night, 22 November, at Liverpool University. The Bandits had supported and a full house awaited as Joe Strummer & The Mescaleros took to the stage and opening with *Shaktar Donetsk* and completed the set and tour with *White Riot*.

The band and crew went their separate ways for a few days. One particular crew member, Stumpy, was the drummer from The Almighty. After the tour he went back to The Almighty for their Christmas tour.

After a few days' rest Joe & The Mescaleros headed for Monmouth, Wales and Rockfield Studios to start recording the next album.

Martin Slattery: "That's where we cut *Coma Girl* and did the vocals for *Ramshackle*. We cut *Midnight Jam*. We didn't get a vocal on *Get Down Moses* but we did some more work on that."

As well as the new album, plans were afoot to play in South Africa in early February 2003 and to support Pearl Jam on the first leg of their extensive American tour in May 2003.

Joe Strummer very sadly passed away on 22 December 2002, at his home in Somerset, aged just 50.

The album, *Streetcore*, that Joe and the band had been working on before he died, was finally released on 20 October 2003. It was mixed, produced and engineered by Scott Shields and Martin Slattery.

Also released was the single *Coma Girl*, in three different variations, on 6 October 2003. It reached the position of number 33 in the British charts.

A cover of Bob Marley's *Redemption Song* was released as a single on 15 December 2003. Like *Coma Girl* it came released in different formats, including two CDs and 7in vinyl, all with different live tracks. Unfortunately *Redemption Song* failed to chart.

In a press release issued to coincide with *Coma Girl*'s release The Mescaleros' line-up was described:"This last Mescaleros line-up had settled as Martin Slattery (keyboards, guitar, sax), Scott Shields (guitar, also occasionally drums and bass), Simon Stafford (bass) and Luke Bullen (drums)."

It is fair to say the intense work undertaken in the producing of *Streetcore* took its toll on both Messrs. Slattery and Shields.

Today (late 2004) Martin is in a band called Half Cousin along with Mescaleros Luke Bullen and Jim Hogarth who together with the very talented Kevin Cormack are starting to get the sort of reviews such talented musicians deserve.

Scott Shields has never played live since the last date at Liverpool. Scott is at present writing and producing scores for television and film.

Tymon Dogg is currently writing new material and is looking to get a band together and go back on the road.

Simon Stafford now works for the Royal Mail in his home town of Sheffield. Also plans are afoot to have his own studios in Sheffield.

Pablo Cook is currently taking a year off from touring mainly with Moby and enjoying the peace and tranquillity of Gloucestershire.

Smiley is currently drumming with Archive, who are very big on mainland Europe.

Every now and again in English towns up and down the country, you may also see "Smiley's Heroes" advertised on a billboard.

Antony Genn. the man who got Joe to put a guitar round his neck after such an absence, is today producing and writing for films and numerous top artists.

John Blackburn is mainly recording and touring with Skin.

Andy Boo is as always very much in demand by top musicians as a back-line tech.

Martin Slattery

"Boston was mental, it was a proper pogo night that. It was kinda like that one at the 100 Club where you were stood on geezers heads basically as they passed out on your pedals."

Martin Slattery

I'd worked with Ants (Antony Genn) with Robbie Williams, strangely enough. We met on that and started hanging out. Ants goes around London kinda picking up friends really. It's amazing how he does it. Whenever Ant had a track to do he'd give me a call.

Then I left London for 18 months and went to LA with Scott. When we came back I did a gig with my mate Paddy and bumped into Ants. I had spoken to him and certainly not seen him for those 18 months.

Shortly after that he called me up and said, "I'm doing this thing with Strummer; we're doing this album. I want you to come down to the studio and do what I do, bring my keyboards."

Just prior to this I'd done a little thing with Pablo and Ants, a tune called *All Kinds of People*, a little funk thing. Prior to going to Los Angeles I couldn't play guitar but while I was out in LA I learnt to play because there is fuck all else to do there.

So I took my keyboards and my horns to the studio and Ants said, "I want some guitar in this but I can't really do it." So I put some guitar in it and it was like, "What the fuck you doing with that in your hand?" I said well, I was a bit bored out in Los Angeles and Jimmy showed me a bit.

I went down with Ged and just hung out. The Black Grape thing was still fresh in the mind and Joe had been hanging out at Black Grape gigs. Ant then talked about needing some bass, how it was going to happen live. It was gonna be a definite transition for Joe. Part of doing the first album was to get Joe back into the fray and that would definitely mean doing gigs, particularly as he was being managed by Simon Moran, one of the biggest promoters in the country.

So then I took Scott down. Scott went back and did a couple more sessions, got involved. Him and Ant got on. Joe liked him. You had to fit in with the firm-type thing as well. It's no good just turning up, doing your bit and fucking off. That's not how it works.

When we were in the last throes of doing the record, Ant started to talk about how we were going to do this live. In Battery studios, as well as Studio 2 where we were working, they have a big studio so we set up in there. Ant was like, "This is fuckin' great, opening the show *London Calling*." Handing out all the tunes for everyone to listen to.

Listening to The Clash was something I had never really got into. It wasn't whether I liked it or disliked it. It was something I had never got into.

We started working out the Clash tunes before we started getting into the studio stuff, mainly because they wasn't quite finished. Scott was bass, Ged was going to play drums but ended up getting a gig with Marianne Faithfull. I think he just jumped ship from what I remember, so then we had to get a drummer.

I remembered about Smiley from the Robbie Williams sessions. Somebody else must have known about Smiley as well. I know a lot of drummers down here, some I've known a lot longer than Smiley. So Smiley came down and we started blasting through the tunes.

Scott was bass, I was playing keyboards, Ant was going to play some guitar but we needed a kinda lead guitar player as well. Ant couldn't do it, Joe couldn't do it, so I did it. Having never ever done anything like that in my life before, just kinda got thrown into the mix and everyone seemed to dig it.

Ant had pilfered a load of crew and sound from Pulp, which included Andy Boo, and off we went.

At that early stage Ant was always wanting to use technology. I kinda went along with it but I like to play stuff, me, I don't like mixers with loops on and shit like that. I can't be arsed with it and it always goes wrong and it's no fun. When we first started doing *Yalla Yalla* I'd be pushing buttons. Well that's no fun.

The tunes that actually developed the band ironically were the Clash tunes, 'cause it was just about playing the tunes. Particularly in the early stages everyone was enthusiastic and everyone was totally living the rock 'n' roll lifestyle, inspired by Joe leading the way. There was definitely a feeling of togetherness. Showing up at venues that were full houses every night and getting rave reviews, the rot of not wanting to play those tunes any more was years away!

We were having great fun playing them even if it was to middle-aged men as opposed to younger people.

After a while playing festivals is, well you're rushed on, no soundcheck. It's all line check; you're miles away from each other unless you've made the conscious effort to set up like you would normally do in a small club. The sound's always crap.

At Glastonbury Joe didn't want to be there anyway. I go to Glastonbury now just as a punter and I totally know what he means. He would have his whole camp back there. To be honest playing at it was probably more of a pain in the arse. Hence why he went a bit mental, I think! I've been for the last two years just as a punter and each time the last thing I would want to do was play there. I'm not trying to be throwaway about it because it is an amazing thing to play Glastonbury.

We didn't know Joe as well at this time... he's the kinda guy who does take a hell of a long time to let you in. At that point we were all just still the band

and he was Joe Strummer. You'd never get near him after a gig anyway 'cause there's loads of people that want to be there. We did start meeting the crew around him, the people that would always be there, people like Bob Gruen and his missus, Josh Cheuse and his missus, the kind of New York set and the LA set. Joe's friends who would always be there and be supportive. Obviously for us it was just totally exciting. I don't think any of us were like, "We're playing with Joe Strummer". It was like we're doing a band with this guy and fortunately we didn't have to do much work to build up a basis of supporters because he had hundreds of thousands of them all over the world anyway.

It was a real buzz for us; it was none of that toilet tour playing to two people that I'm doing at the moment with that band Half Cousin that I do. There's no showing up in Liverpool Barfly and only two people being there.

Everywhere we went it was rammed whether it was Sweden, France, London or New York. Even some of the midwest stuff we did later on, which is a fuckin' spooky part of the world. Always people there to see Joe. We never had to worry about anyone being there or not, all we had to worry about was being great. We had great players.

By this time it was probably the start of interband kind of probably getting bored, not bored but wanting to change things and get this. Ant would be on at Smiley to take a couple of toms off the kit. So the band kinda started being a band and having these minor divided loyalties.

To all intents and purposes you had people like Terry (I don't even know his second name) going, "So you're in Mick Jones' shoes then" and things like that. I'd only been playing on the Clash as far as the tunes, not Mick's part. They'd be going, "You didn't play Mick's part right there."

I still don't consider myself a guitarist, I'm a keyboard player and a horns player and that's what I spent my formative years doing. Guitar is still a fairly alien instrument to me so I was always really conscious of that. Instead of going out and enjoying whatever city we were in I do remember that was always my main focal point.

I do remember, particularly me and Scott would always be incredibly nervous before we went onstage in the really early days. Scott was playing bass in a band, which he had never done before. He had always played drums in bands, big bands at Wembley etc, so he was confident and safe behind the drums. Even though he is an awesome bass player. You've got all these specific parts that aren't yours, that are someone else's, that you've gotta try and put across.

I do remember being very nervous for quite a long while in the beginning stages before each gig. Making sure the sounds were right, wanting it to be good before you begin and every venue the sound changed. At that time I didn't know what to do straight away to change it. It was a real virgin area for me as a musician.

Even now prior to a gig the adrenalin kicks in a bit. I think it has to really. Scott would be puking up. Scott puked up before a gig for years into it. He was still puking up when we had that run in Los Angeles at the Troubadour. He was still puking up in a fuckin' bin before a gig at that stage. It was stage fright if you like. I think most of us had kinda got over it by then. There was that tension and you're still wondering – Is Joe happy?

It's always hard to differentiate because we would have a routine every time, do the same routine which would be show up, do the soundcheck, get some food, then before you know it the show's on yer, get psyched up for that, do the show, generally from good to fuckin' amazing. Come off and get hammered. Quite a regular routine.

You had quite a lot of caners in that band, Pablo, Scott. We all got up to quite a high level of having it. Ants at that time was the ultimate caner. It was do the gig, stay out till the last man drops, get up the next day.

When you've got Joe as your guiding beacon there is no one that can outlast that guy; he was the man for the late nights.

What was it Bob Gruen said? "If you go out with Joe make sure you have a pair of sunglasses on yer, 'cause you'll still be up when that sun comes up."

I think when we did the American tour in November was when Joe started getting agitated. I remember that being really tense. Trying to keep that same routine and momentum that sometimes meant finishing the gig and only having a couple of hours and then having to get on the bus. Maybe it was that that pissed him off. I know Gary Robinson had a hard time.

Boston was mental, it was a proper pogo night that. It was kinda like that one at the 100 Club where you were stood on geezers heads basically as they passed out on your pedals. Geezers everywhere reliving their youth.

By that point we were probably starting to immerse ourselves in Joe's world. To be perfectly honest from time to time the lifestyle almost became a bit of a chore. It would get to the point where it was, "OK who's going out and getting Strummered tonight?" It became, "Oh fuckin' hell I don't think I can handle it."

I suppose it must have happened with Black Grape as well, that you just get on this roll and that's what you do. Where you have this delirious free time at home for a week or so and then you're off again.

Everyone would have been really looking forward to the Big Day Out 'cause everyone knew what it was like. Its nickname is Big Day Off. You do, like, eight gigs in a month. We knew we were going out, Primals were going out, The Chemical Brothers. We knew it was going to be an amazing trip and it was. I lost a stone on that tour through not eating and getting high all the time. I was about eight and a half stone when I got back.

Ant was really into Talking Heads and the drummer and percussionist were at the Bowery Ballroom. He met Tina Weymouth and Steve whatshisface the drummer. Again as is his way – doesn't care who it is. – just go up to them and introduce himself and more often than not become friends with these people. "Tina Weymouth's invited me over to her studio to do some work." It was, like, there's no surprise there, Ant.

I always feel it was just feeding off of Joe's energy. I never imagined myself ever to be in that position. It's not where I came from. I was working with Johnny Marr when I first started working with Joe and I can remember him saying, "You're gonna have to start learning to pogo and play at the same time."

I never thought, right, I'm being Mick Jones now. I'll do it how I want to do it.

Joe's intensity was incredible and his commitment to the fans, to putting on a show, whether: Is it suits? Is it all in black?

There was a thought process to everything. The look for the band for a long time was the all-black look. I think it was Luce who said you would all look good in black Ts. It kinda worked.

Maybe it was just that thing about hanging out with each other and the frustrations you come across being away from home all that time, being on the road and just having that hour and a half to offload it all. I think that was probably why we went a bit mental after each show. Blitz the gig, offload the energy, come off high already!

When we were playing those gigs me and Scott were always getting the crew to roll us up a joint. Me and Scott would always be puffing through the shows. By the time you got to play *White Riot* or *Tommy Gun* or whatever, your head's going.

By the time we played Jesolo there was definitely an animosity between Joe and Ants. It kind of created a distance between the band and Joe as well. Everyone had divided loyalties. Ants was my mate. I do remember Ants not making that show and I'm sure Joe was incredibly pissed off about it.

When you look at the setlists it's no wonder we started to get pissed off about being a Clash covers band. I can understand why Ants was getting pissed off. I don't know why Joe was doing that. It's weird because he started doing it again on the last British tour we did.

I probably felt then like Ant did there. What are we doing? What are we? Why are we doing this? Just Clash tunes. Ant said it to Joe – it was probably part of their falling-out.

I'm sure part of it was purely to entertain, giving the punters what they wanted. It was weird at this time. Maybe Joe just felt like we only had one album of new tunes at this stage. I know Joe wasn't enjoying doing *Yalla Yalla* – he wasn't enjoying doing them with the tape machine. He wanted it to be organic. He felt a bit uncomfortable with those tunes, like *Techno D-Day*.

Ant wanted to do it a certain way and Joe wanted to do it a different way. The thing was really brewing by this point. You can tell Joe was annoyed and unhappy just by looking at the setlists.

It's bollocks really, because you can't get a new band together, doing new stuff and creating a new band and then ask them to be a covers band. The whole point of getting in with Ant and getting a fresh new band as opposed to just getting a few of his compadres together – I'm sure the Pistols' drummer would have done it. I'm sure they would have all got together and done a little super band. But Joe didn't want to do that, he wanted to move forward. In retrospect it does seem ridiculous.

Even on the bus during the V2000 festivals Joe started making noises about me and Scott doing the next album. It was always really uncomfortable for me 'cause Ant was my mate and he got me in on the gig in the first place. I had grown really close to Ant and used to hang out with him in his darker moments as well.

There would be times when he would be trying not to do stuff, get off everything. Which would mean leaving the dressing room straight after the gig, not being around any funny business. Sit on the bus listening to CDs. With a bag of pharmaceuticals desperately trying to kick the situation. I would go and talk to him. It was pretty sad.

But at the same time I've got Joe coming up to me going, "You and Scotty do the next album." Obviously I wanted to do it. In terms of my own personal wants, co-producing and co-writing and playing on Joe Strummer's next record. Come on, bring it on.

The thing with Ants had to be sorted first. It's a ruthless business, to be given an opportunity like that to work with a legend. You want it to be as good as it possibly can be.

Just before the Who tour Scott lost the plot. That was kind of a weird time 'cause I felt it was kinda all down to me at that point. It's in my nature to want to help to sort things out. Up until that point it was always somebody else's responsibility.

Ants was a huge character. He always drove those rehearsals etc no matter how off his head he was; he would always be there sorting things out. The lifestyle took its toll on Scott at that point and it was left to me to sort it all out. It was odd because we were doing new tunes, totally different to the other album – *Bhindi Bhagee* – never heard anything like it in my life, don't think anybody has.

Then we go on the Who tour with these tunes fresh out of the box with a new band. I felt the pressure personally. We had Tymon who was new to the band, we had Jimmy who was new to the band and Joe really liked Jimmy. Then we had John.

When we started on the next record it was, like, we'll meet you in the Battery on Saturday and we'll be there two or three days and see what happens and you come out three months later. That's what happened with Ants on the first one and that's what happened with me and Scott on *Global A Go-Go*. This was probably the most mental time I had had in my whole life in terms of your life being turned upside down

I think Smiley's a great drummer but we just wanted something a bit different. We didn't want loads of drummers coming in and out. We knew we wanted to do something different with this next album. Joe had a real soft spot for Smiley.

For most of 2001 we had two weeks on, a week off from the studio. At that time me and Scott were really getting on well. No record company bothering you about what's going on, a 24-hour studio and a drug dealer at the end of a phone whenever you wanted him.

We basically lived at Battery studios. We were really excited 'cause we would work on an idea and Joe would come in occasionally. Joe had this idea of it being a collective production even though he knew someone at some point had to steer the ship. He had this idea of everyone putting in their ideas and everything would be split equally.

It's a bit of a utopian idea that doesn't quite work, unfortunately. We were doing ridiculous things. Joe would say, "I don't want to start with drums, no drums; you can use dustbin lids if you want but no drums." We were, like, "OK?"

So he had these little mad ideas going. Me, Pabs and Scott really were the ones chomping at the bit to make it happen. Flacky was there as well. We didn't really know what we were doing. It was bizarre. We were writing and producing all at the same time not really knowing what the fuck was going on.

Then there was the issue of Smiley. We felt we didn't really need him 'cause Scott can play drums. Scott loved that lifestyle. It burnt him out. But he was very good at it. We were basically fuckin' about.

Joe was always going on about throwing off the shackles of The Clash, not in a way that he wasn't proud of his past, just that he wanted to move on. He wanted to move forward and I think that was always his dichotomy. He himself wanted to move forward but his passion for the fans and what they wanted was always there as well. I think that was always a push and pull for him.

Joe would come in to the studios full of praise for what we were doing so obviously that spurs you on. It was highly drug-fuelled and booze-fuelled (apart from Flacky).

A fair amount of schnifter. Pablo loves all that kinda shit.

We would do seven or eight days straight, take a week off. Joe lived at the studio, so would Scott, so would Pabs. I never once stayed at the studio; I'd always go home even though I lived in Battersea at the time. I always got a cab home – go to bed get up and back to the studio. We could never have done a month in the studio. We would have been dead. Joe would go home and spend some time with Luce then we'd be back in.

Then it started coming together. In the initial session we wrote four tunes. Joe really drove it. He called it all really.

By this time me and Scott had been working together for a lot of years. We just decided we were a really good team and so we decided to try and become a kinda production team on the back of this album. We got a studio together at 2KHZ on Scrubs Lane where we started writing for other people as well and that's where we bumped into Luke who was doing a session down there.

With the gigs coming up we needed a drummer. I already had Simon Stafford in the back of my mind. I had met him through Ants. He was another multi-instrumentalist. To me Simon was a perfect choice and was available.

Particularly after those instore gigs and we were back on the road, Joe would come on the bus and be like, "We're really doing it, we're doing my dream." We had two albums now of original stuff to call on, we could just throw a few Clash tunes in and that was probably the most exciting time for me and Scott. We were fully ensconced in Strummer-world; me and Scott were in the bubble.

For you to become Joe's mate you had to almost prove that you were there for him. As committed to him as he was to you. When Pabs suddenly couldn't do a couple of gigs, because he was touring with Moby – better money, he was thinking of his family – Joe was getting a bit pissed off about that I think. So that was teetering, Pabs' kinda position in the band was teetering a bit. Then after the Brian Setzer gig Pabs went on the road with Moby and that was the end of that. It was Pabs' choice. He has a wife and two kids.

So out of the original band there was left me, Scott and Joe. Me and Scott were really intense – for a couple of years I saw more of Scott than I did Kirsty.

In a way there was a certain ragginess lost, a certain rawness lost but as far as I was concerned it was becoming a better band. That was a brave move for Joe to change. When I think about it now I feel pretty proud to think that he had the trust in us to pull it off with him, which I think we did.

What Joe wanted to do within the band was accommodated as opposed to fought all the time.

When you're a 50-year-old legend if you can just keep doing it, it's the ultimate existence. Spend time at home with the ones you love and spend some time on the road, visiting all these places. Joe would always have the map and be at the front of the bus. He would always want to get the bus somewhereas opposed to the plane. Joe loved the whole being on the road thing.

And we were playing our tunes; as any band being onstage playing your own tunes is the best feeling in the world.

It was amazing when we flew into New York just after 9/11. Joe's got a lot of friends in New York and they all said the same thing "God, we need something like this." So many bands had pulled out of getting on planes basically. We just took the bull by the horns and went straight out there.

They were almost grateful for us being there. Something to take their minds off it for one or two nights. Also in the back of everyone's mind, being away from home, everyone's talking about the threat of more attacks.

I remember being in LA with Joe and there were rumours about LA being next whilst we were there. A couple of Joe's mates had bought chemical warfare suits for their kids just in case. It was like, fuckin' hell, what if it goes off here?

Joe and Dick Rude took a taxi down to LAX to see if they could spot any Muslim people getting on planes to leave!

This was the plan because we couldn't formulate a plan; some people were saying, oh fuck it! So Joe said: "This is the plan. Me and Dickie will go down LAX and if we can see any of those people getting on planes then we're getting on the next plane outta here."

Anyway they went down, nothing happened and we carried on doing our shows.

That was the point where me and Scott were on the road and you're not just on your tour wages. So I just ignored finances – $250 bar bills.

We were in this posh hotel and the guy just kept the bar open till five in the morning, which just doesn't happen in LA.

Absolutely completely committed to being in a band and everything that it entails. It was great and Joe was loving it, he was fuckin' loving it, loving the gigs, loving the band. Dickie was out there filming it.

We all wanted to do DVDs of it. We recorded all the Troubadour shows. To try and get some kind of thing together. The band was possibly a bit ropey, but we were all so fucked.

We had just done the album, been out on the road. We were pretty mashed.

It was probably more raucous when we had played, say, Montmartre with Ants, Pabs and Smiley, but it had more finesse about it at this point. Luke's a fuckin' amazing drummer – he drove that band.

We had this Tymon thing going on as well, which created real tension in the band. But when he was on it there was this new dimension to the band, which could be amazing. Actually, to be honest, for the most part he was hard work as well.

We were one of those bands that had never ever been totally happy, I would say. There's always been something. Maybe there always is, I don't know. You're living with these people all the time, you're getting on each other's tits, don't yer from time to time.

The five nights in Brooklyn was a real pinnacle point in terms of the band and being able to be excited about being in The Mescaleros. It felt like it was a whole band now – we didn't feel like it was Joe and us. We felt like The Mescaleros was the whole thing.

In Brooklyn we were doing a lot of our tunes and doing the Lou Reed thing. That time in New York was fuckin' awesome, absolutely awesome. People came down to see the shows... we hung out with them. That was a great little trip. Everyone was getting on well. We knew the band was good. There was no weak links in the band.

It was a fuckin' good band. Then you've got Strummer fronting it with that amazing energy. You just could not fuckin' beat that. No one could say anything against the band then.

The Fleadh was probably one of the worst shows we had done – it was shit. It was five days after my kid was born. I was all over the place. It was all a bit weird for some reason.

Hootenanny was great; Joe brought Lolla and a mate of hers along. We were playing good again on that tour. But it started getting back to playing more Clash. It really threw me. I didn't understand it.

At one of those gigs I was playing and Joe just turned around to me and said, "Shut the fuck up." I was like ... it really freaked me out. For the first time, afterwards I said, "Listen, don't fuckin' talk to me like that onstage, I'm not having it. I'm serious 'cause I want to do it. I'm not a fuckin' paid monkey, I do this because I think I'm part of it and I love it. I would never do that to you, don't fuckin' do it to me."

As it goes, Joe was embarrassingly apologetic.

But we had that moment on the last one of those where we did *Yalla Yalla* and at the end of it Joe had tears in his eyes and it was like a real beautiful moment.

At Shepherd's Bush we ruined *Willesden To Cricklewood*.

When we went to do Paul Heaton, I remember talking to Joe about it and I felt really weird about that we'd just taken off. I think that probably freaked Joe out more than he let on. I don't think he minded us doing the album with Paul. We took the whole band and did the Heaton thing and I think that pissed him off. I felt so bad about it that I spoke to him about it and kinda asked him what he thought. He was cool. But thinking about it he obviously wasn't. I enjoyed it apart from me and Scott being a bit nifty with each other, it was a good band. It was a lot more middle of the road than what we had been doing. I like Paul, he's a good bloke.

When we went to Japan, in my mind that's the best the band ever was. We had had that bit of weirdness at Hootenanny. Just little things with Joe that we had never had before, arguments I suppose, and disagreements about stuff which you're inevitably going to get. The Japanese tour picked everyone up again and got everyone fired up to do some more recording.

I don't know what it was about that trip. We always got really well looked after out there by the Smash people – wonderful, wonderful people, really look after you. Take you out, sort you out with anything you need, lovely meals etc.

We went to this bar called JB's and there's this Japanese guy who owned it. He was a huge James Brown fan. He had met James Brown in the 70s and James gave him this video that was not on general release of a live concert. He played it for us in this bar. It was amazing and Joe was like dumbstruck by the show that he saw, by the way James conducted his band. It was an incredible sight just to see on film. Joe seemed to get immersed in the show somehow.

When we played Tokyo, Joe came in with this riff before the gig; he had written this song about Harajuku. When we jammed it on the gig it was like fuckin' amazing. It was such a buzz. It's one thing getting a buzz from having a big crowd when you're in a band, because that makes your life easier. If you've got a thousand people loving what you do you get your buzz from that.

Everyone was just buzzing after those gigs. Musically as a band that was amazing. 'Cause as well out there, the Japanese don't go mad while you're playing. They're a really respectful audience, dead polite, when you're playing – it's like theatre gigs – but when you finish it's like loads of noise so loud... then as soon as you start the next song it's shushhhhh...

I remember in my mind thinking, this is a fucking great band. It's then that we started talking about the next record. We were really into the idea of writing sessions of rough sketches of tunes, then going on tour, playing the tunes and getting them together on the road. Then go into the studio and record them in a retro style, how it used to be done. Having an organic band basis for each tune and then working the productions from there. Joe was excited about it. His band was good enough (when focused enough and not twatted) to do that.

We said, "We don't want to make the album like we made the last one because it would kill us." Joe was like, "You fucking Jessies." I said, literally, "Joe I can't do it like that again."

He agreed to this way of doing it, which in retrospect I don't think he was 100% happy with. But we were writing tunes... we were going out on the road and writing tunes.

Then it started getting into playing more Clash tunes again.

My dad had been to a few shows and when we did that last run he came to the Blackpool show and there was a lot of things going on. Scott went back on bass and me and Simon did *A Message to you Rudi*. There was a real diversity in the show, a real musicality in the show.

We had a great gig but in the back of my mind it was a bit uncomfortable about the way we were going.

That whole kinda retro thing at Acton was just like being catapulted back into the 70s. Maybe I'm just being a grumpy twat?

My mate Chris, he's a Clash fan and he came to a few Mescaleros gigs and him and his brother were there that night. Seeing Mick and Joe onstage to them was like – Wow! That's not where I come from and I can't help that. I have total masses of respect for Mick but me and Scott were trying to get into doing this new record. Yet all around us was this kinda retro kind of paling of what was.

Joe was always going on about, "I'm moving forward. I'm throwing off the shackles of the Clash and I'm establishing myself as an individual." Then all this happened. It was nice but it didn't make any sense of what we were trying to do.

I remember the gig in Newport. I was just so unhappy with it all – we were a Clash covers band again. We had been having pretty mixed audiences with young people coming down, people getting into the band. Then we were doing this real retro. I kinda could understand Joe wanted to do something for the fans but I didn't understand it. So Joe and I fell out again at that gig in Newport. I was well pissed off. We spoke about it but we never really sorted it out.

The essence of my thing at this point was the exciting times for me were Brooklyn and Japan when we were being The Mescaleros, when we were moving forward. When we were playing new tunes, when we were trying to get the super new tunes that were going to be on *Streetcore*.

Playing Clash tunes again kinda took precedence and that confused me. At that point I didn't see the need. At that point we got into this little policy that we were really only doing tunes that The Clash covered in the first place. We weren't doing *Safe European Home*, *White Riot* or *Tommy Gun*.

I've got fuckin' masses of respect for that band. But that's not what we were doing.

Maybe I was a bit too unforgiving and should just be allowing Joe to do what he wanted to do. It wasn't fitting in with what we talked about. It didn't make any sense to me, it was just moronic. Me and Scott would find it quite awkward to talk to Joe about.

I don't think I really realised that Joe was just trying to give something back to the fans, which in my mind was at odds with what we were trying to do with the band. It was incredibly frustrating.

After the tour we went down to Rockfield, which was like it was back on track. We spoke to Joe and said, right, we're going to take the band to Rockfield; we're going to stay there. It was the environment you like, where you can live. Live in the surroundings that we were working in.

That's where we cut *Coma Girl* and did the vocals for *Ramshackle*. We cut *Midnight Jam*. We didn't get a vocal on *Get Down Moses* but we did some more work on that.

It felt like the album was coming together. It was a bit weird because Tymon wasn't really invited down and that was really awkward. We felt that Tymon suited the *Global A Go-Go* aspect of The Mescaleros but not where it was going. So Joe had probably had a lot of pressure dealing with that. He had Tymon in one ear and us in the other. I don't know how that affected him.

We had a great time down at Rockfield, a wicked time doing our thing. Working all night. Being away from home you don't have to exist in reality, you can go and live in the bubble.

This idea of being in a band in the studios as well, really excited me and cemented the whole idea of being in a band. It wouldn't be going back in the studio and just me, Scott and Joe and getting people in when we needed them. It would be we're going into the studio as a band.

That cemented the longevity of it and had what happened not happened we'd probably still be proving that now. It then meant more than just being a musician in someone's band. That's what I wanted. As well as obviously

Joe passing away being incredibly sad, we lost a lot when that happened. We lost everything. Joe really cared for our existence, our welfare within it as well.

There's a bit in Dick's film when we were in LA where Joe says, "I don't want to disappoint the guys, I think they think this album's going to be a mega-smash and I know that it's only going to sell a certain amount. I hope they don't get despondent with the way the industry responds to me now." Joe cared for our welfare within what was going on. We actually didn't give a shit; it was just about doing it. That's all it is about, is doing it.

Obviously it becomes a living as well but we forgot about that; it provided a living. So we could just concentrate on what we were doing. Which is an amazing situation to be in. I just hope I can find that again. There are a lot of possibilities for it to happen again. But that was really special and by that point I was excited. I can't speak for the other guys but I personally was excited about the possibilities.

Particularly for the next album where we wanted to move away again from the eight and ten-minute meanderings back down to two-and-a-half-minute in-your-face tunes. Which is what we wanted to achieve with the next record. We wanted to put a bit of rock 'n' roll back into the band. Move away from *Global A Go-Go* and back to a bit more of what Joe was about. Without in anyway *parodying* The Clash.

That was the premise for *Streetcore*. So the fact that you can do it live with a band and prepare it in that way added to the whole motions. It was all going to plan. There were a few gripes here and there, but essentially it was going to plan.

When Joe died it was a massive shock as it was for everybody. It took me a while to realise how massive an effect it was going to have on my life. It was four years up to that point. Four years of my life with Joe. Four years of moving forward as well. There was quite a wide variety of music made in that time. As you say, 160 gigs – that's a big chunk of time.

It was heavy realisation when you realise you've lost your mate, you've lost your livelihood, everything, and we still had to finish the record.

I hope that record reflects the spirit of what we were trying to do, tracks like *Coma Girl* and ironically enough of what Joe had done with Rick was very much in the spirit, a bit raw, focusing on Joe's voice.

The beauty was, over that last year or so I really felt that Joe's singing had kinda gone into a new stratosphere. His ability to sing complicated melody and carry it off. Maybe he could always do it... maybe it was just a confidence thing. Early days, he was paranoid about being out of tune at gigs. He blamed it on Mick's guitar being too loud in The Clash. All the time he really worked on it and in those later recordings he's on it.

Musically as a band we were always pushing for it to develop and Joe was as well, but like I say he had this dichotomy of his past, balancing the two.

Whether that be tunes, whether that be Clash, even his relationship with

Tymon and his relationship with us, constantly balancing a couple of worlds going on around him.

He did like the cat amongst the pigeons, definitely. He loved Scott and Tymon's battles. I lost my rag with Tymon in rehearsals at the Depot like totally, like I have never done in my life and never will do. I totally lost it. I came back in and apologised and Joe said, "Don't apologise, it was great."

And that's that. Re the future:

It looks like me and Ant are finally going to do something along the lines of Help.

Scott Shields

"Our first gig at Sheffield I remember London Calling started. I started pogoing and then I suddenly stopped and just realised what the fuck am I doing?"

Scott Shields

We were working right up until the first gig, mixing and just putting finishing touches and redoing some things. I played on a couple of tracks plus we were rehearsing at the same time in the studios. We'd rehearse during the day then Ants would be up all night doing his thing. Once we'd decided to get together we were there or thereabouts for most of the time. There wasn't an awful lot else going on. It was quite good fun being in the studio. I was quite enjoying it; it was quite a creative place.

It was good just to be doing something again; I hadn't been in a band or done anything like that for a while.

Our first gig at Sheffield, I remember pogoing at that! I remember *London Calling* started. I started pogoing and then I suddenly stopped and just realised, what the fuck am I doing? I never moved again onstage or tried to dance again. It was just, it was really exciting; it was great to be finally playing onstage and doing it.

It was good to be standing onstage, because before I had never been anything but a drummer. It was totally different to stand on a stage than it was to sit behind a drum kit.

Playing Glasgow was great, all my family were there. Good vibe, terrible stage, King Tut's – it's really hard to get a lot of people on it. We had a few sound problems but it was good.

The trip across the channel to Amsterdam was rough. I remember Martin throwing up that morning. He just walked out the bus and threw up this green stuff.

Playing Elysée was great, it's one of my favourite venues.

Before the Swedish festival we went out in the boat. It was solar-powered – you go out with the captain. We all decided we would jump in the water. Maybe about half a mile out into the lake, we jumped straight into the water, naked, and the water was only three foot deep. We stood in mud and clambered back in the boat. He didn't tell us it was really, really shallow. That was a really nice day.

Finland was a strange one, it was weird – a strange stage, hot, middle of the day. Strange bikery crowd.

When we played Glastonbury I was fucked. I had been in the studio with Ants the night before doing a remix. We left about seven in the morning, drove to Glastonbury. As soon as we arrived there we went straight to bed on the bus.

It was quite scary and Joe was obviously batting people about with his mike stand. That time he went off at the cameraman.

Glastonbury wasn't great musically but it was good. It wasn't the biggest gig I had ever played. I had played 100,000 stadiums in Europe supporting the Stones.

Milwaukee Summerfest was unusual – mothers and daughters and sons, very family-orientated that festival, I remember. Don't remember much more about it to be honest.

Playing the Fillmore was always good, it was another one like playing Elysée. Every time we played there it was good – good vibe, good sound, good crowd.

Los Angeles the Palace was a good gig – that was a good one except I got a nosebleed. I turned round, wiped the back of my hand under my nose. I had a white T-shirt on and my hand was absolutely covered in blood. I just thought, oh fuck! That's me, I'm screwed now! There was a good party afterwards; we went to the Viper Rooms afterwards.

Fuji Rockfest was wicked. All the bands stay in the same hotel. It's like a ski resort in the winter – don't know what it is in the summer, lovely big hills. It wasn't actually at Mount Fuji this time.

I got really wasted on sake the night before. ZZ Top was headlining and they asked us to headline because they were going to miss a flight or something. Joe was just like, "Nah, fuck off."

That was the first time I had been to Japan. It was an eye-opener even though we didn't really see Japan properly 'cause you're taken straight in there and then it's straight back out.

The gig was indifferent really... it was all right. I don't remember any catastrophes. Most of the time the gigs were of a fairly reasonable standard. It depended how fucked you were feeling from the night before or how many nights you'd had on the trot, how you felt at the time. None of the gigs were a real disaster I don't think. I can't remember any really bad ones. But I'm sure you'd remind me if there were.

The Free Wheels festival was terrible – that was where we were advertised as a Clash tribute band. "A Tribute to The Clash: Joe Strummer & The Mescaleros." Joe didn't see it; the tour manager at the time told them to take the posters down. He basically went round telling everyone to get those posters down. "If Joe sees that he'll fuckin' go nuts" and he would have. Plus the crowd gave Andy Boo a hard time because he was black. That was really surreal that place.

Portugal was a weird one; they were all heavy metal bands.

In Dublin they wouldn't let us off the stage. Joe had to go out and say, "Please go home! We can't play any more." We were all offstage eating our dinner and Joe came back and said we got to go back on. Ants had to pull himself out the shower, get his shit together and go back on. The crowd just refused to leave, so we played *London Calling* again.

Belfast was one of those very hot ones. Joe kept opening the fire exits so we could go out and get some air. It was one of a couple of times where Joe was curled round at the bottom of my feet just lying there going "Urghhh, Urghhh, I'm dying!"

As Joe Strummer was really big and he hadn't been about for ages it was inevitable people were going to see him at least once. We knew the fanbase was there in the first place.

In Munich we got pelted with all sorts of shit. I got hit by a Lit CD. Joe was going to fight this guy. I felt a bit scared because once I saw the size of this guy I thought Joe was going to get a fucking pasting. Joe kept saying, "Do you want a fight?" This guy's going, "Yeah." This guy comes up and it's like a fuckin' mountain. Joe gave him a load of abuse because I think he thought he' got no chance.

It nearly started a riot. It made me angry. I'm usually quite het up before I went onstage. The slightest little thing sort of makes you snap.

When we played Bologna I got pelted with an egg – first song this egg fuckin' smashes on my guitar all over my black T-shirt. That was the first of a few eggs that came up that night.

It wasn't that people hated us; it was just one guy being a prick.

The egg seemed to cook on my bass underneath the lights. It was all over my guitar. I turned round to signal to the crew and they were laughing.

On the British tour Manchester Academy was a good one. I remember seeing the woman that plays the woman that had a sex change in *Coronation Street*, Hayley, she was moshing down the front, pushing people about. She looked up at me and said, "So what!"… then continued pushing people about at the front.

When we played Barrowlands all my family and friends came. I felt like a bit of a star that night.

That was the night the bus driver took offence to the Manchester Crew being on the bus. The driver felt a bit threatened by some people telling him to fuck off after he asked them to get off the bus.

He pulled over and left us there. Joe was chasing him down the street, jumping up and down grabbing his windscreen wipers in a rage.

On the American tour Anaheim was a weird one. It was all tables … it was "chicken in a basket".

The Pietasters who were supporting us were good guys; they were funny. I remember they were quite mad. We had a good relationship with them. They were a very entertaining band.

Playing LA was always weird because there was always Joe's entourage. It's like playing London. The equivalent number of people that are friends with Joe over there. You always felt a bit outta place at those ones. Not a lot of people weren't really that bothered about you. I think I'm right in saying Gene Simmons from Kiss came to that one. Steve Jones was also there.

Hard Rock Hotel was another strange venue to play. When you go to Las Vegas it's not to go and see bands; you go there to gamble.

All the midwest places were weird. I remember all the midwest Bible-belt places were weird. Strange crowds coming, it wasn't a good time for us.

Chicago was always good. Playing the big cities you're not scraping together to find an audience that's right for you.

Boston, The Roxy, was nuts, I was fighting people off the stage. I felt a bit scared at that one; I felt it was a bit out of control. It was just too many people on the stage. They were all grabbing at Joe. I felt a bit pissed off that all these people were on the stage and not watching the music. On reflection, it was a punk moment, but at the time I was pissed off. People were bumping you out of the way and grabbing your guitar. It pisses you off because it wasn't really that kind of band any more. It was a little bit more mature than that.

In New York Joe threw another wobbler, kicked his monitor onto the floor or something.

Most of the time on tour you kinda go into automatic pilot really, you don't end up seeing a lot of the places. I never got exhausted on the road. I got more exhausted in the studios making a record.

There's no real pressure when you're playing live but when you're trying to create something there's a lot more pressure and you're inclined to stay longer, work longer, which is not always the best thing to do.

I had a good show in Philadelphia; I had just met this girl called Dylan. I think her mum was a friend of Joe's and she had been to a couple of gigs in New York. I just got talking to her, got friendly and ended up staying at her house. She drove one-legged Tim and me to Philadelphia, which took fuckin' hours. On the way back to New York the bus broke down. We got terribly lost, didn't have a clue how to get onto Manhattan Island but we still got back before the rest. They had to get a limo to take all the stuff. They were waiting about for a long time and were well pissed off.

Suppose there was a bit of a divide as well. Joe and Ants were getting less friendly, conflicting with each other quite a lot. Anything Ants said Joe would say the opposite even if what Ants was saying was right. Joe would just have a conflict with him all the time. It was still fun, though there were times when you'd turn around and think I wish I was doing something else!

It felt great coming off at the end of the Paris show in December. The crowd weren't going mad throughout the whole show but at the end we'd got them. It was the best ever Mescaleros show.

We did Japan then went on to the Big Day Out. That was great except I got busted for drugs and strip-searched on the way into New Zealand. One of The Pietasters had put a hash cookie in my bag and it had all crumbled up but I had scooped it out. So on the way into New Zealand the customs dogs were sniffing all over my bag.

At the end of it one of the customs guys went, "You'd be crazy to bring weed in here mate; we've got great stuff." They let me go on my way.

We went to this beautiful place when we arrived in New Zealand. We went to the countryside, to this woman who was building her own house and had a caravan. It was dark when we got there and we had to find our way in by torchlight.

When we woke up next morning we found we were in an amazing area with a massive lake. The place had quad bikes. We had great fun. Then we went back and did the gig the next day.

It was definitely a holiday being in Australia, everybody hanging out and partying together. We were hanging out with Primal Scream and The Foo Fighters. It was just fun, there was no stress involved at all.

The gig at Richmond Corner Hotel in Melbourne was fuckin' outrageous. That was a good one – low ceiling, really fuckin' hot.

When we were flying to New York for the gig at the Bowery Ballroom Ants missed his flight. He was supposed to be picking me up so I had to get my own taxi. It was a nightmare.

In New York Ant just turned up all bleary-eyed and walked onstage. Before he arrived we thought we were doing it without him. We only played a short set to a strange crowd.

Jools Holland was good. I had fun doing that. We played *Louie Louie*, which is shite.

After the gig in Lido de Jesolo was when I got my first tattoo in a field by the festival. There was a point where Joe lost his bottle a bit about playing his own songs and playing the Clash songs. It was safe to go to the Clash songs; we always got a better response at the beginning. Joe gradually backtracked away from what we had started off doing which was mostly our own. Again this was a rebellion against Ants, not wanting to play the new songs because Ants wanted to play the new stuff.

It had got to the point where Ants would drop a setlist in and Joe would drop another setlist.

I remember feeling really pissed off when we were going out playing Clash songs all the time, thinking that's not why I'm here. We're here to promote Joe's new record, not to be a Clash band. It was getting beyond a joke.

Also some of these places, when it was the first time we had been there people are kinda entitled to hear the Clash songs once, twice even. So I think in the territories we hadn't been to before you'd give them more of what they'd be looking for really. On the second time you'd face it more your way; we'd say all right you've seen that, you've had your try at it, now see what we're doing now.

When we did V2000 it was Ants' last gig. I wasn't upset to see him go, as he was a pain in the arse at that point. It was just a bit too far-gone. Too much bad blood between him and Joe.

I don't think we were sad to see him go at the end especially as Joe had been sort of hinting, dropped a couple of hints in there to show us the band was going to continue without Ants.

He wasn't any less of a friend. As far as the band was concerned it was just too antagonistic between Ant and Joe. They just weren't agreeing on things. I think that's why Joe took it upon himself to say, "All right, see yer."

There were things going on in my body that I didn't know what was happening and I was told it was all psychological and yet there were very definite physical symptoms, like playing the drums on *Bhindi Bhagee* I literally fell off the drum kit. They kept the tape running and eventually I managed to get up and started playing again. Afterwards I had to go for a lie down. I was bad at that point.

Just the constant late nights and drinking and that combined with the fact you've got a shitload of work to do, so it's not as if you're just partying. You're doing all these things and working through it. Then the physical symptoms... it was just too much.

I checked myself into a private hospital. Basically I was just saying, look, what the fucks wrong with me? At that point they were still treating it as if it was psychological/psychosomatic, putting me on different drugs to see if it would alleviate the symptoms and it actually wouldn't.

I was getting a kinda electric shock feeling running up and down my spine every time I moved my head. That just wouldn't go away and that was what eventually led them to think right, we've tried all these things – if this isn't working then it must be something else.

I went on making the record before I knew anything about it. I had pulled myself together a bit. Eventually I got to see a neurologist and he told me it was MS that I had.

Because I had got no information from anybody I had thought: Was it cancer? Was it AIDS? I hadn't had a fuckin' clue what it was. It wasn't a big deal to find that out. I remember feeling quite happy when they said you've actually got MS. Also at that point I didn't know what it fucking was about. He told me it could do this, it could do that.

But I think deep down if I just sorted my life out, changed my eating habits, changed my life-style habits that I'd be able to control it.

So far that seems to be the case. It knocked me out for a wee while and I've had one recurrence which was quite bad but, touch wood, the last two years, nothing really.

I don't really know what my dad's take on it was. My dad's quite hard to flap – he's been through so much himself that he doesn't really get himself in a panic about anything.

I think if it progressively got worse and I was showing signs of deterioration then perhaps people would be concerned.

It's kinda forgotten about really. I'm all right. I'm left with certain physical side effects from it. The scarring on my brain, my hands don't move ... they don't have the co-ordination they used to. I'm not as good as a guitarist as I used to be. It used to be a lot worse but I've found ways round it. You forget bad things easily I think. It's quite hard to actually pinpoint what it's like when it's actually having a recurrence or maybe I don't like actually thinking about it.

I came back for the last show at Wembley Arena though I didn't actually play. I think I was going to play but I didn't.

It was my first time co-producing an album; it was just music before. It was my first time major-label-backed. I had never been given that freedom before, put it that way. I had tried to make my own album with the Bond project but that was a totally different ball game, just because of the whole way of going about it as well. At the beginning Joe insisted that we don't start off by doing drums; we always do the music first and then we'll think about the rhythm later.

Gamma Ray, for example – we construct this clever percussion part but not actually out of a drum kit. We went through most of the record trying to keep that ethos.

Joe was just sick of hearing dum dum dum dum and wanted to try and take a different approach to it. So that was just the main criteria; make your music without drums. A lot of the time the drums were just a little snare drum or hitting a bit of paper with a brush. It was quite a different approach to doing everything really. *Shaktar Donetsk* we set out to try and make the weirdest piece of music we had ever made and that was the only criteria on that and I think we did!

I think once we made the record we were worried about how the fuck we were going to play it live because it was such a piece-worked record, so bitty and all put together with the aid of a computer. We were just frightened how we were going to pull it off live. As usual we started off by running lots of samples and lots of things on tape triggering things. Gradually that just fell by the wayside. Joe was always anti-technology onstage because he felt it restricted him. What was happening was, we were always fighting to get the sounds and the samples off the record. Joe was always fighting to have it more organic and just played live and if we can't play, we can't play it. So what tended to happen was we'd start off with the good intentions of triggering all the sounds on the record. By the end of it you'd have a few key sounds and gradually phase them out one by one.

I had plenty of sleepless nights but I don't think I ever felt the pressure that this had to be finished. I don't think that pressure was ever put on us.

This was because of the way Joe made his records, which was self-financing. He always made his records on his own and then got somebody to buy them off him. So there was never the restriction of the record company saying, "No you can't do that", or "You can't do this", so it was always completely free creatively.

Pabs, Joe and Tymon were there; we all turned up to do a cover version of *Silver and Gold* and ended up staying there. It was never planned to make a record, it was just go on, show us what you can do, write some songs. You never got the feeling somebody was looking over your shoulder. You never played music to anyone that wasn't finished so nobody could judge it or make a comment on it. It was quite a free experience. There were no rules.

Roger Daltrey was under the assumption that he was coming to write with Joe but we had the track all prepared with certain parts for him to sing. I think he felt a bit put out that he wasn't involved in the creative process of writing a record.

Joe would get you in a situation, i.e. Roger Daltrey or Paul Heaton, where he'd sort of introduce you and then just fuck off. He'd go oh this is blah blah blah and then go and disappear in his little room and let you get on with it. Maybe he didn't feel comfortable in the situation. I can't speak for Joe what his reasons were for doing it but that was one of his things.

So he'd leave it to you to explain to Roger Daltrey, "This is what you're singing. No, no this is what you're singing, we've already worked it out what you're singing, this is it." It's kinda interesting. Roger did it and at the end of it, it was good.

I just remember him singing the parts and I would sing parts to him how he would have to sing it and it was kinda like, "Who the fuck are you?" That's what it felt like; maybe it wasn't that but you're dealing with somebody who's got great history, great track record somebody who's a musical genius and you're trying to tell him how to sing your song. You don't feel right really telling somebody of that calibre what he should be singing.

When we played the instore gigs it was quite stressful at that point because we hadn't done it before. It was stressful. You're in a record shop, you're not in a gig, nobody's drunk, everybody's just standing there. You're not sure of what you're doing, you're not in your routine yet. It was quite weird that, doing those gigs. I don't like doing it instore. I didn't like the American stores either.

I like suits but I don't feel there's a place for them on a rock 'n' roll stage. I never felt comfortable. There were certain clothes I could wear that I'd feel comfortable in, baggy trousers, tight top and a pair of sandals. Wearing a suit restricts your arms and I felt it was a bit cabaret. I felt it was a bit too much and Joe was kind enough to let me get away with not doing it. It's not for me; it reminds me of my days when I was in a wedding band when we used to wear a fucking suit all the time. I just felt, nah, I didn't want to be in a fuckin' wedding band any more. As soon as the first song was over I took my jacket off, "Can't stop me now."

Doing the Letterman show is an acclaim, something to say you have done.

When we did the Viper Rooms it was too intimate, I preferred a bit of distance and anonymity really. I wanted the audience to be anonymous. I didn't really want to see them picking up on a mistake that I had made. I wanted to be a shape in the distance. I felt a bit uncomfortable when it was a small venue like that. It's just my take on it. I never liked it when it was small; I never liked it when there were people in your face. I always preferred a bit of distance when you were up on a high stage. I think when people are really close to you it's harder to pretend to be an image that you are.

Martin and I were of the mindset that we didn't want it to be so fuckin' messy this time. We were so fed up with what it had been like before when it was lots of parties and debauchery. We wanted to try and get some work done on the road, try and write some songs. Try and do some things, which inevitably never happened – we just fell back into that partying way of life, which as it transpires I think you have to do. Just to get over the monotony of being on a bus with fuckin' 12 other guys, you have to lose it. Well I do.

I think Pabs was a wee bit pissed off that we were saying: "Look, it's not going to be parties on the bus, it's not going to be this." We were kinda stressing that it's not going to be like it this time if we have anything to do with it. I think that, combined with the fact Moby was coming up and a few other things, I think Pabs just felt he had had enough.

We were not young punks, we were more mature people than that.

It sometimes seemed a little bit false to me to be doing this punk thing all the time. It used to piss me off to see 40-year-old men at the front. We used to sing this song to the tune of *No Woman No Cry*, and it was "No Woman All Guys" because there was never any fuckin' women in the audience. So there were limits to what you could do afterwards! Guys with no teeth?

When we played Atlantic City Joe tried to drum up an audience on that one going round touting people saying, "What are you doing at 9.30 tonight? You want to be at the Trump Marina." Then he went to the radio station and pressing the buzzer going, "it's Joe Strummer from The Clash, can you let me in and give my song a spin? Yeah, used to be in a famous band."

It's all on Dick's film. Actually, it's quite touching. He's out there – "Would you play our new song?" But they were more interested in talking about the past.

Joe would sneak off with Dick Rude and do the side footage. I never knew about it until I saw the film and thought it was quite touching that he was actually out there working his balls off trying to get people to come and see us. He didn't have to.

When we played New York I think everyone was glad we had gone over because everyone else had cancelled. They was nothing to take their minds off of what had happened. There was a lack of ways to switch off. Playing New York was touching – when we played Minstrel Boy people were crying at the front.

When we really got the feel was at the end of the tour in LA when Joe started going on about the threat of a chemical attack. I felt perhaps he was winding us up. We were sat round at a hotel, talking about this threat. Do we want to go home? Do we want to stay? I wanted to stay really. Joe told us he had drove to the airport and was seeing if all the Middle Eastern people were leaving. If they were then they would have had a tip-off. We were all not sure at the time whether to believe him or not, whether to take him seriously. I think at the time he had sown a seed of doubt in the back of our heads.

It might just have been a moment of madness. Joe occasionally had moments of madness. Joe's point was, if it goes off who do you want to be with? Do you want to be here touring with the band or do you want to be with the ones you love, your family?

I loved playing in Japan because the crowds weren't all old people. There was an element of people that were fresh to it. They knew who Joe Strummer was but they probably hadn't seen him or weren't massive Clash fans. They would probably talk about one of our songs in the same way as one of the Clash's songs. I always felt it was more relaxed, further from home.

The way I used to approach a gig when we were close to home, I felt that people might know me or might know who I was and I'm not really pulling the wool over anybody's eyes. So it was always very different onstage when I played a British show.

When you go to somewhere like Japan and there's just no chance that anybody's ever going to know you – they don't know what you're like. I know it's silly to think like that but you do what you have to do to get by onstage. If you're not comfortable with your normal persona... if you're meant to be a rock guitarist and you're just standing there it's not very interesting for anybody.

I felt quite often when I was on home turf a bit more withdrawn, careful about what you do, do less, less happy to take a chance like playing a weird note. So I always felt like going to Japan, where the language is completely different, there's no familiar cultural issues. I always felt it was quite relaxing to play out there.

Unless you were bad it was unlikely that the fans would fuckin' give you a hard time really. The funny thing was, every time we went to Japan we were all really fuckin' good. We always played well as a band. It was always at the start of a tour or end of a tour and it was a breath of fresh air to go there and the professionalism of the Japanese people.

I had changed from bass to lead just because on the record I had played all these guitar parts – somebody had to play them. It's like you either fuckin' teach somebody else to play them or you just do it yourself and you get somebody to play the bass which is a bit more straightforward.

Maybe I just always wanted to get further up the front of the stage or something. There was definitely an element of that. It probably came around because I knew all the parts and it was easier to joint move on the band with Martin as a guitarist.

When I played bass my presence onstage was very different to when I played guitar. It used to fuckin' piss me off because the lighting guy would never put light on me. It used to really annoy me. There was always light on everybody else. I often had a word with him but there's no fucking excuse for it!

Do you stand in the middle or do you stand on the side? I was always in darkness. When you stand in the middle you're going to catch all the light that's there to catch Joe. The thing that pissed me off was Martin was always lit and he was on the opposite side of the stage. I thought what the fuck's with that? Is it just the white suit? He's not that good looking!

When you play bass it's like a cool instrument. You didn't do a lot of movement when you're playing the bass but when you're playing a guitar part you have to be a bit more angry. You change your character as time goes on.

When we were flying from Thessaloniki to Athens I got bitten by a cat. I was trying to feed it. It was a cat that was actually walking about in the airport, that's how fuckin' weird it was. I gave it a piece of my sausage and it dug its tooth into my finger by mistake.

I was absolutely shitting myself because of rabies. When we were driving past places I'd see a sign with a big Alsatian dog's head and a red line through it. I'd go "What the fuck's that?" Everyone would go, "That's the rabies sign!" So eventually I called the doctor and he gave me a tetanus and I asked him about rabies and he said, "We haven't had rabies in this country for fuckin' years."

I had been crapping myself. I had a hangover and was just quite easily impressionable and they were all fuckin' pissing themselves. I was cacking myself.

The Athens gig was great, a big basketball stadium.

We never went to South America because it just was not financially viable for us to go there. I was fucking looking forward to that one. I was looking forward to the week in Cuba at the end of it.

Brooklyn was great – you know what you're expecting the next night. I have good memories of that. I remember one time in particular sleeping in. We were about 45 minutes late when we woke up; we were meant to be onstage in half an hour or something. We had to get from the hotel in Manhattan to the venue. Martin and I had both fallen asleep in our rooms and nobody had woken us up, just assuming that we would be there.

That was a bit of a panic, I remember rushing there, rushing onstage, right go! It was a really good gig because you don't have time to worry about it. You don't get nerves or anything.

I used to get really bad nerves before going onstage. I suffered quite badly. I'd get myself really wound up and the slightest little thing that went wrong I'd go arghhhhhhhh.

By two or three songs in I was always all right. I always had a joint break round about middle of the set. That just came habitual. It got to the point where you wouldn't smoke during the day because you'd be worried about the sort of head space it would put you in before the show. But I'd always succumb because I'd see Martin or Joe smoking a joint. I'd take a puff and as soon as you'd have it your hands would be shaking. Quite a lot of the time when I'd go onstage I'd be so nervous but when I came offstage it's such a relief that it's done and it was good that it would take a good half hour to 45 minutes to even just come round to being a fuckin' normal person again. It affected me that strongly. It would get me so wound up that I'd really have to go and sit in a quiet room.

Joe always liked to fill the dressing room with people five minutes after we'd come off. I just couldn't deal with that. I wouldn't want to talk to anybody. That's what it takes to get me to go on a stage. The last thing you want to do is look stupid.

When I was with GUN I was a drummer and it never bothered me then. I had been a drummer since I was five so that was no big deal. I knew the stuff inside out; with GUN we had rehearsed and rehearsed and rehearsed.

But Joe always liked to keep this element of, you can't be over-rehearsed, you can't know what you're doing too much, you gotta always have that air of just scraping by the skin of your teeth. That's the way Joe liked it. He would never do a song ten times over just to get it right. He would discourage us to warm up at soundcheck. It's just on/off. Keep the energy and keep the tension for the show really. Everybody's sitting on edge – "What the fuck's he doing?" We would get to see the setlist about five minutes before we went onstage. That's just the way he liked it. Joe liked it quite ragged, Joe liked everybody on their toes.

I'm the opposite – I like everything to be in perfect control and know what's happening. I wasn't so bothered when I was the bass player. I wasn't so bothered when it wasn't my songs.

It's not that you want to be better. I'm a guitarist – it's something I'm not hugely familiar with and yet you're further forward. More people are looking at you and you've got to make a conscious effort to get it right. It's a combination of different aspects.

There was a point where I was throwing up before going onstage. Nerves, just threw up and shitting myself. I'm quite a nervy person anyway.

The Fleadh was terrible; it was a really rough show. Don't think we did enough rehearsals. At that point I used to live about half a mile away from Finsbury Park. There was just something about it. I didn't enjoy it.

One reason why I most probably didn't enjoy it was because it was the first time we played *Guitar Slinger Man*. I just didn't like the idea of *Guitar Slinger Man*. I just thought it was silly. I didn't like the title. It was a Johnny Rivers song. It was originally *Secret Agent Man*. We were approached to do it as a movie soundtrack. We did a version of it, which subsequently didn't get used. Then Joe thought it was so fuckin' different from the original song why don't we change the lyric as well and make it *Guitar Slinger Man*. I didn't want to do it. I just didn't feel we'd got it right. I didn't feel the music was right – it made me feel quite uncomfortable. It was a bluff onstage – we were up there bluffing it.

Hootenanny was weird again, on in the middle of the afternoon, sun beating down on yer. It was a strange, strange crowd, very rockabilly – not my scene. When we were there I got a new tattoo, fell down a wall and scratched it the day I got it. We broke into a swimming pool and I fell down a wall. It scratched all the ink out of it. Luke got his first tattoo in Las Vegas.

What else did we do?

When we played at Shepherd's Bush Empire and we did *Willesden To Cricklewood* we hadn't rehearsed it, we hadn't practised it – Joe was singing it in the wrong key. It was a disaster. When you're onstage you definitely know when it's not going well. The show didn't feel right to me. It might just have been me on a bad day.

The Move, Manchester, was another terrible gig. All my equipment was fucked. It probably wasn't as fucked as I was making out.

When we played T In The Park we just got a good buzz. It was the only place that time in the day where it was dark. I prefer playing in the dark. It was a nice slot. We were kinda worried – would the people be there? Then all the people came in and it was good. I enjoyed that one.

Paul Heaton initially wanted to write with Joe but because Paul and Joe basically did the same thing – they're both lyricists – I think Joe felt he would just introduce Paul to the team. So again he introduced him and then fucked off and went down the pub.

We did a couple of songs with Paul in the studio – a demo tape. He had a couple of songs he had already written and we co-wrote a few more songs.

I often wondered whether Joe felt a bit pissed off with that, that Paul took the full Mescaleros pretty much.

It got quite difficult. But it was good, it was nice to do. It was nice to pull in all these different musicians. To work at a nice big studio... I enjoyed it.

I never thought we'd end up playing. I think the album came out and it stiffed because Paul wanted to put it out before the Beautiful South's greatest hits album but the record company wanted the Beautiful South to come out first. As the result of that they didn't really put any promotion behind the Paul Heaton album. It got a few plays on Radio 2 but nothing much. It was a surprise that they relaunched the album after the Beautiful South's greatest hits and Paul decided he was going to do a few shows. Quite a different show, a lot quieter, more mellow but it was nice to play.

When The Mescaleros went to Japan was when we had the rethink about the album. That's when it hit us that what we had been doing was wrong, trying to put this studio project together and really what we should be doing was trying to capture elements of the live band because it was a really good live band at that point and we were exceptionally good in Japan. I think it just made everybody feel, right, OK we should try and capture this in some way, whether it's a live record or changing the way we're approaching this record. That's when we booked Rockfield. As soon as we came back from that we decided we were going to go into Rockfield.

I really enjoyed playing at the Royal Opera House. It was toffs that were yeahhhhh! We were the first rock band to ever play there. We had a good party afterwards.

I didn't enjoy the BIABH tour that much. I didn't think that was great. I was quite happy to do it but once we got to the venues and saw what we were dealing with and how stripped back it was... I'm a snob but I like the set to be good, the sounds to be good and the lights to be right but this was just exactly as it was advertised as – Bringing It All Back Home, low-budget tour, test out new material.

We experimented in Japan and it went down really well, playing jams onstage, trying out new songs, but you can't do that on the BIABH tour even though that's what it was initially designed for.

Because it was small venues the only people who were there were diehard fans. All they want to see is Clash songs and the hits. It just wasn't cutting it for me. We were trying to get new songs on the set and we didn't get them in until close to the end. Shitty places, out-of-the-way towns. It just wasn't very nice to do.

Acton was just another gig to me. The fact that it was just around the corner didn't really help. It's funny when you go home after soundcheck, have your dinner, and when you turn up for the show, you're not intact. Then just drive down at show time. It just didn't feel like you were on tour. The Mick thing, I don't know! It just wasn't to me what it was to a lot of people. I could hear what was going on, what he was playing and what he was singing. The visuals are great but it didn't sound very good.

I'm not taking anything away from what happened. It was really, really good that they reunited and buried the hatchet even if it was a bit impromptu and not on the cards. It was totally unorganised – Mick was just feeling that he had to be onstage and Joe sort of shouted him on. It was good to see it happening but it really overshadowed what we were trying to do. It was frustrating as the MD of the band.

I didn't like TJ's, it was rough, people hurtling all over you – I don't like that. Hastings was dire. That was an error from the word go. All these places were off the beaten track so that we could experiment, which never happened. So we just had to please the few people that came to see us.

The last night in Liverpool was a good one. It was quite a relaxed show. This is still the last time that I played on a stage.

Had we been given the chance to tour this album I thought it would have been good. I felt really confident. We had satisfied people's needs for the Clash songs, had built up a moderate new fanbase, and I thought it was all in place to be the album to go off and do.

Rockfield was good but again at the end of that it was, OK see yer after Xmas, nice one guys.

No big goodbyes or anything like that. We were to take it all up after Xmas.

Tymon was excluded from the whole project because the band was moving in a different direction and the *Global A Go-Go* thing – that was another time and a place. That doesn't always mean we're gonna write songs with fuckin' violins in it. He was a showman, Tymon, and he wouldn't be a team player – he was out there on his own. Some people liked that, some didn't. I just found it difficult to deal with.

It wasn't on a personal level at all. I've got no personal problem with Tymon Dogg whatsoever. But musically I do have a problem because he wasn't prepared to do what everybody was doing to make the greater good. I just felt that he went off on his own, he didn't really listen, he didn't really play as a team player. That got progressively more and more frustrating for me. That's why we ended up not really talking. Joe felt the same. The amount of conversations I had with Joe about "what are we going to do with Tymon?" Joe couldn't bring himself to distance himself from Tymon. I don't think Joe wanted to let him down or to dump him.

So we tried to figure out a way that he could still be involved but not as involved. I don't think Tymon was happy to take that on board really. He just saw it as a personal slant on him that we were trying to muscle Tymon out of the band but that's not the case. Because we'd always need him to play the songs that he was an integral part in making. So that's his choice.

Pablo Cook

"I was playing London Calling for fuck's sake, it was so great. We were truly excited about being in a fuckin' great rock 'n' roll band."
Pablo Cook

What Ants comes in and does is make it exciting. To actually try to put a band into motion can actually be a bit bland, you've got to do this, you've got to do that, get a manager etc.

Ants not only makes it exciting but also has the capability of putting it into motion. He knows so many people; he knows how to get a manager, plus he's artistic enough to know how to write the tunes to back it up. Ants has got the mouth and he's got the talent.

To me it was just fuckin' about, you know, Joe's a good friend, it's nice being with Bez, we're doing loads of drink, doing loads of drugs we're having a great time ... but Ant kinda grabbed it.

Before, The Hand of God were really just grooves with Joe and Bez just shouting over the backing track. He listened to what we had put together and said, "This is fuckin' great, but let's try this tune."

We had been down the studios for a fair while and Ged had left, then come back...

It was quite a long day; basically we were pissing around with it. It was along the lines that with Ged, if the part's been written then he will play the parts, whereas if it's rock 'n' roll and you've got a fag in your hand and it's basically entertaining then that's fine. I think what tipped the scales towards Smiley was that Smiles has a bit of that Keith Moon swing, shoulders down, enjoying himself, whereas with Ged it's a part.

I think there was a vote on it at the Battery; we struggled with it as everyone sat on the fence. As Joe said when you take out the drummer you struggle. It was a very stressful day. It was left to Ants to decide.

I first met Smiley when he was with Robbie Williams. I thought, hey he's a tasty little drummer, big smiles and all of that. I received a call and they said, "Robbie wants to use you as a percussionist, so can you come and audition?" I said I don't really do the audition thing and I'm a bit snobby like that. Listen, I'm not queuing up in a hallway, at nearly fuckin' 40 years old with loads of other percussionists.

Listen, the way this is going to span out is I'm going to come in, I'll do what I do, you'll hire me, it will cost you a lot of money and I'll be your percussionist. After some debate, I said I'll tell you what I'll do, I'll get the boys to bring my gear in, I'll whack out the songs and you're going to go "He's my man" and then we'll move forward from there!

So I turned up, had a little chat with Smiley, then I was told right, we're going to do this song now, I want you to play along to this, it's a song called *Mr. Keen*. I want you to come in on so and so, go out on the middle section and chorus ... do you think you'd be able to pick that up?

I said, "What are you talking about man? I fuckin' wrote it." Inevitably I didn't get the job, I was way too fuckin' cocksure. I was auditioning my fuckin' song. I think Smiley sussed it.

I was being told what to do on my tune.

Joe always conducted the band from behind his back with various hand signals; *Straight to Hell* was the most obvious with the highs and lows. With *Straight to Hell* it's a tune that either drags a little bit and you know you've got to get out because the tune itself is so intense. I personally think, and this is one fucking proud statement, that we played it better than The Clash.

If people have got their shoulders down and they need to have something else, then just kill it off. But more often than not, when we played that tune, Joe would drag them in. I was never really a big fan of that tune until I worked out the height on it.

Once Joe had drawn the crowd in you could have been there all night on just that one tune.

With touring you can basically judge it by the days of the week – be careful of those Tuesday night people!! They've had a long weekend, do they really want to be watching Joe Strummer and his bunch of "young students" doing that tune?

You get an angle as to how it's going to react. But if you take a Friday night at Sheffield Leadmill, fuckin' full house, just throw everything into the pot.

Joe was a great crowd controller. You've just got to be careful of those Tuesday nights. When I'm with Moby and we play Utah on a Monday/Tuesday, no drinking, Mormons, it's a case of do the hits, no jammin', knock it out and let's get the fuck out of here. On the whole touring is great; you get a few problems, getting stopped at cross-border customs etc. Actually Joe's theory was not to totally clear the bus out, but leave a little bit as they expect to find something, so why disappoint?

We had a lot of great fans; like that time in Japan, I was really surprised to see you there man – I just laughed. I just did not expect to see you there!

Willesden To Cricklewood was a programmed track – that means if it's programmed you had to rehearse it.

The bear brunt truth is if you're looking after somebody that is dependent on drugs in a band, you carry a lot of weight. You've got to remember that Topper Headon was the same with The Clash. When you take that element out of a band, next thing you know you've got two keyboard players.

There was no doubt that Ants' drug intake had spiralled out of control. I think Joe had really had enough of it – when you have a drug addict on tour with you, you know you've got to allow for him all the way down the line. I was always big on drugs and I would follow Ants' lead, but there are occasions when I would just think, that's out of control.

Timmy Tim would step in and he would look after Ants. There was a certain stage when I would look after Ants, get the drugs. I never treated drugs as a need for my music.

There's a part of Ants' character that just tipped it over the edge a little bit. The relationship between Joe and Ants, Joe just had to lose him because it was derogatory to what Joe was up to. Everything from timing to turning up on time, rehearsals, losing gigs, playing certain songs.

I think the split came when Joe thought, we've got to be our own musical directors because Ants can't do it.

Given the choice, we should have kept him on, should have paid for him to go to the Priory. We should have done that.

These types of decisions are quite heavy decisions; you're talking about somebody's life here. A lot of us were cokeheads, heavy drinkers. Everybody has their own problems. At that particular time Antony had a real problem and the mistake I think Joe made and I think I made as well, I think we made it with Smiley as well, was we should have taken it on board.

What we should have done is, fuckin' hell, can we put Ants into rehabilitation? What does that cost? Five grand at the Priory, and Smiley's overdoing it because of this or that – can we not get him to do this?

You're always forever adjusting what you think you did wrong, which is what I'm doing now, but you can't do that at the time – you can't see it.

But at the time I think somebody in a neutral position, no need to have been a psychiatrist, would have said, right put Antony into rehabilitation, somebody needs to speak to Smiley and we would have still been playing in the band today. At that particular time we just didn't know.

Getting rid of Ants was a bad mistake. It was fucking bad. Two mistakes – Smiley bad mistake, Ants bad mistake – and that's when it just hit the slippery slope. I mean, I'm sure the latter part of Joe's career was fantastic, but there was something about The Mescaleros at that particular stage. If you look at the photos you know, we're sweating, sweating on it – fuckin' musos.

The one thing I got from Joe at my last gig in LA was the fact that we didn't seem to be working hard enough.

Smiley and Ants were quite an integral part. Antony Genn's departure is not just a flick of the switch; it was quite a large step. I don't know what your opinions on Joe's career after that are? What do you think?

They had flown me over to LA. I had that plastic fuckin' surgeon, pissing around with my eye. I turned up at the gig; it was lovely to see the people. I knew there was something up anyway. Joe was pissed that I had left. But he knew I was a fuckin' prostitute anyway, he didn't mind that side of it – he knew that I have to supply my family, fair enough.

But when I turned up there and it was all that acoustic stuff, I thought what is going on here?

I think there are certain parts of Joe's set on the latter which Martin and Scott did, which really highlight what Joe was really after. Certain parts I thought were really good – music can be sensitive. You can do a version of *White Riot* as a folk song... you can do it. But your average punter says turn that fucker up.

I didn't ever think Joe would ever get into that. We did some gigs where we did that tune, we knew it was cool, but to do it as a band I don't think worked and that's what turned me off.

We needed to turn it up – we needed to get going. That's where it sort of grew, with the loss of Smiley, the loss of Ants. I've said it to you before, that digression for me, Joe knew it anyway. I just looked at Laura; my missus is a good judge. Acoustic guitar on *Rock The Casbah* and we'll say no more about it!

Joe knew what was going on but I think that with the latter part of The Mescaleros, without sounding too philosophical about it, I think he was directing himself more in a sort of Neil Young-type way. He was trying to get songs out where all you need to do is play them.

I don't think that version of The Mescaleros was the version that was his original idea.

His original idea was hard and core. We replicated The Clash to a certain extent, which sounded great as a band, the middle part of it; the folky thing just didn't happen.

The latter part of it where Joe was no longer with us would have probably been in my eyes (and my ears) – would probably have been just very, very simple, just Joe on his own, That Neil Young in a truck thing. It would have been very simple. I think that's what he was heading at. I just didn't get that bit in between.

On reflection I wasn't really thinking it, I just had a sense for it, that that whole section was probably where Joe was working towards the realisation that he could do this. Again it's the Neil Young thing. I'm the songwriter, I write the songs.

The bear brunt reality of it is, if you listen to Joe singing *London Calling* or *Nitcomb* on his own, it's going to blow your fuckin' head off – it's going to blow your FUCKING HEAD OFF.

I was at the studio with Keith Allen mixing and stuff; Laura called me up and said, "I'm coming round to the studio straight away". Normally when Laura rings when I'm in the studio it's about kids' stuff. I'm thinking, oh my God, the fuckin' kids, one of them has fallen over and broken their leg. Nobody ever comes round to the studio whilst I'm there because I can't handle people around me. Laura said, "I've got to come round to the studio." I said, "Listen don't come round the studio and don't bring anyone round," so Laura said, "Joe's dead, Luce has just called me!"

I said, "What? What are you talking about?" I said, "Laura you need to chill out." I put the phone down and carried on mixing. That was the angle I took.

Although Smiley describes it much better than I could, I was just rattled.

It gradually hit me that Joe had died. Laura kept saying, "Are you all right?" I said, "Yeah," I was trying to hold on.

I called Slats and Scott, you know people I hadn't spoken to for ages. I said something's happened here, we need to speak to each other. So we all spoke to each other, nothing to do with The Mescaleros.

Keith Allen came into the studios. Keith had heard, he had bought some beautiful bottles of wine with him. We had a drink and then that's when I cut up. From that I don't remember anything until the cab driver dropped me off.

When I got in I just said to Laura, "He's dead." That was it. That was the end of it. We had to go through the whole thing with Titus, as Joe was his godfather.

From the moment I heard Joe Strummer had died, musically I was prepared to take on the whole thing but as soon as Keith came onboard my whole musical thing went out the window.

Smiley

"Joe Strummer was a legend when he put out *Rock Art And The X-Ray Style*. Those same people gave him a couple of stars and said he was an old has-been churning out a load of old stuff. Those same people are now jumping on the bandwagon about how great he was.
Joe Strummer was always fuckin' great.
   Smiley

When I joined on day one, I didn't really know a lot about Joe, the timing of The Clash... I missed it, just that bit too young. My mate Phil showed me the cover of *Earthquake Weather* and I can remember thinking what a great cover it was, with Joe standing on the diving board. So when I got this call to go and play at the Battery, which was through Martin and Scott, the thing that hit me was how slapdash it all was, so disorganised.

It wasn't like I had the sense, "Oh I've got to get this gig." I did a bit of drumming with him and then I did some recording of *Techno D-Day* for them to check out whether they were going to use Ged or me. I left it with Ants, with me saying, "Thanks a lot. Look don't sweat over it. If you want to give me a call, great; if not, no problem, let Ged do it." I had only been there a day, I saw Joe and said goodbye and hopefully see you again and he said, "Yeah, you will."

The story goes that Ants, who was living in a house opposite the Battery, was going to make a decision. When he left the studio he had chosen Ged and by the time he had crossed the road he had changed his mind and he had chosen me. That was the official line, so then he gave me a call.

I had no idea of what I was going into. We started rehearsing at the Battery, simultaneously to recording the album. Most of the drums had been done, but Joe said I think we should really let him play on at least one song, which was *Forbidden City*, which I did in one take. That was a really decent thing to do. He didn't have to do it actually. To this day I only played on that one track, did all these gigs but only played on one song. The only benefit for me was they put this compilation album together from the Big Day Out and the song they picked was *Forbidden City* which was a bit of a blessing to me.

When we started off, the early gigs were tiny venues. It wasn't until we got to America that I suddenly realised who it was that I was drumming behind; seriously I didn't really have an idea who this guy was. I just thought it was a guy who used to play in The Clash and not many people particularly knew him and not many people were particularly arsed about him.

But when we got to America, the vibe over there was incredible. People were coming up to me and saying, this guy (Joe) changed my life, and wow man! You're playing with Joe Strummer. When this started happening dozens of times every night, you suddenly realise who it is I am playing for.

I think it was when we went back to America to do the big tour in November 1999 that I suddenly did really realise it and I had started to get to know Joe as a person as well. It was one night, 'cause Joe used to love to go out to just a bar in the middle of nowhere and he would just get to know the locals, that was his thing, and I remember going out to this bar, God knows where – it was some small city in the middle of America. It was me, Joe and Timmy, we got free drinks all night, everyone sitting around chatting and they took pictures of me and Joe and the crowd of people. I know now that somewhere in the midwest of America there's a picture of me and Strummer on the wall of this bar.

When we were playing places like Los Angeles, San Francisco, the Fillmore, places like that, it was incredible. The Fillmore has got massive framed photographs all the way around of people who have played there; it blew my mind because every legendary act ... ever! had played there. We played there a couple of times and we filled it out.

The other thing that gave it away was when we were playing festivals, all the other bands – Catatonia, Offspring, Foo Fighters, Chilli Peppers, Primal Scream – Joe was the focal point, the one all these bands wanted to meet.

The two main ones for me were Glastonbury, which was incredible. We were on at about 4.00 in the afternoon and I was just walking around the site near the main stage and Billy Bragg was playing and Billy said, "The only reason I'm here today is because Joe Strummer's playing," and everybody cheered. I thought of all the people playing here this weekend, Manics, Stereophonics, they were all desperate to come and see Joe.

I remember at V2000 I went over to say hello to Paul Weller like some starstruck idiot, and he was saying to me, "Where's Joe, I'd like to see him." Paul Weller giving me respect for being Joe's drummer...

I really started noticing how everybody else was falling over themselves at festivals – big names, your Noel Gallaghers and Paul Wellers, they just couldn't get enough of him. As Noel Gallagher said, "You're Joe's drummer."

The biggest crime for me was the Big Day Out; they put us on a very small stage in comparison to the others. You see the Big Day Out had two massive stages side by side. As one band walked off on one stage, the next came on the other, but we were on a really small stage right away from the main stages. But every night we'd have Primal Scream there, Chilli Peppers would be in disguise at the side of the stage... Dave Grohl and Chris Shiflett of Foo Fighters would be there.

To me, Joe should have been on the main stage, without a shadow of a doubt. There was a thousand people watching us. He should have been one of the main live acts. To me, still to this day that's still the biggest mistake that happened; they just didn't realise who he was.

It just grew and grew on me that he wasn't just formerly of The Clash, a band from the 70s and 80s. It was very much in the professional circle, the music circle, that he was worshipped.

When we did the May 2000 tour, to me that was when it ended. Brixton Academy was the best ever – we were brilliant that night and to me it went downhill, it never was the same, there wasn't that good vibe between the band any more after that.

I really liked Ants – I've a lot of time for him, he is such a talented man. But Ants had become a real arse. I had a couple of run-ins with him. What used to happen was, because he was musical director, he felt it was within his power to kinda point things out and instruct people. For some reason I became his scapegoat. He would say something to me after I had played a night really spot-on and he would pull me for something so minute just to assert his authority and it had started to get on my tits after a while. We had a couple of shouting matches. I told him I weren't interested, he was just trying to prove a point and I wasn't having it. I had had enough.

There was one point when I just thought about quitting. We had played Milan – it was an amazing show and after the show, the crowd was baying for an encore. We were just sitting in the room, just about to go back on, and he said he thought I was dragging all night, playing everything slow. Fuck me, I had just played *Safe European Home* and *Tommy Gun* full on. I pulled everyone in the room and said, "Do you agree with him?" And of course they were all very tight. You got to remember that I was on the outside a little bit because Ants and Pabs, Scott and Martin were a little gang and they were very hard to penetrate. They all put their heads down and agreed with him. So I told Ants to fuck off, poke it up his arse and just walked out, did the encore.

Joe asked me, "What's the matter, what's the matter?" I just said, "No it's cool Joe, honestly, don't worry about it." Gary Robinson saw it – I played the encore with a face like thunder, finished the last song, just walked off, walked past the dressing-room. Gary said, "Stay there a minute, don't move." He grabbed his coat and said, "Come on, you and me are going to a bar somewhere and grab a drink." He sat down with me and said, "Look, I've just watched what's gone on and you were absolutely right." That was the lowest point for me.

Being in a band is like having five wives, you've got a lot of egos going on. It's not healthy to put 14 men on a bus for 28 days, it's not a healthy environment in any way, shape or form.

When you have got the drug thing as well, people go downhill. Plus, if you don't take drugs, which I don't, you are on the outside the whole time and it becomes quite lonely. Joe saw this a lot – he saw me on the outside. I never used to whinge about it and there was a night on the bus, I was just sitting alone with a glass of red wine and a cigarette, and I remember him coming up behind me and put his arms around my neck and said, "You've got the right idea, you come offstage unwind, get out and about in the cities, have a look round."

The reason that I stayed so long was because of Tim; I had someone to hang out with. When we went to New York, me and Timmy went out, looked around, visited the sights – Statue of Liberty, baseball stadiums etc. Look, I realised how fortunate I was. I was being paid to be in America, I made the most of it and I am really glad I did. Also Joff the T-shirt man. When we were out in the midwest, me, Joff and Tim used to go and find pool halls, drink beer and play pool for hours. That was the division between the band and me in a lot of ways.

There was a period when certain people didn't know what day it was, it was ridiculous. Pablo could take it or leave it; if he wanted to go on a three-day bender he would, but then Pabs could be straight for five days. I used to room with Pabs a lot. I found him fascinating – really interesting character, lovely bloke, really top, top geezer.

Pabs was clever because he could put his foot in either camp. He could quite easily go to a museum, go and see some art gallery. He wasn't addicted to anything.

Pabs was Joe's boy, no doubt about it. He was the one who had the closest cling to Strummer, but he was also the closest to Ants. He pulled more strings than you think.

Ants liked to think he pulled the strings. Pabs had Joe's ear.

Joe liked me as a person; I think he liked Martin and Scott creatively. The biggest compliment I ever got was when Luce let it be known I was her favourite. Joe's daughter Jazzy also told me, after I left and I went to a gig in Brixton, that she was gutted when I left. From my point of view that's lovely.

I had a really good relationship with Joe, but my relationship with the boys was hard. I gotta say I struggled with Ants. Ants is one of the most intelligent people I have ever met, but he could also be so bombed out and I found that quite hard to take. Pabs I loved to bits, but I knew when to leave Pablo alone, when he was going on one.

Martin and Scott are Martin and Scott!! Martin I love, Scott I love, but Martin and Scott together, they were like one person, joined at the hip. I found them together quite hard work, but on their own or when they were sitting either side of me, smashing.

You say you are due to meet Scott later. Give him my love; I have nothing but love and respect for him. They were quite overpowering as a pair – they are incredibly talented those two. Scott's an amazing drummer, so when you are drumming in a band and you know there's a person who can take your place at any second...

I'm trying to give you a balanced idea here that it wasn't kinda all roses and amazing.

I can remember Joe going off on one when we went on the American tour in November 1999, first few days. He hated it, because Andy Boo wasn't there. Gary Robinson, second gig, threatened to quit – he was out of there, didn't want to stay.

There was a terrible vibe, because we got there and Des couldn't get in on his visa; it was basically just wee Gordon and that was it on the roadcrew.

Joe didn't have his mate Andy to sit with because they were really very close.

I said to Gary, if you go I'm going with you.

I ended up sharing with Joe Campbell on that tour. I really love that guy. Band and crew don't usually share, but with five in a band, work it out – who the odd one out is? Timmy Tim didn't officially have a room; he just used to jump in with anyone.

Looking back, I loved all of the crew, Justin Grearly was a lovely guy, little wee Gordon was smashing, Des was smashing, bit of a big old brutus of a geezer but ... Dave the drum tech ... I liked them all.

On that tour we had an American drum tech, TC. Everyone loved him, Joe loved him to bits.

Joe's original guitar tech at the beginning of that tour was an American guy; Joe just met him in a record shop and just said, "Do you want to come and tech for me?'

He was awful – the crew hated him!

When Andy Boo came back, that's what put Gary in a really bad position, because Gary had sacked him and Joe changed his mind. Gary had to get him back and Andy Boo wasn't particularly cool about it, he kinda rubbed Gary's nose in it.

I was actually getting on really well with Martin at the time, which is strange because there was a lot of bad vibes going on. I actually got a lovely text from Martin the other day; I do like him, he is great. I also think that if I went out for a beer tonight with Scott I'd get on really great with him. But together!!

It was actually Martin and Scott who took this all away from me, because Scott played all the drums, even though I was the band's drummer. They were producing, they had the budget.

There was one night that they used as the real chance to get me out the door. I was playing down the road from the Battery, in Willesden, with another band. We didn't finish until 2am and I said I was going to pop into the studio, but this is where the misunderstanding comes from. I had heard all the drums were down for the album, so I didn't want to go into the studio because I thought it would embarrass people, so I didn't go in. Joe took that as a snub – he thought I didn't want to be part of it all.

When it came to going out on tour they just thought, we've got to get another drummer – he's not interested, because he didn't turn up on that night. It was just one of those things.

If it was about me as a person I could take it, because everyone is not always someone's cup of tea. But when it comes to drumming I knew I had played drums with The Mescaleros the best I could have done.

So the time had come! I have really great memories of it. When I went to see them at Brixton that was when I realised I wasn't all that gutted.

I remember when I lost the job with Robbie and I went to see Robbie play it broke my heart.

Luke is a great drummer; I must say that, lovely chap.

To be honest, if you're going to go out, Wembley Arena supporting The Who is a pretty good place to go out as opposed to Margate in front of 300 people. I had no interest after that to be honest. I learnt so much being with Joe. I found Joe Strummer one of the most genuinely loving, attentive, intelligent, compassionate men I have ever known in my life. I knew him as Joe, not Joe Strummer of The Clash the rock idol, just Joe, and he was a genuine lovely fella who I adored.

It did show me a lot about life, because life goes on because people like yourself, Nyle and Timmy all said, "Oh, I can't believe it, you're not playing any more, it won't be the same." But the next gigs, everyone's at the gigs, you're all enjoying yourselves, having a great time.

If I could put it into an analogy with football, when Zola played for Chelsea, everybody loved Zola – fans, players etc. I'm not blowing my own trumpet but I always got on so well with everybody. I was Joe's drummer. I got on with the fans, they were always lovely to me. I like to think I was lovely to the – it was great.

I like to think the fans would still remember me because I used to give them time. I'm just a genuinely nice guy same as anybody really.

But life goes on. Joe Strummer didn't stand on the stage every night and go, "Nah, it's not the same because Smiley's not behind me," because he had Luke behind him, who's a great drummer. Same as Robbie with Chris Sharrock.

You all went to the gigs and you got heavily involved, doing the site. You were genuinely lovely to me, all of yer. When I did go to Brixton – it was fabulous, it was a great last thing to do – even Giuseppe, all of you were genuinely lovely and decent to me and it was great to see you all.

It shows you what Joe was like. I hadn't seen him for ages and as I went into the dressing-room, he went, "Smiley, grab us a beer" and that was it.

To sum this up, you don't realise how good something is until it's gone. You don't quite realise. The two examples are, I never realised whilst I was drumming for Joe Strummer how good it was, how lucky I was and what a legendary figure I was part of, which I will remember to the day I die.

Look, those DVDs you've just brought me (from Sukwoon). You haven't got a clue how much that means to me, you really don't know how much having that forever now means. An account of my life where I was lucky enough to play with one of the greatest frontmen in rock history. Me, Smiley. I still go and play in pubs every week. I'm truly blessed to have done that and I never realised how lucky I was to have also been a friend of his.

The other example to prove that is, now that Joe is not with us any more, suddenly everybody realises what a legend he was. Because when he was alive all those journalists now who rave about the last album, "Oh Joe Strummer is a legend, Joe Strummer is a legend."

Joe Strummer was a legend when he put out *Rock Art And The X-Ray Style*. Those same people gave him a couple of stars and said he was an old has-been churning out a load of old stuff. Those same people are now jumping on the bandwagon about how great he was.

Joe Strummer was always fuckin' great!

When you lose somebody you realise what an incredible person they were.

I'm very proud to be in this book as well, a book documented when I was an integral part of something like this. I'm very flattered; I can't do enough for yer.

I can't tell yer how impressed I am the way you're doing it, the reasons you're doing it, because you should be cashing in on this and you're not and I think what shows me the kind of person you are is, you went from a fan to an integral part of the band's life.

It should be applauded that it shows that the good guys do win sometimes!

I'll always remember the time in Japan, they're moments that I will never forget and you were a big part of that. I've never known anything like it. I've told this story hundreds of times in the pubs where this guy just turned up – he just turned up!!

No hotel, no tickets for the gigs, no passes and was shocked that we invited you in the dressing room. For goodness' sake, you had come all the way from the other side of the world.

It was nice to become friends with you as opposed to you're a fan of Joe Strummer. You're my mate, you're one of my best friends and now that it's all finished and Joe's not here any more, you'll find that people like Martin, Scott, Pablo, Ants, me, you, we're talking... that was then, this is now. There's no bad feeling towards anybody.

I think it's great that you're seeing Scotty tonight – pass on my regards to him, I hope he is doing well. I'll be really interested in what he is doing now, same with Martin. I keep meaning to ring John Blackburn.

I must stay in touch with all those guys. They were great people and they were a great band.

When you said you didn't want any money for doing the book, one, I thought that was typically you, two, you mentioned doing it genuinely because it was four years of your life that meant such a lot.

I know you bandied about some ideas about what you wanted to do with the money. But when you mentioned about the kids, that to me is the most amazing brilliant gesture, because it's like Strummer's legacy is being given to our next generation and my daughter Georgia will benefit from the fact that I played drums for a living legend and she will get the benefit out of that and when she is older she will know where that came from. Put in the back of the book the next generation of Mescaleros, pics of the kids.

What an honour for my daughter to be in a book about Joe Strummer. He is going to be a legend forever.

It's like a legacy from Joe and if he's watching now, bless him, he's most probably sitting with Jimmy Hendrix and John Lennon having a chat and a brandy. He'd be going "Yeah, I like that."

I'm still drumming, mainly drumming for Archive – just done my fourth album with Archive who are an amazing band and will hopefully get the recognition here that they get in Europe. \they are massive in Europe. I've got a lot of touring coming up with them this year.

Had a nice little tickle with The Mock Turtles last year, *Top of The Pops*, touring, the best of album, that was great – I love those guys.

Done a few other albums with various people. Carried on playing in the pubs, cover bands, done a few nights on my own, just me and my guitar.

Now I'm going into song writing. I've just sold a couple of songs to a pop star in Spain – *Sell Your Soul* was one of them. Me and Johnny (Wilks) look like we're going to get a publishing deal to sell our songs.

I'm writing for television. I've got a song coming out in a Hollywood film soon, *See You On The Way Down*, a Chevy Chase film.

I'm writing a BBC theme tune at the moment and hopefully that will lead on to other theme tunes.

I'm just trying to find that balance between writing and playing. Life's good at the moment.

Tymon Dogg

"That song (Minstrel Boy) was always a bone of contention in the band.

It had been a bone of contention in The Clash and ended up being a bone of contention in The Mescaleros as well"

Tymon Dogg

I met Joe and Pabs at the Poetry Olympics at the Astoria in October 2000. I just bought a ticket and went as a punter. I met up with Joe and said "hi" and he said, "Where's your instrument? Do you mind if you play with us tonight?" I said I didn't mind because I owed him a gig anyway.

The last time I'd seen Joe was at the Acklam Hall in 1999. I hadn't seen him for several years, I turned up late and he wasn't ready to play when he turned up. I hadn't expected Joe to come up from Somerset. I said, "Let's go and play on the stage. Have you got your guitar?" Joe said "no", so I said, "Let's go and find one." It was a memorial concert. We got a drummer; Clive Timperley from The 101ers was there. We did *Lose This Skin, Junco Partner* and stuff like that. It was great because I don't think Joe had played for a while.

So when I met him at the Astoria and he said, "Where's your instrument?" I thought "Ummm, the last time I met you I made you play." So this time I said sure, I'll go and get it from the car.

When I came back Martin Carthy was coming out of the loo. I introduced Martin to Joe. Joe said to Martin, "Do you fancy joining us?"

We went on stage – did four or five numbers; *Silver And Gold* was one. When we came off it was a shame because we had just got going. Joe was really getting into it.

I think it was that moment when Joe said, "I think we should keep going" that we both started thinking about working together. Joe said when he came off stage that "that was the most enjoyable gig ever because everyone was listening to me. I never felt like that before."

Afterwards we went to the Groucho Club and we played music all night until about seven in the morning. Jah Wobble and John Cooper Clarke were there.

Before we got going on *Global*, we did talk about just Joe, Pablo and me touring.

A couple of days later Joe called me and said, "Do you fancy coming down to the studios?" So I went down and it was just Joe and Pablo there. They were working on *Gamma Ray*. A few hours later Martin and Scott turned up and the first thing we did together was *Silver And Gold*.

We were knocking out basically from scratch a tune a day. I was sleeping on the couch at the Battery. I wasn't even in the band; I just popped into the studio. Five days later or five tracks later I left.

On the last night we all had a Guinness before we were going our separate ways and Pockets had brought this Irish songbook. Me and Joe spotted this song and we both started smiling because we remembered this particular song had been a bone of contention in The Clash as Joe had wanted to play this song when he was in The Clash, but Mick hadn't been that keen. The song was *Minstrel Boy* – it was the first song I ever learnt. My mum used to sing that song to me all the time when I was very young.

Joe said, "Let's go back to the studios and pop it down." So me, Martin, Joe and Richard went back to the studio. I just played the violin on that song and that version that's so long with me just playing the violin is actually me teaching Martin the song as he didn't know it. I got kinda bored actually, so I started messing around. I didn't think any of it would be used but Richard Flack, who is just amazing, used it. He had this way of getting us before we knew what we were doing.

Joe and I actually said, "We could put out an album every six months." We had such a lot of songs.

I was leaving and Joe said to me, "Hang on, there's this big showdown on Sunday." This turned out to be the day *Bhindi Bhagee* was written. Me, Pockets and Joe were wandering about on the street trying to find a café to get something to eat. As it was a Sunday, it was difficult and we went to a lot of different cafés. This guy called "Stretch" did actually come up to Joe and said, "Are you Joe Strummer?"

We met Stretch again just after we recorded *Bhindi Bhagee* and we took him into the studios to listen to it. He went "Wow." Joe did say, "Sorry about the mushy peas!"

Joe said, "Look, we're going so good now, I don't want to stop these songs. Let's not do the Who tour – let's blow it out?"

I said, "Go along and I'll help you out and we'll play these new songs."

Joe said, "OK, we'll do that then, but on one condition – you start with *Minstrel Boy*." So when we played at the 100 Club we opened with that song.

Something happened to Scott and he missed the Who tour, so we were really missing electric guitar. But this then opens up other possibilities. Later we had a similar problem with *Mondo Bongo*, which has no electric guitar on the record. For some reason Scott insisted we had electric guitar onstage for that song, but it never really worked. It wasn't an electric guitar song.

I don't play without enjoying it; I feel I owe that to myself and the people that have come to see us and made that journey. Something me and Joe had learned, approaching 50, was that without people listening or dancing you wouldn't even be there.

I wouldn't put a note on *Bhindi Bhagee* until I had heard the lyrics. Martin was getting a bit anxious but I said, "Not until Joe's done the lyrics." Once I heard the lyrics it was: right, now I can think Indian.

Joe put the tune of *Johnny Appleseed* to a mandolin, I wasn't sure why he was waiting so long to bring in the voice. It was because that little tune started.

I wrote *Mondo Bongo* on the way to the studios, which isn't really what I normally do. I like to write the tune in the studios when we're working together. Joe said to me, "I want to do a song called *I Caught You Dancin'*" which I wrote in 1974. Joe said, "I remember you playing it on a Spanish guitar in Eastbourne."

I replied, "Let's leave the past right where it is and let's do some new stuff. We can always go back there."

After knowing Joe for nearly 30 years I was still really impressed by the fact that he could come up with lyrics to a tune like that.

There's a lot of history with me and Joe, we had been through a lot together. Joe didn't start playing until he was about 22, three years after I met him. When I first met Joe he was an artist, at St Martin's. I went down to the college with him. He was having his work assessed and he had been up all night doing the picture and whilst Joe's work was being assessed he fell asleep – he was snoring. His assessor was actually Frank Auerbach. Joe left a short while after that.

When we did the first instore gig Joe's guitar strap snapped – he'd had it from 1976 – and at the same show my pre-amp conked out which I had had from 1976. The record store gigs were good, though it is a bit funny to see people's heads popping over record racks.

When we did the Brian Setzer gig it was a bit cold for us really. It's such a big place and not all the people were in. Pablo did a gig with us, which was nice. I think percussion was an important part of what Joe was doing and wanted to do more of in the future as well.

When we went to New York, we did the David Letterman show and the following morning I got up quite early and got the subway down to Ground Zero to have a look around, to get a feel. When I met up with Joe later in the day I told him I had got the subway down to Ground Zero and he said, "So did I. I got up early and got the subway down." He wanted to get aware of what had happened.

Everyone on the David Letterman show seemed to be in a state of shock. Even the woman doing the make-up before the show had a baby in a pram which she was rocking and had a big dog by her. The whole place was in such a state of shock, you could get on the subway and it would be virtually empty. If the subway stopped between stations you could feel the panic. The high buildings, where they used to be a symbol of power, were symbols of vulnerability.

We only did the Letterman show because some other band had pulled out. We went because you can't back down when the going gets tough. You might as well stop your life right now, if you're scared to go somewhere. Tragedy always happens at the least expected time. I think it was not only a case of we had the balls to do it; we had the minds to think through it.

We opened with *Minstrel Boy*; it was pure coincidence that song had been taken on board as the fire brigade's tune.

When we got to Los Angeles the papers had caught on about *Minstrel Boy* and one had done a bit of a spread. So when I got to the dressing room I just left the newspaper open at the page. That song was always a bone of contention in the band. It had been a bone of contention in The Clash and ended up being a bone of contention in The Mescaleros as well.

I grew up with that song – the lyrics were very special. It shouldn't really have gone in *Black Hawk Down*. It doesn't fit with the lyric of *Minstrel Boy*. It's about the poet who goes to war with his harp and never wanted the instrument to be played by the enslavers and smashed it before he died. Joe said to me, "That's you."

I just kept a low profile. I'm not anti-American; I actually like Americans and I could quite happily live there. I don't generalise about any people.

I lived in America, that's how I came to do *Sandinista* I was living in New York. If it wasn't for family commitments I would have stayed a lot longer.

One of the great things about Joe was he sometimes he didn't think and did something which gave him a lot of energy. He didn't deliberate too much. Joe was a cosmic rocker.

I really enjoyed the tour in Japan; it was my first time there.

When we played at the Concorde, Brighton, the sound was weird with all the glass sides. We didn't do a proper soundcheck as a couple of the lads couldn't get there early enough but as we came offstage the guy who owns it said, "That's the best gig we have ever had here. We really enjoyed it."

I loved the Glasgow gig; it was a particular nice feel. I played with John Cooper Clarke who was supporting. At Brixton, I was not too sure about playing with John, because of finishing John's set with a violin solo and we were starting with *Minstrel Boy* in our set. I said to Joe, "You don't mind me playing with John, do you?" Joe said, "Nah, nah, course not."

I said to John, "I don't know whether I can make it." John Cooper Clarke replied "Tymon, do you want me to beg?" I said, "OK, I'll be there – the idea of you begging, no way!" I do like John; he's a good lad. Joe loved John Cooper Clarke.

Mick Jones was there that night and I said to Mick, "You can't be replaced, you know that, Mick – there's no way that you'll ever be replaced."

I've known Mick since 1976 and I worked with Mick separately after The Clash split. I had a whole different relationship with Mick and I could see how there were a lot of differences between Mick and Joe but I also could see a hell of a lot of similarities between them.

Brixton Academy was most probably one of the most theatrical gigs we did. Andy the lighting tech even had a little x on the stage where I would stand to hit the lights. They pulled all the stops out.

When we did Five Nights I loved it.

I never wanted to hoist my own strengths at all. It was the anniversary of recording *Sandinista* at Electric Lady. Joe said, "It's the anniversary of *Lose This Skin* and I said, "If we're going to do it, let's just do it." Joe wanted to do it. The only lad that was interested in doing it was Martin; the other lads weren't interested in doing it at all. Scott said, "It had nothing to do with the band and nothing to do with The Clash and why don't you do a G.U.N. song?"

Anyway, I just put it to them and said, "Look, I don't care who does it, I'm going to do a solo," Joe said, "I'm going to do it." Martin said, "I'm doing it." So it was just the three of us and when we started the crowd erupted so much, Luke suddenly appeared so fast behind the drumkit. Strangely enough, my D string broke – it's in the key of D and the string broke in the middle of it. Before the show me and Joe were working out the chords in the dressing room and I remember Eddie Izzard was there and he was most probably thinking we were a pair of weirdos. Joe and I had played it together at the Acklam Hall in 1999.

The Hootenanny was a bit strange, like country and western rallies, but I enjoyed them.

When we played at Shepherd's Bush, I had parked my VW outside on the yellow lines. After the gig when we were about to get the bus up to Manchester, I said to Joe, "I've got to deal with the VW." It was like two o'clock in the morning. He should have really given me a bollocking for leaving it there. Joe said, "I know – Hilton car park." So I drove over there. It was full, so I came back. I was trying to find a place where there was no line. The bus was following me all round London. We got separated, so I thought, "Oh well, only got myself to blame. I'll have to get the train up in the morning."

Then all of a sudden along came "Plank" saying, "We've been sent out to find yer." Joe had sent him out to find me.

When I got back to the coach, I sat down and Joe and I had a long chat about "Internet Anthony". Joe asked what did I reckon about the internet and the site. I said, look, I told Joe I had heard about Anthony with his credit card getting to Japan that time and coming back with a box of chocolates and getting them thrown in the bin. I said, "look, these guys are so chuffed to be doing this." Joe sat there all excited and said, "I can see Ant now bringing those chocolates back and getting them thrown in the bin and then doing the internet." Joe was really laughing and kept saying, "I keep seeing Ant going to the bin and getting those chocolates out."

Joe trusted a man that would do all that to see the band.

When we played Cambridge, it was great for Joe; he loved Bob Dylan, Woody Guthrie, and the whole folk thing. I can't speak for the other lads but it meant a lot to me and Joe, playing there. The whole folk tradition. Joe loved that tradition. Its one of the biggest folk festivals in the world. He was being welcomed into the tradition. When we walked offstage Joe turned to me and said, "We earned that!"

In 1974 I wanted Joe to get on with what he wanted to do. I was writing a lot of songs, Joe wanted to get the The 101ers together, they were playing straight *Route 66* Chuck Berry songs and by that time I was writing very different things.

Joe was left-handed and he was playing on my guitar right-handed. He got it together and his enthusiasm, his charisma meant a lot of musicians joined him. I never joined The 101ers as a person. I'd get up and play with them now and again, such tunes as *Dog Dirt On My Shoe* and another one called *Too Late For Me, Minute Too Soon*. The 101ers were a retro rock band and I didn't think at that time we could work together, not like we could with The Mescaleros.

Before I worked with The Clash, Joe had come round to where I lived to try and get me to play on the second album, *Give 'em Enough Rope* on the last track. At the time I was living with a couple of members of The Slits in Elgin Avenue. I had been away and when I got back Paloma said Joe had been round looking for me.

It was actually Mick who got me involved in *Sandinista*.

When we talked about the Bringing It All Back Home tour, I can remember Simon Foster saying it's so mad it might just work. With such short notice of the BIABH tour, without the internet site nobody would have known – the places would have been empty.

When we played the Opera House, it was difficult for me because when we got onstage my gear was just a pile of wires – nothing was plugged in.

When we played at Acton we were sitting in the dressing room and I don't think the people running it knew what a "rider" was. There was just a bottle of cider vinegar there and I think maybe a Kit-Kat. Joe had asked for some cider and he just sat there looking at this bottle of cider vinegar.

When Mick came on during the encore, it reminded me of when I first saw them play together at rehearsals all those years ago they would always play from the same amp. That night I looked down and Mick had gone into Joe's amp, and I thought, you've ended up exactly where you started.

Afterwards in the dressing room Joe was sitting there and he looked over and said, "Bloody cheek, he just came on and played." Then he smiled.

On the bus that night there was a strange atmosphere and I said to Timmy Tim, "All the other lads are sitting there looking a bit down, you know. What's the matter with that lot?" Timmy Tim replied, "They're feeling a bit redundant."

We all had been playing Mick Jones' compositions for the last few years and making a bloody living on it.

When I was 15 was the last time I played a lot of somebody else's songs, like Bob Dylan and Paul Simon, and if they would have came on and joined in matey, I'd have... Well I'd have bloody died of ecstasy. It kinda made me wonder, hang on! Where are we all going from here then?

To me, you have to be secure absolutely in what your position and your reasons for playing is. Whether you learn that over the years is hard to say but there is a very different reason to play at 50 than at 25 or 30.

I sometimes had to stop and think about it from those lads' point of view. Like John Blackburn who played bass with us – we were in a lift once and we both forgot to press the button and we missed our floor. We were having a chat and John said, "I never listened to The Clash until the day before yesterday." Basically he had put headphones on and learnt the songs.

He wasn't born until 1976. I loved John, he was great, was a great bass player. He was just kinda trying to say, "Do you realise where I'm at?"

Young people should have their own revolution. They can't have their dad's revolution, they can't have their grandad's revolution.

I saw The Mescaleros as a band to invent new music, whether it was *Cool 'n ' Out*, *Johnny Appleseed*, *X-Ray Style* or whatever it was. Antony Genn has a great overview of music and his interest in music is very, very broad. He wrote great songs with Joe on *X-Ray Style*.

Scott said to me at the Bridgwater gig, "You're pushing us all right over the edge." I said, "What are you talking about?" He didn't understand I had been stroking them like they were babies. I was absolutely amazed.

Scott said, "It's that banging on the violin." It was really troubling him that I was turning the violin round and hitting it with the bow. I was being really careful with the band, that I wasn't making them push, because I knew they were about 30, had a few worries, trying to get mortgages etc. They had families, what we all go through at that age. I was always trying to remember what it was like to be 28, you know? What it would be like if I was playing with, say, Tony Bennett?

I realised it was going to be hard to keep up the output. The band produced very few songs since *Global*. In 18 months very few tracks were put down. Joe and me could knock 'em out – we had very few problems.

I said after Joe's funeral, "Keep the band together. The Mescaleros stay." I said that to Luke and Simon. I said, "We keep playing or we are nothing but tossers hanging on the coat tails of a great man," and I said: "And I'm not that."

I said, "We play and we stand on our own feet." Joe would have wanted us to keep going, write new songs.

You write the future from the present. They might not know, but the past started from nothing – Mick and Joe banging away.

I actually shook hands on it with another Mescalero. I said, we honour Joe with our music. That included playing live, whatever. I'd do it tomorrow.

When Martin very kindly offered me work with Paul Heaton, I didn't want to do it. I thought, well, I don't know the guy I don't know his stuff. I said to Joe, OK, Dylan, Van Morrison, Bruce Springsteen or the unheard-of guy next door who knocks the block off me – because I think he's a genius, I'd play on his record for free. There is no price tag on my work. My music to me is something that keeps me healthy. It's something that you keep close to your heart.

I have to be honest because people know when I'm working I am giving my heart. I wrote on the contract "My heart and my soul and my conscience."

I didn't get a lawyer; I just scrawled across it what I was actually giving them.

I said to my mum on her deathbed a couple of weeks ago, "Look out for Joe."

Antony Genn

"I just said to him, 'You should be making a record, you're fuckin' Joe Strummer, for fuck's sake'."
Antony Genn

I remember walking into the room where Pabs and Joe were. I listened to their music. I think the verse was major and the chorus was minor. I just said, "Why don't you change those round and make that major and that minor?" Looking back, Joe would have been well within his rights just to think, who the fuck is that? Telling me what to do, the jumped-up fuckin' whatever!

But somewhere in that he obviously thought, fair enough. I never really spoke to Joe or anything.

The next time I actually spoke to him was when Joe was with Keith Allen, who was a mutual friend of both of us. Joe was playing some guitar for him on one of his daft comedy records. Alex James was there from Blur and a few other people, and I remember thinking to myself what the fuck. I was probably thinking what the fuck am I doing here, but certainly thinking what the fuck is Joe doing here.

I remember saying to Joe at that session "What are you doing? You should be making a record." It wasn't said in a big way.

The next time I saw him was in a place called the Pharmacy, a bar in Notting Hill, which is owned by Damien Hirst who is a good friend of both mine and Joe's and a lot of other people. We just ended up getting really drunk. Me and Joe got involved in very deep conversation about music. I just said to him, "You should be making a record, you're fuckin' Joe Strummer, for fuck's sake." He kinda called my bluff on it and said, "OK, I'm gonna call you tomorrow, me and you are going to go in the studio." I just thought, course you are!

Of course the call come, he called me. Then within two weeks we were in the studio. After two days of being in the studio and writing a song we wrote together which was *Techno D-Day*, Joe just said, "Let's book the studio for three months and make a record."

That's kinda how it happened, instinctive. That's something what Joe was, 100% instinct. He didn't really give things too much thought. He went with his instinct.

At the beginning of *Westway to the World*, the opening line is Joe saying, "It seems to me that origination is about instinct, not intellect." That's Joe all over.

We got in the studio. For most of the time making the record it was just me, Joe and Richard Flack. Richard Flack came in the first day and said, "I'm your assistant." I said, "You ain't the assistant mate, I don't know what I'm fuckin' doing. I can't work at a mixing desk. You're the engineer." Before that he had just been an assistant making tea. We both cut our teeth on that record, we learnt a lot.

It was all instinct, I didn't know what I was doing, he didn't know what he was doing.

Joe obviously knew what he was doing but also he had to leave a lot to me. Joe's talents aren't in musical arrangement; Mick Jones did all that in The Clash. Joe's the blood and guts, the instinct, the lyrics, the poet.

Joe Strummer was a poet. All Joe's songs that he writes are very straightforward, three little chords that go round and round, like *London Calling*. Mick Jones was the great arranger in The Clash – he's the one that pulled all the great songs. *Safe European Home* is like a symphony with all those chords.

So it was a lot on my shoulders with all those songs that weren't written. Joe just let me do what I want with those songs – *Tony Adams* which I wrote the music to in five minutes, with that tympany sound which was too quiet on the record because I was smoking too much crack. I was deluded whilst we were mixing and kept telling Richard to turn the tympany down because I thought it was too loud.

We would just bash everything down quite quickly, then get the band in to play on things. Ged Lynch came in and played drums on *Techno D-Day* and *Yalla Yalla*, although there is a lot of programming on that.

I had met Martin on a session with Robbie Williams; Danny Saber had bought him in because Danny knew Martin from Black Grape. We hit it off straight away and I realised what a talented musician Martin is. Martin is still my favourite musician I have ever worked with and I've worked with quite a few good ones.

When me Joe and Richard were making the record, our typical day: I would be sleeping either in the Battery house because I had nowhere to live or the overdub booth in studio 3. Joe would be asleep in the vocal overdub booth in studio 2.

We would get ourselves up at about 1.30, have a little shower, sort ourselves out then go up the boozer called Katie O'Gradies on Willesden High Road. Really good Irish pub that knew how to serve a pint. I was on the cider, Joe was on the Guinness. Then Richard would come and join us. We'd have three or four pints. On the way back to the studio we would stop off at an off licence we christened Al Rashid, which is famous from the song *Willesden To Cricklewood*. Then go and have our tea in the Battery café. Paul the chef would make us a nice little bit of steak (not for Joe obviously).

We would start about 6.30; Joe didn't like to work in the studio when people could phone him. He liked to work at night because no one phones you.

Joe already had a handful of songs, *Forbidden City*, *X-Ray Style* he had already written.

Yalla Yalla was already written. We kinda stripped apart and built it all again. It was a hard song to work on, to get right. I was credited as additional production, because Richard Norris had already been the producer on it.

Joe had also done *Diggin' The New* with Richard Norris before, but that had been done in a totally different style and I wanted to make it more rocky. For most part I was playing a lot of guitar, bass, backing vocals, bit of keyboards here and there. When Joe went home at weekends, me and Rich would stay and carry on working.

We did one song which never made it on the record, *Ocean of Dreams*. It was a track of mine. Steve Jones was downstairs seeing someone in Battery studios and he came up and played guitar on it. Brilliant, he was amazing. Some people seem to have got a copy of it in America. I've been struggling to find a copy of it myself.

Martin had been the first call; Ged, having been with Martin in Black Grape, was the next call. Martin then brought Scott along who though I had met a few times I didn't really know. Pabs was already there. I was very good mates with Pabs, had been on tour with Pulp with Pabs, Me and Pabs had a lot of crazy times together before then and during The Mescaleros!

Basically Ged got offered a tour with Marianne Faithful. Then we got Smiley in. He played on *Forbidden City* and played well. That's how it started.

Decisions like Ged or Smiley were never left just to me, it was me and Joe. Me and Joe just couldn't decide really. I called Ged and he said to me, without me saying anything, "You've decided to go with Smiley, ain't yer?" I said no actually, we're thinking about going with you.

Ged said, "Oh, I thought you were going to go with Smiley, because I've promised so and so I'll do something else. I was sure you were going to say you were going with Smiley."

It was very touch and go. I think Ged thought we were going with Smiley because we had been so very indecisive. Then we went back to Smiley and Smiley came in. Smiley was a solid enough drummer. Smiley was a good kid, hasn't got a bad bone in his body. We played some great gigs with Smiley.

We were still making the record when we started rehearsing. We'd rehearse in studio 3 and Richard would be working in studio 2. We had to learn the Clash songs, learning the new songs.

At the time it was hectic and put on top of that I was a full-blown heroin addict at the time, taking a lot of drugs. I was a long-time drug addict; it wasn't like I was taking drugs and getting off my head. I had to take drugs to be normal. To be any use to anyone I had to be on a certain amount of drugs.

Bill Price got bought in to mix the record. Bill Price had mixed *London Calling* and was the engineer for Guy Stevens. He came in, he was a lovely guy but it just didn't work out. The mixes didn't seem to be tough enough for me. He had mixed *Techno D-Day* and *Yalla Yalla* and we weren't really happy. No disrespect to Bill, it was a different thing. I wanted them to be drier, punchier and more aggressive. So we kinda took the reins back and mixed the record ourselves.

Joe had gone on holiday to Almeria in August, which is when we mixed the record. Or should I say Richard mixed the record and I mostly took heroin and crack. I'd be in the studio watching *UK Gold*. I had the sound from the studio plumbed into the stereo system, I'd be watching TV and then just click on to what he was doing.

It says on the record mixed by Antony Genn and Richard Flack. Really, knowing what I know now, Richard mixed it and I produced the mix, which I think is what every producer should do. It was an interesting time.

We started at The Leadmill in June, obviously my hometown. There were plenty of people there. The first song we played in public was *Techno D-Day*, which never really worked. Joe never really learnt the words to *Techno D-Day*. He never quite got to grips with learning the words, ever. Also it was a bit slow, because we played along to loops. It should have been faster. Live, it really dragged amongst all the others.

We used to change the setlist pretty much every night, flip it round a bit here and there. Until you get it right or make it more interesting.

We did a fuckin' mad concert in France at the biker festival.

When we played Köln it was Joe's birthday, so we bought him some Marilyn Monroe lights and an oil lamp.

I also met Cerys in Köln. We started seeing each other after that and got serious pretty quickly. I had my little team, me and her. I don't think Joe took to her particularly well. Maybe because he thought, not that she was a bad influence on me, I was a bad influence on her. It was somebody outside of the group.

There was two amazing nights playing with Joe, Paris and Dublin Olympia. Dublin was the greatest gig I ever did; everybody refused to leave.

When we played Kuntspark in Munich, Joe said, "I didn't think you meant it literally."

When Offspring were onstage, after three songs they stopped, brought a sofa onstage and said something like, "We love Joe Strummer and you should love Joe Strummer. We won't play any more songs until you chant 'We Love Joe Strummer.'" So all the crowd sang "We love Joe Strummer." Joe loved it.

A lot of it is a blur to me. Around that time it is fair to say we weren't exactly the cleanest-living band in the universe. I hold my hands up and formally say I was the worst culprit for bad behaviour, but a lot of the boys didn't need too much persuading, especially uncle Pabs! But we had a lot of fun.

I remember Nottingham Rock City, 'cause my dad came to that.

At the time of The Astoria gigs we were good. We were firing on all cylinders at that point.

I remember opening up in Manchester with *Ishen*, the dubbed-out, tripped-out reggae tune, because Joe thought they were hip enough to get it in Manchester. We can just come on and do that if we want. In the dark without any lights.

I remember Glasgow, Wags, Cresser, and Winker all came up with us to Glasgow. The driver thought we were all animals. After that all the bus companies banned us.

The American tour was pretty mental 'cause Cerys came out. There was a fuckin' lot of drug abuse going on there. At that point I was seriously into the twilight zone. But we did some great gigs; we did the Fillmore, and the amazing Boston gig. It was like '77, no barrier. At one point two pints hit me, thrown from the crowd within a split second of each other. It was quite incredible, pure rock 'n' roll. It was the first night we did *White Riot*.

The first night we did *Police on My Back* in Japan, Joe had been playing it on his ghetto blaster in the van on the way there.

The Big Day Out in Australia was an awesome tour, with the Primal Scream lads. The Big Day Off it should be called – you just turn up, work once every three days and get thrashed out your head.

It is important to know by this time I was pretty much out of control. Me and Joe weren't really speaking. Not "not speaking" but we weren't really communicating like we once did.

I just degenerated into becoming such a drug addict that the only thing that really mattered to me was drugs. Also I had hooked up with Cerys – Sid and Nancy they used to call us, and to be truthful they weren't all that far off. A lot of drugs, I was very big into heroin and crack.

Wherever we went on tour that was the first thing I had to do, so I'd be gone off into the night. Everyone would be like, "Oh my God! Where has he gone now?" That would cause a lot of problems.

Joe is not a confrontational person. But by this point he was thinking, "I've seen this movie before" with Topper. It only ends one way.

At the Bowery gig, I missed my flight, had to get another flight, and brought Cerys with me. Missed soundcheck, turned up late. I was out of control at that point.

I didn't go to Jesolo – drugs, drugs. Basically I just phoned up the tour manager Neil Mather and said I couldn't go because me and Cerys had degenerated into total Sid and Nancyism. I think we went away somewhere, living in the vain hope of getting off drugs.

At that time I was spending a lot of time down in Cardiff with Cerys. To all intents and purposes my creative input into the band was over at that point, I'd say. It had probably been over for a while. I think we'd been as good as we could be, I think, at that point.

Even now, I would say I naturally get bored with things like that. To be honest it wasn't exciting for me any more, that coupled with all I wanted to do was take drugs.

Joe called me up one day; it was a sunny morning. We probably hadn't really had a proper conversation for a long time.

Now my behaviour was undermining the stability of the band. He said, "I think it's about time we parted company."

I genuinely thought he was saying that the band should split up, for some delusional reason. I then realised what he was saying. So I said, "OK! But I'd like to do these V2000 gigs."

When we did the gig in Leicester, by the time we went onstage I had drunk 12 pints of cider and had ten valium. What the fuck I was playing on there I had no idea.

When we came off, Martin Slattery said to me something along the lines of "You're a fuckin' disgrace." Which for Martin to say something like that is quite a big deal, because he's not the kinda guy who says stuff like. But he was right – I was a disgrace.

At that point I also had had a Naltrexone implant in my side to stop me from taking heroin. It's an opiate blocker. It stops heroin working. So, I was caning so many prescription drugs – Rohypnol, Temazepam, a drug called Largactil which is just like being hit with a sledgehammer, Clonodine, Thioridazine, all these drugs, Blexidrine, prescription speed to get up in the morning, loads of cocaine and just a stupid amount of alcohol on top of it. I was just out of control, totally out of control.

When we did those two V2000 gigs I said to Martin, "I'll only drink five pints before I go onstage," which was not much for me. So I did that.

At the Chelmsford gig, I drank the same before we went onstage, then six cans of cider onstage during the gig. Which was only 45 mins long and you've only got a moment's drinking before you go on to the next song.

There was a lot of tension between me and Joe at that point. I remember we went onstage and his guitar wouldn't work, so I played the riff to *Brand New Cadillac*, do, do, do, do, do, do, do. He turned round and went, "Stop, stop, that's my riff!" I sauntered over to him and said, "I'll think you'll find it's not!" He went, "Damn, you're right" and laughed.

That night was the last conversation that me and Joe really had until years later when I sorted myself out. We sat downstairs on the back of the bus, just me and him talking. I was off my head and he was drunk. He started talking about they were really putting pressure on him to reform The Clash and what did I think. I was trying to be reasonable about it, so I said in a way I think you should do it, because if you want to get the money for your kids or whatever, then it's a good way to do it and then essentially you kinda think about selling out. We've played so many Clash songs now, it's kinda like selling out anyway. We do so few of our own songs.

I did say, well, if you need the money, and Joe's answer to that was, "Yeah that's what I'm worried about. What would they do with it?"

It was something that he was constantly asked over the years. When you're constantly questioned and offered that money you've got to keep answering it.

That was the last conversation me and Joe had in that scenario. When I got off the bus at Islington, I went off into the night. I was twisted, not sad. I'm sad now thinking about it. It was sad because of the state I had let myself get into. I was totally out of control, probably not a nice person to be around. Totally unreliable and always a liability.

Me and Joe were very tight for a while; you have to be when you're in a creative environment with someone. We were writing songs together; the guy hadn't written songs with people in a little partnership for a long time. I was very privileged that he chose me.

Essentially it became a very different band when I left, because it was a much more muso event. I'm not a muso. I can't play like they can play.

The Clash used to draw a line across the room, between musicians and buskers. There was Simmo and Joe on one side and Topper and Mick on the other side. If we had done that in our band, certainly me and Joe would have been on our own, because me and Joe were the laymen as it were.

I'm the only one in that band that comes from that music. I'm the only one in that band that grew up listening to The Clash. I'm the only one that was there. I was outside the Top Rank in Sheffield on the 16 Tons tour with my brother, trying to get Joe's autograph. Seventeen years later, or whatever it was, I'm producing Joe Strummer's record.

I made a note of all those songs, that's what I grew up on. My brother was seven years older than me, I went to see The Stranglers, I went to see The Damned and I went to see all those bands.

So that's what runs through my blood, so for me to play *White Man In Hammersmith Palais*, my brother had that on 7in with the fuckin' gun sleeve when it came out. The others had never seen that record or probably only heard it years later. That was the difference.

Years later it was great to play *White Man* onstage with Joe Strummer. Well the thing is, it never felt like that, because Joe Strummer never felt like a superstar to me. Maybe even contribute a bit of that to my drugs haze. You can contribute a lot to it, to the kind of man Joe was; he was not the kind of man to make you feel that he was better than you. We were equal. Me and him were an equal partnership; it was my band as much as it was his. It was always his band to a point, but we were playing my songs as much as his, in the new songs.

He didn't know those guys before he knew Pabs. I got those guys in. We did it together – we made something together. It kinda run its course and that was that for me.

It couldn't have gone on much longer for me anyway. If I wasn't so on drugs I would have been more together and gone off and done something else. So either way there was no way I would have carried on being in that band. I would have gone off and done my own thing, whatever it was: producing records or playing, or whatever it is I'm into at the time.

They're a lot more complex; they complicated things a lot more than I would have ever done.

I'm into riffs, strong powerful riffs. I think that *Tony Adams*, although we could have mixed it better ... I think if that were a Clash song it would have been a great Clash song.

I think that is a really great song, *Tony Adams*. Why the fuck it's called *Tony Adams* is stupid.

One thing's for sure, there's no guitar solo's on *Rock Art*, there's a little bit from Slats on the track *X-Ray Style*, on a little Spanish guitar. Because it's not me, it's not my vibe, it's not Joe's vibe and we made the record.

It is quite simply two different bands. I didn't really like *Global A Go-Go*, it's not really my bag. Some of it was OK!

The last record was good, I think *Coma Girl* is totally amazing; I like *Ramshackle*, I love *Get Down Moses*.

I think if Joe had been alive that would have been a really great record. It wasn't to be, unfortunately.

Willesden To Cricklewood was the one for me; it was just a perfect moment. Joe went off to Cricklewood to score off Cricklewood John. He had walked from Willesden to Cricklewood and he walked back. When he got back I had been fiddling about with this little idea – it sounded like fuckin' Camberwick Green or something. Not the sort of song Joe Strummer would ever sing.

He came back and said, "Yeah man, I like that, keep going," then he would walk round the room with reams of paper then he would wander off. When he came back he said, "OK, let me sing you this song." So he sang me the song and it was beautiful. A very simple song. I never realised how much he loved that song.

I did apologise to him, but Joe wasn't into confrontations – he wasn't into opening up big cans of worms, it wasn't his style. I had seen him in the street outside the Groucho Club on Dean Street, I gave him a hug and he gave me a hug, it was kinda little bit funny. I said, "Look, I just want to say sorry for my behaviour and how wild I got."

He was like, "Yeah, don't worry about it man" kinda thing like I said, sorry I didn't give you that 10p I owed you kinda thing.

About six months before Joe died, about the same time I was making the UNKLE record. I was again at the Groucho Club one night with Damien and Joe was there. James Lavelle had been on at me saying, "Let's get Joe Strummer on a track, let's get Joe Strummer." I didn't feel like I could ask him because there was too much unsaid between Joe and me. That was the past. I didn't want to just use it because he was Joe Strummer. It wasn't what I was about.

Eventually I did call Luce. I called the house and Joe was in America working with Johnny Cash. I told Luce what I wanted to talk to Joe about. The conversation finished by me saying I'll speak to him later when he gets back. Anyway I never pursued it; never spoke to him about it.

When he came into the Groucho Club that night Joe went, "I've got a bone to pick with you!" I was like, what? He said, "Come up to the bar" and said, "I thought we were going to do a track together?"

I said, "What do you mean?" Joe replied, "You and me, you spoke to Luce about some track that you want me to do. You never called me, what's the matter?" I said, "Well, you were in America, I knew you were busy, I was busy. I knew you were doing your stuff, so I just didn't get round to it."

Joe went, "**TWO HOURS**, I live two hours away from you. You call me any time and I'll be there in two hours, that's all it's going to take me to get there. You just give me a call, I'll do anything you want me to do."

That was Joe's way of saying me and you are fine.

That same night, we had had a great night, great chat and Joe started telling Dougie from Travis and his wife Kelly MacDonald, who was an actress from *Trainspotting*, about that song *Willesden To Cricklewood*. Joe was going, "It's like Mozart, you've gotta hear it."

I was shocked and privileged when Luce chose that song for Joe's funeral. Of all the fuckin' songs he had ever written, they chose *White Man*, which is my favourite Clash song, *Coma Girl*, which I think is as good a song as The Mescaleros ever did, and *Willesden To Cricklewood*, which is a very special and different song. Both how it sounds musically and how it's sung.

The bit where Joe sings:
"Thought about my babies grown
Thought about going home
Thought about what's done is done
We're alive and that's the one."

Very reflective, he'd just walk down the street and he was just looking at people. He's getting older, sees things differently. It's a beautiful song, very sentimental piece of music.

We wrote and recorded that song in 12 hours. We finished it on my birthday: 19 March we started to write that song, because the next day was my birthday. We started at 7 o'clock at night and finished at 7 o'clock in the morning. That's it, what's on the record, done, mixed, finished. I tried to re-do some stuff on it but Joe went, "You're out of your mind."

Looking back, the chemistry of me and Joe together was good for all of us. For whatever reasons my bolshie, don't-give-a-fuck attitude was good for something. Because I had got Joe to put a guitar round his neck again. That did make a lot of people happy, made him happy I think.

Wherever he went Joe was revered, particularly outside of this country. I felt it more in other countries, particularly America.

At the festivals all these other bands would go, "Oh my God, Joe Strummer." Which we could all understand, but it's very difficult when someone's a normal bloke like Joe to get past that.

When I look at Joe Strummer in The Clash that's not the Joe Strummer I knew, that was the young, feisty punk rocker.

The Joe I knew was a much wiser old owl, not without his faults, of course, like anybody. He was a very special man.

I'm not ashamed of my past; I'm not ashamed of anything. It's what made me the man I am today, all those experiences.

I'm thinking of doing some more stuff – make my own record. I'm going to do some stuff with Martin, it's been a long time coming. I want to play live.

I also do films now and production.

Me and Martin have definitely got some plans to start playing some gigs, just small gigs. I think me and Martin could do something good together.

It would also be nice to play those songs just one more time. I'd love to play *Safe European Home* one more time. I loved playing that song and *White Man*.

Luke Bullen

"Washington was the first time I had walked on and everyone there went mental. That will forever stay in my memory. That kind of response was phenomenal."
Luke Bullen

It's still a bit vague for me really, as to when it felt like I became a Mescalero. I was at a studio over in West London where Scott and Martin had a production room and I was playing on someone else's record. They stuck their heads round the door, introduced themselves. They said, "We've finished the *Global A Go-Go* record and there is talk of going out and promoting it. What are you up to? Are you around to do it?"

I said, "Yeah, that sounds cool."

I didn't hear anything for a couple of months and then, all of a sudden, in the middle of a rehearsal in Shepherd's Bush, I got a call from Martin to say "Are you up for it then?" We were to start rehearsals the following week.

So we rehearsed for a couple of weeks and the first gig was at HMV, Oxford Street.

My position in the band was very vague to start with. They had made *Global A Go-Go* and Simon and I weren't involved in the recording process. They needed to go out and tour it and they needed a couple of musicians to do that.

No one established what it was going to be. When we first got involved it was like "Would you come and help us promote this record?", not "Would you become a Mescalero?". It just kind of developed slowly. So we did the first rehearsals and the first instores in the UK, and it went pretty well.

The first time Joe mentioned anything to do with our position in the band was when we did the Virgin Megastore in New York. Up until that point it was just the four of them signing records after the instore gigs but there was a bit of a rapport being established, everyone was getting on, so Joe said, "You and Simon come and get involved. Come and sit in with us for the signing."

I think the first one we did was in LA, but Joe definitely mentioned it in New York, from my memory.

It was never, in the 18 months, "You're a Mescalero." (*The fans said you're a Mescalero.*)

Yeah, but that needed to come from Joe, really, or from the band! Then our position changed when we started to record the third album. I think when you are involved in the recording process the songs mean more to you as a musician. You've been there; you've had songs you've struggled over. You've been present when someone's written the lyrics or sung them. You understand where the music has come from.

But when you join the bus halfway along the journey it's not as personal.

When we were in New York doing the Megastore gig, this guy – I think his name was Chris, a really tall, quite loud American guy – started the "Luke, Luke, Luke" thing. I thought that maybe there was some connection with having played in New York with another band.

That day we did the Conan O'Brien show, then jumped in a van and flew over to the Megastore, so my head was spinning anyway. It was so amazing.

Wandering out to set up my drums and then hearing someone shout out my name, being so many thousands of miles from home, that was really weird. I thought that someone was booing but once I worked out they weren't it was all right.

The instore performances are totally different to gigs, you feel like a performing seal! You are playing at the wrong time of day, usually afternoon or early evening. That's always a bit weird. You've got lights on, so you can see every face in the audience. The whole time I was sitting on the edge of my seat – it wasn't so much stressful, it was just really challenging.

What was always quite difficult was that there were two bandleaders, two people that were directing the musicians: Martin and Scott. I would often be looking at both of them and getting conflicting information.

Also, I had Joe explaining that there was a certain signal for going quiet, a certain signal for going to the chorus etc. So I've got three people to watch and learn the set and get blown away by playing with Joe Strummer and by meeting all these incredibly friendly people and getting used to being on the road with a bunch of new people that I don't really know. There were so many things to take in, my head was just overloaded. It was never a negative experience but always a challenging experience.

The Viper Room gig was just so much information to take in; one of The Ramones had turned up to see Joe and a member of The Chilli Peppers was supporting. Just being in that environment where people that I had read about or whose music I had listened to were showing up at a gig. It was all pretty mind-blowing.

The Viper Room doesn't stick out to me as my first gig. It still felt like part of setting the tour up. The first gig for me was Washington, at the 9:30 Club.

Up to that point it was all quite short shows. It was always a taster; even the Viper Room was quite a short show because we didn't have a lot of material rehearsed up.

From Washington onwards the shows became two hours long. I remembered that show because that was the first time as a musician I'd walked onstage and got that kind of response from an audience.

I'd done big shows before but that was promoting a new band. Washington was the first time I had walked on and everyone there went mental. That will forever stay in my memory. That kind of response was pretty phenomenal.

I felt a bit more confident at that point – we had done all the instores and it was good to have got to know everyone, hanging out on the road together. I had played the 9.30 Club before with my band Addict, but we were the support – no one knew who we were although we got a good response. But to go back to the club and do a sold-out headline show was great.

The after-shows were amazing. I said to Joe, "I don't know how you do it," because every single show he would have so much time for everyone. He was there for them without fail.

I can't remember one occasion where he said, "I don't feel like doing this tonight." He was there for everyone who wanted to speak to him and that was absolutely incredible.

I didn't have the same energy. There were nights, and I think this applies to all The Mescaleros, where you just go "I can't do it tonight, I'm exhausted, I need to just go and have a drink with the boys on the bus or chill out for an hour!"

It was just full-on. Speaking personally, I've only got so much capacity for that. Having done a two-hour show, having given his all every night Joe kept going – he had incredible stamina.

The two nights in New York at Irving Plaza were amazing. We opened with *Minstrel Boy*, and there was a connection with that song and the New York Fire Department. That was pretty special, they kept the lights dimmed; Joe was huddled down pointing to Tymon who played the song on his violin.

The atmosphere was just amazing in New York. This was two weeks after 11 September. I remember walking along the street and these two old guys just walked up and embraced each other in the middle of the street. You don't often see that kind of display of emotion on New York streets.

I couldn't go down to the twin towers site, it just felt wrong. It just felt macabre to actually go down there and look at the hole in the ground.

Boston was a great show; that was where Joe said to take away the barriers, get rid of the security guards at the front of the stage. We had more fans onstage than we had band members. I think Champ and Timmy Tim were throwing people off the stage. It was just a constant stream of people getting onstage then get chucked back in, the whole gig. I spent most of the gig laughing. It was hilarious.

Seattle nearly broke me. That's the only time I thought, "This has beaten me". I got sick, flu or something, and had very little sleep; basically it was get on a plane, check in, soundcheck, do the gig, another couple of hours' sleep, get on another plane etc. I felt absolutely awful. I remember getting to the hotel in Seattle and I just thought, get me to my bed. Just let me get over this.

Joe knew we were all shattered at that point. Everyone was exhausted, crew, band the lot. But we did a great show.

We then did five nights at the Troubadour in LA, which was a fun week.

The Japanese tour was my first visit to Japan. Japan made me feel the most alien I have felt compared to other countries I've been to. There's no similarity in the language. Not a lot of English in terms of street signs etc, and the culture is very, very different. It was fantastic to be able to go there and check it out.

They worshipped Joe in Japan. It was a totally different atmosphere. I remember a signing we did at the record store in Tokyo, this girl came up with a guitar for Joe to sign and she just fell to pieces when she saw him. She just crumbled.

Manchester was a really great gig; it's a great venue. Birmingham was all right, Dublin was cool, Bristol was fine.

Brixton Academy, now that was pretty amazing, because that venue was one on my list that I had always wanted to play. Plus my parents and my sister came down – that was the first Mescalero show they had seen. It was a great moment for me to have my family there. They've always really encouraged me as a musician, bought me my first kit, set up a room in the garage for me to practise. So it was great to invite them down.

I remember seeing them sitting on the front row of the balcony when Joe introduced the band. I stood up to take the applause and saw mum and dad up there. It was a bit of a moment, from being a 12-year-old kid wanting to play the drums to being there in front of that amount of people, doing a good show. It was great personal experience.

The time in Greece was mental. Because we knew it was the end of the tour, after the Thessaloniki gig, the penultimate gig, we couldn't wait for the last night and we went out and got absolutely trashed. It was a proper rock 'n' roll night out. I remember at 6.00 in the morning, the hotel fire extinguishers were going off, luggage getting emptied into baths, it was just chaos. Everyone falling about.

We had to get up at 8.00 in the morning to get the flight to Athens. It was like some nights when you get absolutely hammered, you wake up and think you've got away with it, but really you're still drunk. Slowly everyone's starting to go, "Ohhhh God". We felt absolutely awful. When we got to the hotel in Athens I didn't know whether to see it out or go to bed. I felt like death.

We did the soundcheck, went back to the hotel, got another hour's kip, got to the dressing-room, and I'm still feeling absolutely rough. Ten minutes before we went on the hangover just went and we played a blinder. It was one of the best gigs we did. Before the show everyone was just holding their heads and thinking, "How are we going to get through this?", but we just rose to the occasion.

The five nights in Brooklyn were a phenomenal experience. We soundchecked for the first couple of days and after that all we did was turn up and play. There was usually a car to take us to the gig but New York's traffic is like London's, a nightmare. So after the first night, I just took the subway down to the Manhattan Bridge and walked across the bridge to get to the gig. It is an incredible view from Brooklyn Bridge especially at night.

As I crossed the bridge each night I would think, "This is my life, I'm playing with Joe Strummer and the Mescaleros in New York, for five nights, getting paid, hanging out with loads of great people. Fantastic." After the gig we would always go to the bar just up from the venue and that would kick off the rest of the night.

The last night we stayed up until the sun came up. I went to so many different parties that night at different places across Manhattan. Such a great time.

At the time of the Fleadh gig, I was going through some personal stuff so I wasn't completely on it. I was in a bit of a daze at that time. I was in the thick of it and it was pretty tough.

Joe had all his hand signals for different cues in a song. We had rehearsed up a new song, *Guitar Slinger Man,* and we had done it exactly the same way with exactly the same ending all the time.

The Fleadh festival was the first time we had played it live. At the end of the song, we were rockin' out on the outro and a few bars before we normally ended the song, Joe gave me the gun sign. That was his sign that at the next musically appropriate point it was the end of the tune. From my point of view as a musician it made more sense to go on another couple of bars and finish at the end of the cycle of the tune.

Well, that wasn't what Joe was thinking. He wanted to finish where he stuck his hand up in the air and I had kept going.

I had my head down rockin' out. The only thing I knew when I stopped and looked up, there was this microphone lead lying over my shoulder, and the mic's lying on the floor behind me. I remember thinking, " Whats that all about?" I think I'm quite a philosophical person, it takes a lot for me to lose my temper and snap.

I just let it go. People were coming up to me, "Are you all right? That was completely out of order" I knew I didn't have to do anything, say anything. It was obvious.

He was wrong and he knew he was wrong and everyone else who I cared about on the stage or was involved knew he was wrong. So we came off and I walked to the dressing room, kept myself to myself and Joe came up and said, "We still mates, right?"

I said, "Yeah." I didn't have to say anything. Because I knew the type of guy he was and he would be gutted. That was enough for me.

When I became involved with The Mescaleros, I knew about The Clash but I was too young to have experienced them first-hand. It was when I started getting involved in the signings and meeting fans that I could see how important Joe was to other people. But when I joined The Mescaleros, Joe was Joe. He wasn't an untouchable rock hero to me. Joe was an ordinary guy and an extraordinary guy all at the same time.

Everyone had a good grasp that Joe was why the audience were at the shows and The Mescaleros were the next part of his career. We all hoped it would become something in its own right and we were all aiming towards the day when one or two Clash tunes would be in the set, but it would predominantly be Mescaleros material. That was what we were all aiming for.

T In The Park was phenomenal. We played in a tent that was so rammed we couldn't believe it. The audience response from the first note was just awesome. They were into everything, both Clash and Mescaleros material.

The highlight for me was playing *I Fought the Law* because I started the song with the drums and when I went into the fill at the beginning, a lot of people recognised it straight away and the place erupted. Getting that response from the audience just blew me away.

The gig at The Royal Opera House was good fun. We played *Shaktar*, *Global* etc and I remember Joe wanted to play *White Riot*, despite the auspicious venue. I remember Bryan Adams and Brian May watching at the side of the stage, which I found amusing.

The British tour followed; Edinburgh, Newcastle, and Blackpool were all good gigs.

The Acton gig was a very special night. I remember when Mick Jones came onstage for the encore. I remember looking at Joe when Mick came up and Joe's face said it all. It was a very youthful smile. He looked genuinely pleased to see him. Afterwards in the dressing room Joe said in dry humour, referring to Mick, "Bloody cheek, coming on our stage at my gig."

After the tour we had a week at Rockfield Studios in Wales and that turned out to be the last work we did as a band on *Streetcore*.

I last spoke to Joe the day before he died. I had rung up to say that John Squire had asked me to be his drummer on his British/Irish tour starting in Belfast in late January.

This clashed with a proposed date in South Africa with Joe & The Mescaleros, so I said to Joe, "No problem, I'll contact John Squire and tell him I can't make it." Joe added, in his usual dry and witty way, "Tell that John Squire I'll kick his head in for trying to poach my bloody drummer."

Simon Stafford

"The five nights in Brooklyn at the time was probably the best week of my life.

The first day, you do the soundcheck, do the gig. Then every day we made that journey over Brooklyn Bridge. It's a fantastic journey to do at that time of early evening."

Simon Stafford

I knew Martin through Ants. We did a session for *Nova* magazine. Ants had got this idea to do *Jungle Jim* which is from *Midnight Cowboy*. Ants got me to play bass, another guy from Sheffield to sing, Martin to play keyboards, Chris Sharrock on drums. We did the song in a day, real garagey jam song. They just wanted a similar version to the original, just a slightly different one so they didn't have to pay the same royalty rate.

When Joe & The Mescaleros had finished the album and they needed a bass player and drummer, they got Luke. Martin remembered me from that time and asked me to play bass.

Before the gig I had a joint backstage with my mum. She was back in the dressing room for a bit and it just came up that she was next on the joint.

When we did the first instore in Oxford Street, I was still playing with Richard Hawley and we had a gig on the same night. The second it finished, I legged it out and there was a cab waiting to take me to the Spitz. The guy didn't know where it was, so I jumped out and got a taxi instead. I got there ten minutes late and they were all waiting for me.

At the last rehearsal before the HMV gig, I just mentioned, "What do we normally wear?" I said I had to do another gig on the same night and with that band we normally wear suits. No ties, just dark suits.

Joe said, "That's a good idea – everybody wear suits." Scott didn't really like the idea because he only had one suit which was a shiny grey wedding suit that was really short on the arms and wasn't particularly flattering. He only wore it for a couple of gigs and then came up with this idea that everyone can wear suits if they want to or ripped T-shirts if they want to.

For me it was so I didn't have to get changed between the gigs, so I could just run straight on to the other gig.

Martin had that fantastic white suit – that was his excuse to wear it. He wore it at every gig we ever played. I can't remember when he didn't wear it. Joe really enjoyed wearing that suit – it made him look respectable.

The American instore gigs were fantastic; we started to really get our teeth into them. It was an odd type of gig apart from the Viper Room gig. Even though we only did seven gigs we were away for over two weeks.

Pablo flew in for the Brian Setzer gig. There was no bad vibes or anything but it was obvious we were going to do gigs without him because he was away with Moby. It was a bit awkward for him to come in on tunes he hadn't rehearsed on.

The thing about that tour was all the gigs were weird and different and that kinda set precedent, because that's how Joe liked it. Doing three gigs in the same town over a week means you had a couple of days off and that was a great way to do it.

When we did that later on in Brooklyn, you turn up in town, do the soundcheck, get the first gig over and from then on you're kings of the town. You've got a residency. It's much better than flying in and flying out. It's a real good way to get to know the town. The same people come some nights; you mingle with different people, cross-sections. It's great.

Joe really liked doing that, playing in a smaller place for more than one night. It's something I'd like to carry on doing in the future given the chance. It can't cost a great deal more and gives you a chance to have a shower. It gets everyone there in the town that couldn't make it. If there are three nights, people come on the first night and think wow, then tomorrow... It works well.

That first tour was just getting to know Joe and the rest of the band. The beauty of it was we weren't doing any Clash songs. I think at the Viper Room and Brian Setzer, we threw a few in. But all the instores we didn't do any Clash songs.

Joe said, "This is like a millstone from around my neck – I never thought I'd be able to do this." I hadn't rehearsed any Clash songs and when we were at the Viper Room, I remember being late for the soundcheck, I don't know what I was doing. Shopping probably, shoplifting down on Melrose.

I walked in on the soundcheck and they were halfway through a Ramones tune, *Blitzkrieg Bop*. Obviously with no bass and they were just making a racket. I stepped onto the stage and worked out what was going on. Then that was it, end of the soundcheck. So I just played through half a tune. There was another couple of tunes chucked in.

That was the first time I had experienced that with Joe. I like that spontaneity. He'd just call a tune we had never played.

The first time he did it with *Bankrobber*. I knew the tune but had never played it. Scott said "I'll play bass. I know the bass line." That's how I ended up playing guitar on that. So every time we did *Bankrobber* after that I played guitar.

Likewise with *Junco Partner*. Joe just started playing that one day. I thought, oh yeah this sounds familiar, wait a minute! We don't play this one. Joe was just kinda testing us, I suppose, like if he just wanted to play something he'd play it, if he was in the mood for it. Mix it up, keep the musicians on their toes.

When we played Help's only gig it was one of those things where we could have done more and we should have. Because Ants had this one gig it was a point of focus. It seemed like once Ants had got that off his chest and done the one gig, it proved that he could do a gig and front a band, he lost the impetus.

When we did the American tour just after 11 September, they were really grateful to see some British people. At first we were very, yeah great, in your hour of need etc. But then as it went on, the bombs started raining on Afghanistan and we had a few difficult conversations, where you kinda hedge it away from let's bomb the bastards. I remember having a discussion with the landlord of a bar. I said more innocent Afghans have died from American bombs in the last week than died at the World Trade Center. He wouldn't have it. I think if I hadn't of been with Joe he would have thrown me out. He was really angry and someone else in the bar was like, "Get out of here."

They just don't get the news; they're very sheltered.

I went to look at Ground Zero, it was just a smoking mass grave, there were loads of tourists there filming it. It was a strange time.

When we were getting the rehearsals ready for the full band, playing trombone and sax was something me and Martin were consciously trying to do. On that *Nova* session I played bass and trombone and a bit of trumpet. So for me to play trombone meant Martin could play some more sax. The idea was to get a section together, because it was on a ska-type tune, there are plenty of sections. We were trying to get several tunes together with that line-up, get Scott to play bass. Joe called *A Message To You Rudy* out, played the original. It's a lot more sprightly, whereas The Specials one is a bit more dour really, a bit more of the Midlands. I don't know where Joe got that idea, doing a different verse in every time depending on what town. Before every gig, before the show as a way of combating your nerves, we would try and get rhymes. Trying to get a few lines in for him.

I always kinda get excited rather than nervous before each show. I don't ever get kinda sweats or real nerves. That first tour of record shops I was just finding my feet.

Playing those instore gigs was like playing a house party, 'cause all the house lights are on.

When we played Atlantic City it was in a casino-type complex. It was one of those where you can't imagine that there'd be anyone coming to the gig. It was like playing in Butlins or something.

I don't know where they came from – out of the woodwork.

We started opening with *Minstrel Boy* because it was the New York Fire Brigade's song. It was Joe's idea of a little musical nod in that direction.

Joe more or less steered clear of saying anything on the topic of the war, the bombs, the WTC. He'd occasionally say something for the Fire Dept. He'd make sure he was saying something pretty universal rather than specifically on that topic. It's a right can of worms.

It's very easy onstage when you're hyped up to say the wrong thing or get misunderstood. Joe was making sure he wasn't going to fall into that trap.

It was because we were English and as though we were supporting them,

1. First night, dressing-rooms, Sheffield, Leadmill.
Photo copyright Lucinda Mellor

2.. Joe and Terry McQuade
Photo copyright Propergander, John Zimmerman

3, 4 and 5. Joe
Photo copyright Propergander, John Zimmerman

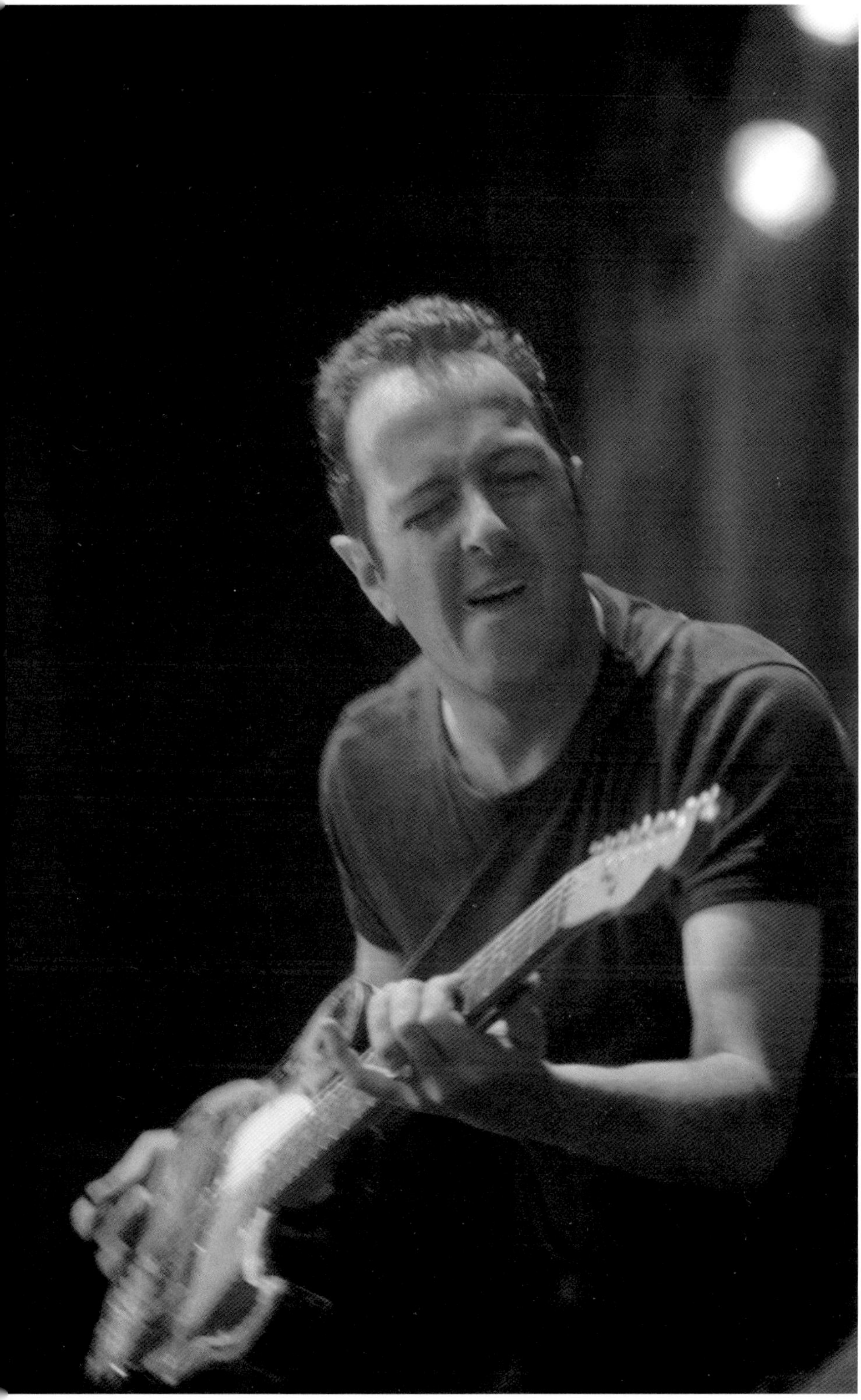

6 Smiley Photo copyright Propergander, John Zimmerman

7 Joe
Photo copyright
Propergander,
John Zimmerman

**8 Joe and Scott
soundcheck**
Photo copyright
Propergander,
John Zimmerman

9. The Mescaleros, Sweden   Photo Copyright Martin Slattery

10. Pablo Cook, Belfast 1999   Photo copyright Anthony Davie

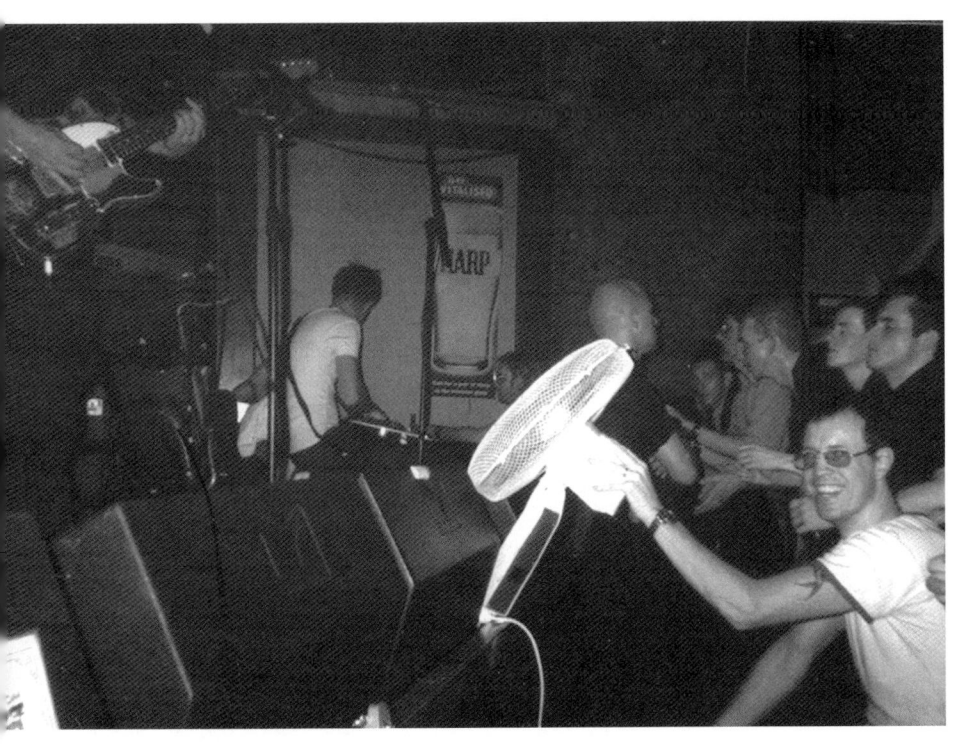

11. Gary Robinson, Belfast 1999   Photo copyright Gary Robinson

12. **Andy Boo** Photo copyright Propergander, John Zimmerman

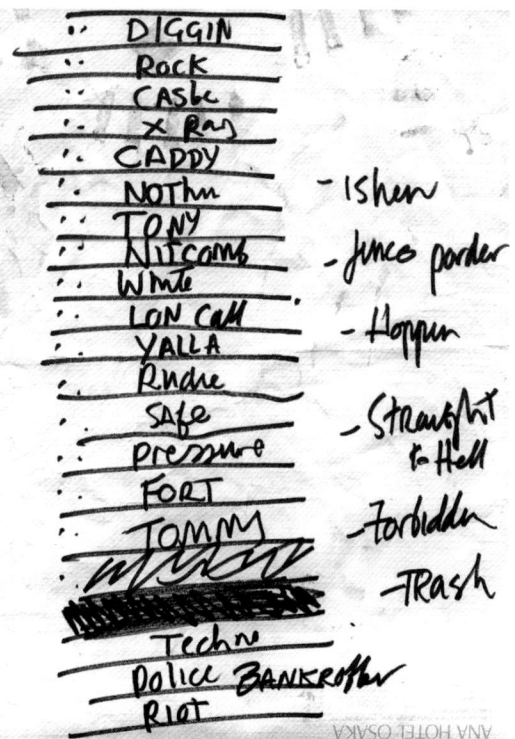

13. Goodnight Paris,
December 1999
Photo copyright Anthony Davie

14. Joe's setlist, Osaka, Japan
Special thanks Andy Boo

15. (top right) Ants, Scott, Joe and Dick Rude, Australia 2000
Photo copyright Lucinda Mellor

16. (right) Scott and Joe, Australia 2000
Photo copyright Lucinda Mellor

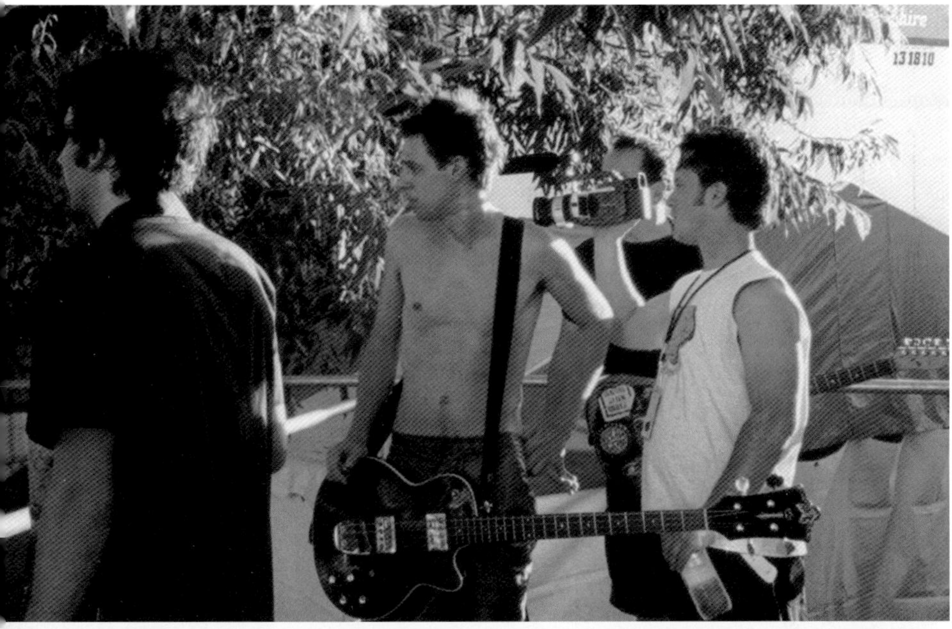

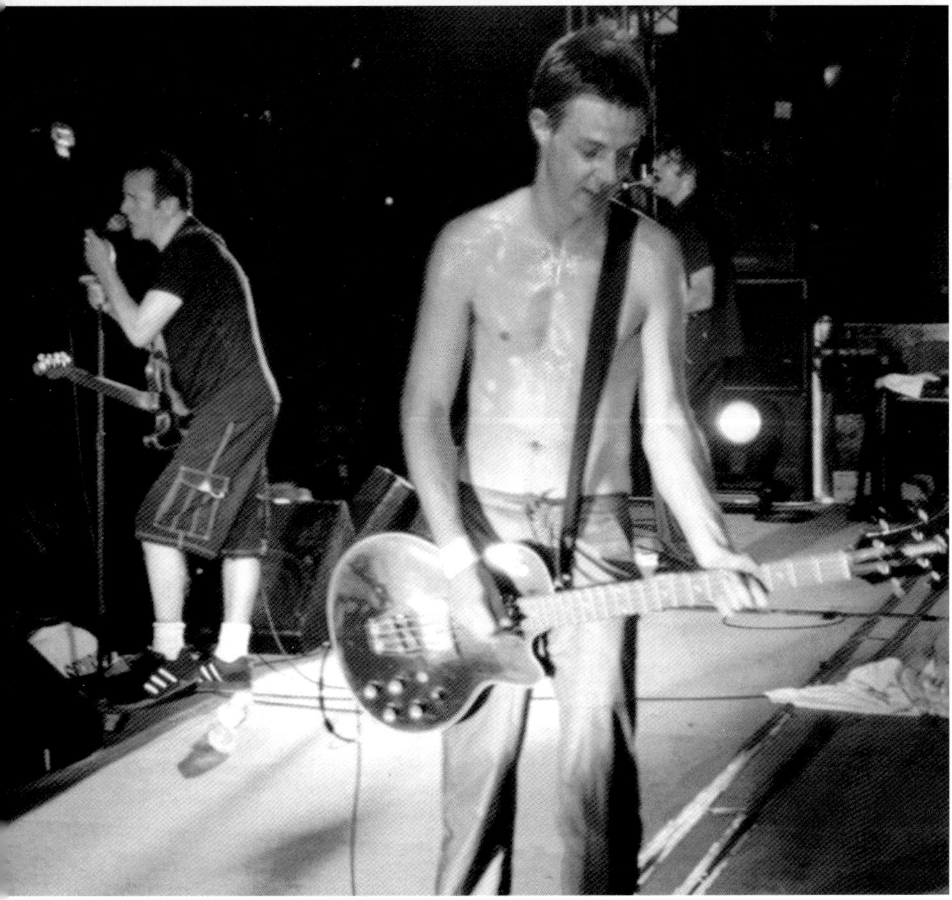

17. Band and crew, Australia 2000   Photo copyright Scott Shields

18. Waiting for the Bus, Jesolo, 2000   Photo copyright Andy Boo

9. Big Day Out, Adelaide
Photo copyright Lucinda Mellor

10. Joe and John Blackburn, November 2000
Photo copyright Virginia Blackburn

21. Antony Genn, V2000   Photo copyright Dave Maud

22. Joe, V2000   Photo copyright Dave Maud

23. **Martin Slattery** Photo copyright Propergander, John Zimmerman

24. Martin and Jimmy Hogarth
Photo copyright Kirsty Slattery

25. Leeds, Virgin Instore, July 2001   Photo copyright Dave Maud

26. Luke Bullen, Shepherds Bush Empire
Photo copyright Anthony Davie

27. Simon Foster 2002
Photo copyright Luke Bullen

28. Simon Stafford
Photo copyright Luke Bullen

29. Tymon Dogg, Japan 2002
Photo copyright Luke Bullen

30. **Joe onstage at The Fleadh** Photo copyright Luke Bullen

1. **Joe** Photo copyright ropergander, John Zimmerman

2. **Mick Jones and Joe, Acton, November 2002** Photo copyright Anthony Davie

33. Joe, Liverpool, 22 November 2002   Photo copyright Anthony Davie

34. Liverpool, 22 November 2002   Photo copyright Anthony Davie

standing shoulder to shoulder with them by coming over and not leaving them isolated.

For us not being scared of flying out, I wanted to do it anyway because I wanted to do the tour. I don't like cancelling tours.

When we played that it always got a big ovation. It is a solemn kinda funeral-style song.

We would come on, it would be an instrumental, it would be solemn, stirring music then Joe would go, "Right now we're going to start the set properly" and go into *Cool 'n' Out*.

I remember walking from the hotel to Irving Plaza on my own. As I got to the place I caught up with Joe and he was carrying the acoustic guitar on his back and he looked like he was really happy, real minstrel in town with just the guitar without a case on his back. It was for the dressing room so we could have a bit of a warm-up. I remember that image – he looked quite cool.

I was just getting to know him then, he was still a little bit of a star then to me. I don't get star-struck. I tend to go the other way, take the piss out of him a bit, and I'd kinda try and rib him. A lot of people would be nervous in front of him and agree with whatever he says even famous people.

You always feel knackered when you fly and do a gig on the same day – you shouldn't really do it. You have spent the whole day travelling, getting sweaty and you're not really in the mood for a gig. That's what happened in Seattle.

Travelling to Scottsdale via Los Angeles and Phoenix was all a bit daft; whoever had done the itinerary hadn't worked out the mileage. So it was a right zigzag around. Bands complain about that. It is a bit daft but it's exciting too. It's better than not doing it.

In an ideal world you'd always do a gig a day apart, have the massage and be pampered. It's hard on the road, but it's not like Guantanamo Bay or anything. It's work, but it's not like work as we know it.

After one of the Troubador gigs, Matt Dillon came in and said, "Who's that trombone player?"

It was a real break when we left America and went to Japan – it was like phew! The intensity of being there, the conversation always went round to the World Trade Centre within ten minutes of talking to someone. It was just a little bit intense and to get a few thousand miles away from that, I was grateful for that.

On the British tour there was a lot of drinking going on.

Our European tour we only played France and Greece. I think the idea was to do a few other places but for one reason or another it all didn't get arranged.

When we drove the coach on the boat over to France we had a big lump of dope. We were just getting up to the customs and we were thinking what should we do with it. Joe just saw on the side this tub of nuts and raisins so he broke up the hash into little raisin-size lumps and mixed it in with the nuts and raisins. They came on the bus to check passports – didn't bring dogs or anything.

Of course afterwards we got on the road we had to empty out this tub to sort out the blim of hash. It was very spontaneous of Joe.

That showed Joe's childish, mischievous nature. He had a sense of humour, you have to say.

In Greece we spent a lot of time making joints in restaurants and public places. Somebody told us you could go to prison for seven years if you got caught with a blim of hash in public places. We were doing our bit to normalise Greece. They were fantastic gigs.

I went to bed about six or seven in the morning after a night's drinking. We all got up two hours later to go to the airport and Joe was still at the bar drinking. He bought everybody a metaxa and coke to see us off to the airport.

The five nights in Brooklyn at the time was probably the best week of my life. It was originally going to be a little tour in America.

The first day, you do the soundcheck, do the gig; the gig went well, staying up all night. Then every day we made that journey over Brooklyn Bridge. It's a fantastic journey to do at that time of early evening. It was a lovely area. All sorts of people turning up every night, ending up in different places every night. I ended up in a lesbian disco at about five in the morning with people I had never met before. It was great!

The Fleadh was rubbish, an appalling gig. We hadn't seen each other for two months. It was awful. I remember after the gig thinking, we can't do that again. It's not the vibiest festival; the sound was poor. I think Scott's amp blew up. It left me feeling really empty.

It was a big effort to get there, set it all up and then everyone went their separate ways afterwards. I lost my bloody car keys; I came back to Sheffield to get the spare key and back down to London on the Sunday morning to pick the car up.

I was pissed off we never played Glastonbury.

At this time it was all a bit bitty. There were no tours, we all wanted to be busier, and things were being cancelled. What we really were doing was putting off making a record, we hadn't got round to it. We had talked about doing it. The record company aren't going to spend a fortune on you doing a tour and the record's just about gonna break even.

We had to come up with odd things to do. They were all clutching at straws, really, just to try and make touring more interesting rather than just going out touring, which is something you're always faced with as a touring musician.

It was the middle of the summer, so we weren't going to make a new album, we weren't going to tour but there's a festival to do.

That Hootenanny was daft, it was all a skata punk collection of bands and us and they were all appalling, making an appalling racket halfway between skittle rhythm and blues and skata punk. We kinda stood out a bit. We just sat in the bus the whole time. We tried not to get drunk before the gig and afterwards sat on the bus.

Again it was a bitty kinda tour. When you're on tour you do go out and drink a lot and feel unhealthy, and if that's all you do, you lose the point of the show to do something new. We were in danger of getting like that at that time.

Likewise with Manchester; it wasn't going in the right direction then. There were good bits about these gigs. But there were a few things out of our control that we didn't like. We were trying to do new tunes, trying to make it less blokey.

When we did Paul Heaton it was all of us together doing something else which was refreshing. I don't think Scott and Martin really ever told Joe in so many words that we were doing it.

I actually just managed to wangle on that. Martin and Scott were going to do it, Luke was going to do it and Arnie who played bass on the record. When Martin was getting everything together he said, "It would be nice if you could come along, though I don't know what you're gonna play. I'll see if I can get it into the budget." So I was like the spare man. In the end I ended up playing acoustic guitar and backing vocals. At rehearsals I ended up playing acoustic guitar on a couple of tunes and I said, "Look, why don't I just play acoustic guitar?"

The music was a lot less intense. It did tighten us up and made us listen to each other.

On rehearsals for The Mescaleros the tendency was just to get stoned and mess about and on the last day knock a set together.

So to have some new tunes to get your teeth into was good for us I think.

At Cambridge it was just funny taking the mickey out of all the folkies.

After the Asagiri gig I had some acid and me Joe and Tymon had a trip each and in the disco Joe was dancing. It was the only time I saw Joe dance – not for very long; he sort of realised he was dancing.

We had all met up at Martin and Scott's old studio 2KHZ to start on some new tunes. Everything was set up and when we first arrived the first thing Joe said was, "Everyone go bonkers." We were looking to him for some kinda direction as to what could we do. So we went bonkers for the week. We had an awesome time, bouncing tunes and ideas off of one another. Joe was going round leaving joints in ashtrays. He didn't do any playing or singing; he'd just come in halfway through a jam and say, "This one's called..." He had piles and piles of lyrics.

Joe loved playing at the Opera House – he wanted to play punk rock tunes at the Opera House.

I loved the last tour; it was typical of Joe to play in all these daft places.

The fire brigade benefit was a great idea. At the time we were all thinking, this is going to be a nightmare. The soundcheck went dreadful. We were thinking of not doing a soundcheck, it sounded appalling in that town hall-type building.

The gig itself was amazing; it was packed.

At the time when Mick came on Joe didn't know anything. The look of shock on Joe's face when Mick came on. Mick said to Mike one of the roadies, "Give us a guitar, I'm going on." He had to plug into Joe's amp, so it was two guitars in one amp. It sounded dreadful from where I was. The enthusiasm and the excitement were undeniable. It was obviously a great buzz to do backing vocals on the same mike.

Afterwards Joe said, "Did you see that guy that came on? He looked a bit like Mick Jones."

Joe wouldn't begrudge it, he made a good show of it, but he wouldn't have asked him on. He certainly wouldn't have said, "Why don't you come on?" That was the only way they were going to get together, by him bludgeoning Joe into it.

Joe was handing out flyers at Hastings, "Come and see a rock show."

Sheffield was the best gig of the tour. It was like the first proper gig. I felt we delivered then.

I had a friend called Simon who came to see the gig in Sheffield. We sat on the bus having a joint before going to Liverpool, the bus started moving, so I said, right, I've kidnapped you now. So he ended up coming to Liverpool and the last gig.

That whole tour was a bit prophetic. Like most tours the second to last gig is the best gig. The last one is like last day blues; you know it's the last one. I remember Liverpool being a good gig; you don't want it to end.

I wanted to get the record done as soon as possible because I was possibly going to be touring in February. We always seemed to do things a week at a time then take a month off.

When we went to Rockfield Joe would go in this backroom and he had this little Fisher Price tape player, a kid's one. Listening to the tunes coming out of the speakers in the background.

Also at Rockfield we played *Get Down Moses* live with the idea that that was going to be on the album release for Japan because they always want an extra track in Japan. In the end that's more or less the version that's on the album. It ended up better than the one we were working on, plus it had vocals on it.

All that's on *Streetcore* is the first run-through of each tune. Joe only spent four hours singing. Some of them there is no second verse, there's bits where afterwards we have had to chop things up, use the same thing twice for choruses. If we had spent one more day, we'd have doubled the tunes on the album.

The last time I saw Joe was at Rockfield. We all stayed up and had a drink on the last day. It got up to 4 o'clock and, as I was walking across the courtyard going our separate ways, I said to Joe, "Nice one Joe today. You don't need to hear it from me but that was great." He said, "No, every man needs a little encouragement. Do you fancy finishing this bottle of brandy?"

So we stayed for another couple of hours, talking all sorts of shit. The last thing Joe said to me was, "Cancel all plans, cancel all plans."

A couple of days before Kate and I got married we had heard the news about Joe. We got married on Xmas Eve. We were knocked for six about whether we should go. But we had to go. I was just in shock. It was losing a friend, a bandmate, someone you respected a lot and also my boss if you like. My livelihood.

Johnny Fingers came on and played Hammond at one gig. Joe knew about it but didn't tell us so we wouldn't veto it. We were playing away and looked around and somebody was playing the keyboards. After the song Joe introduced him to the audience.

That's how we did sets then, we'd do all the new songs and then when it came to the end of the set we'd do new song, Clash song, and when it came to doing an encore we'd do all the old tunes/Clash tunes.

All the time us Mescaleros would be pushing to do more new songs. We wanted to do Mescaleros tunes rather than the Clash tunes, but it was undeniably the Clash tunes where everyone leapt on the stage and went crazy. On the whole I did enjoy playing Clash tunes, but there were times when I didn't. There were times when we'd look at each other and go "Oh God" as we were playing it for the 50th time.

I don't think Martin particularly enjoyed it; probably Scott tolerated it more. Luke always had fun because he was bashing around on the drums. There were times when I was thinking arghhhhhhhh.

I think Martin was just not enjoying it because he's a bit of a jazzer and a muso as well and he doesn't like just hammering away, making a racket. For me it was the repetition.

Sometimes if you look at the audience they're all weight lifters, big muscle-bound testosterone and they're all going warghhhhhhhhh to some neanderthal thing. I don't really want to be involved in that. It depended what mood you're in.

Towards the end of our touring the percentage of females in the audience had gone up from two to six. It was a noticeable increase!

Joe was very much into making a good show. It wasn't just that he liked playing all these old songs, he wanted it to be a good show. We just didn't have enough fast Mescaleros songs, up-tempo Mescaleros songs. I think after the next record would have been made it would have been feasible to play complete gigs with no Clash songs. I think he still would have thrown a couple in; he still would have in the encore.

I think we had a lot in common actually. I really felt like we'd be good friends. I feel we could have been quite close if I'd have known Joe for a few more years.

When Joe died, Kate was on maternity leave so her wages had gone right down, so I had to get myself a job more or less immediately to pay the mortgage. I've recently got myself a publishing deal, so I can carry on writing.

I've got a load of tunes that I want to put on a record. I want to do it with Martin really.

I've got a studio that was an old club that's been deserted for 30 years, so very soon I'm going down there with my wire brush and paints and doing it up. We've got a multi-track. We're going to have to find our feet.

I'm still playing in a couple of jazz bands. I haven't got a rock 'n' roll band at the moment.

I turned down John Squire because I was with Richard Hawley. The only reason I stayed with Richard was I had said to him I was going to work out all his samples. He's useless at technology. If I'd have ducked out of that I'd have really left him in the lurch. Then after all that his tour got cancelled. After that I pulled out with Richard because he had so little work, it wasn't worth my while turning other things down for it. He's still a very good friend.

Actually when I was with Richard we supported Smiley's band Archive in Paris. We never met up for some reason. I only heard about it afterwards.

John Blackburn

"Joe understood how important it was for me to show my parents how grateful I was for supporting my dream of being a musician. After the gig Joe signed a setlist for my dad that read: 'To Big John, The boy done good... Love, Joe'."

John Blackburn

Being born in '76, I was too young to feel the full force The Clash made worldwide when they came out. I would have loved to have been in my 20s then. It hit home when backstage on the tour, you'd see these 40-something, frightening-looking punks who would melt in Joe's company as they had come to pay homage to "The Man." It was fantastic to experience and made me see how lucky I was to share a stage with such a legend.

It was a whole different level to anything I had done musically at that point. My involvement with Joe began by way of Martin Slattery. I knew Martin from playing in a band with him, together with Fil Isler and Guy Chambers. At the time, both Guy and Fil were at the start of working with Robbie Williams so we only ever played a couple of gigs, one of which was at the 12 Bar Club in Denmark Street. We didn't even have a name for the band. It was only when we arrived at the venue that we were asked, "What's your band called? Fil's T-shirt had the word Pornstar on it, so we said "Err... we're called Pornstar."

As it goes, nothing became of the band but later the same year Martin rang asking if I could fill in and play bass with Joe Strummer & The Mescaleros on The Who tour the following day. It's funny how things happen.

"I met up with The Mescaleros (minus Joe) at a rehearsal studio in North London. At the time I didn't know any Clash songs that well and I can remember sitting on the train, listening to my walkman, and memorising the chords whilst travelling across London to the studio. The rehearsal itself was only a couple of hours – then it was off Manchester for my first gig. We did the soundcheck and I felt fairly confident I had learned the listed set in the short space of time I was given.

I was nervous meeting Joe for the first time. It was literally a quick handshake and introduction minutes before the gig at Manchester Arena. The gig went well and I got a real buzz out of basically not really having played these songs before and all of a sudden it's ready, steady, GO!

I did have the privilege to get to know Joe during those couple of weeks with the band. He had such presence and when he spoke, everyone listened. I spent many an hour exploring his CD collection, which he carried everywhere and enjoyed talking about. His music was so diverse and included a lot of Reggae, African, Latin, and Cuban sounds.

Albums we listened to included Ernest Ranglin's *In Search of the Lost*

Riddim and *Funky Kingston* by Toots and the Maytals. Joe's legacy to me was broadening my own personal music collection and always keeping an ear out for new things.

I also learned when you're in Joe's company and he buys you a 15-year-old malt in a bar in Scotland, never ask for a drop of lemonade with it!

The only slip-up I had during the tour happened the following night at Glasgow Arena. Just before we were about to go onstage, Joe said, "Let's do *White Man In Hammersmith Palais* tonight!" and I nearly choked because it wasn't one I rehearsed. Joe was great though. Using a blue pastel highlighter he quickly drew out the chords on a white sheet of paper for me.

Once onstage I thought I had placed it upside down but as I reached to turn the sheet over with *White Man* due to be the next song, I saw with horror that it was blank. I realised the purple stage lighting made Joe's diagram invisible!!! I immediately went over and stood next to Martin on the keyboards and had to watch his left hand for the notes. When I told Joe about it afterwards, he laughed and said it went unnoticed.

I had booked the flight before I had joined up with The Mescaleros and the airline wouldn't let me change it. I knew Scott was returning, and when I spoke to Joe, he was so cool about it. At the time, no one was really sure how long Scott would be absent for and at that point it was pretty much gig by gig.

Two things were perfect about my final night with The Mescaleros: it was such a fantastic feeling knowing I was playing bass for Joe Strummer & The Mescaleros, supporting The Who, and also knowing my fiancée and parents were in the audience watching. Joe understood how important it was for me to show my parents how grateful I was for supporting my dream of being a musician. After the gig Joe signed a setlist for my dad that read: "To Big John, The boy done good... Love, Joe."

Only a handful of musicians were lucky enough to share the stage with Joe during his whole life, and to be a part of that group is amazing. I had a brilliant time on the tour and my last gig with The Mescaleros ended on a high note.

Today I have fantastic memories of the gigs I played during their tour in November 2000. I haven't been in touch with The Mescaleros as much as I would like to. I used to send the odd text just to let people know I was still alive. It's crazy as well because Smiley lives less than a mile from where I live, but we're both so busy at the moment. I only knew him for a little time but I miss his good vibes and humour. He's definitely a good guy.

One person I have met up with again since the tour is my guitar tech, Andy. When I joined The Mescaleros, he knew I was the new boy on tour and took me under his wing. He's a great guy and looked out for me then, and still does now! It's no coincidence that he's currently my guitar tech with Skin. We still talk about Joe and the lasting impression he's left on us.

In retrospect, I wish I could have had more time with Joe and played that last gig. You never know what's around the corner and it's tragic he's gone and there won't ever be another gig where Joe will say, "John boy, you'll do it."

Jimmy Hogarth

"I came back for the last gig on The Who tour at Wembley, Scott was there and I remember him being on the side of the stage laughing at me fighting my way through the songs."

Jimmy Hogarth

Playing with The Mescaleros came about through Martin and Scott really. I'd known them a long time. We were all in a band together in America – me, Scott and Martin and another guy called Steve who were in that band.

When we came back from America Scott and Martin started working a lot more together. They went on to do the production on Joe's records after Antony did the first one. I was still in contact with those guys regularly. When Scott had his period when he wasn't very well, he had lost the feeling in his arm.

I just fitted in, helped them out and did a few shows and got involved as much as I could get involved. Because it was at a period where I was trying to set the studio up at the same time.

I kinda had to choose where my loyalties lay at that point. I don't mean to Joe or to the band but actually whether I was going to go out and be a touring musician or not, full stop. I kinda made a choice at that point that I wasn't going to do it. Obviously you don't pass up the chance to play bass with Joe Strummer very often.

I was drafted in only two days before the 100 Club gig. I did one rehearsal with them before the 100 Club and that was the first gig I did. I had to learn 19 songs, I think, in the one rehearsal. So I never fully got into the swing, into being able to get my head round that whole gig. As much as Joe's songs are fairly simple, they never had more than three or four chords in them. The arrangement is something you've got to get your head round. The way that Joe goes from one change to another is quite complicated. I had Martin shouting out the chords to me most of the show at the 100 Club, which was quite funny.

It was great, I got on really well. I definitely would have done the whole thing and carried on doing it if it hadn't have been the fact that my commitment kinda laid to getting on in the studio and really trying to set that up for myself. I wanted to produce and write – that was my main thing really. It just took its shape.

When I played the 100 Club I wasn't surprised it was heaving. I had been to their shows quite a few times. The Astoria and really whenever they played in London I would normally turn up and watch the shows. So I knew Pabs, I knew Smiley.

It was a very brief encounter with Joe really. Joe really wanted me to carry on doing it. When I told him I had other things to do, it didn't go down too well. I told Joe right at the beginning, in the rehearsals, I said I could only due a certain amount of time as I had writing sessions coming into the studio and I had to carry on with it.

I think Joe respected what I was doing and all that, but Joe's quite hardcore about things like that and he called me "a quitting cunt" at one point, which is very Joe. Martin said it's a sign that he liked me but I'm not too sure myself. Joe used that word quite often.

I had a great time doing it. It was like no other kind of tour that I'd been involved with, 'cause Joe turned it into such a family atmosphere. There were lots of people that were there that were Joe's people. Timmy Tim was always around.

When we supported The Who it was quite weird because they were such big venues. We had rehearsed a lot of the new songs so we were still kinda feeling our way around them. *Bhindi Bhagee* and stuff like that was the first time these had been played.

You have to follow Joe all the time when you're onstage, because he'd want to stop in sections or take it down. I always remember having my eyes on him all the time to make sure I wasn't going anywhere that he wasn't. It was like that in the whole band actually; it was always what Joe wanted, where he wanted. What sections he wanted to go up, what sections he wanted to come back down. Joe's completely for the moment when it's live.

You have got to watch him to make sure you're with him or not at all times to make the show work. I think that's what was good about a lot of the live shows, that there was that communication between the band members and Joe.

I came back for the last gig on The Who tour at Wembley. Scott was there and I remember him being on the side of the stage laughing at me fighting my way through the songs.

I wish I'd have done more obviously; it's one of those things. I don't regret it because it has worked out good for me now, but obviously in hindsight, with Joe passing away, you wish you'd done a little bit more whilst he was still around.

Nowadays I am producing, writing and production, for a couple of artists on Island Records. Have done some stuff for Amy Winehouse. Just produced two tunes for Tina Turner on her greatest hits. Also did quite a lot of Beverley Knight's album as well as an album for Half Cousin and Sia and tracks for Jamilia and Estelle.

It's been one of those things that I wanted to do when I came back from the year in America. If you're not in a band at that point in your kinda mid to late 20s that you've been with for a long period of time, you know that's something that's not going to be an option for the rest of your career. So I decided to get into production. I've never been happier.

I work with Martin a lot; Martin does a lot of my musical arrangements for me, does all the horns and piano. It's nice to have him – he's a very talented man.

Martin is very adaptable; he's also quite sophisticated musically as well. If he doesn't know how to play an instrument you can leave him with it for a day or two and he'll fuckin' know how to play it after that. Martin has a good musical brain. I think that's one of the things Martin and Joe hit it off on definitely. He was very in tune with Joe. I think Joe had quite a lot of influence over Martin on the types of things that he does and doesn't like now in a very positive way. It opened up and broadened his horizons quite a lot. Martin picked up on quite a lot of the world music that Joe was into.

It was a good partnership. He's a great guy to have about, Martin, in any project.

My whole encounter was short and sweet but I feel touched and privileged to have been a small part of such an important man's life. He was an icon to everybody. Everybody that I know, certainly musically, has nothing but respect for Joe Strummer.

Andy Boo

"I was a big man before I went to work for Joe and I'm a bigger man now. I'd still walk that extra mile for all of them."

Andy Boo

Mark Dempsey called me up and I thought he was offering me a gig with Supergrass. He said, "What are you doing between these dates?" I said, "Nothing, who's it with?" He said Joe Strummer.

I remembered reading a few days before in the NME that Joe Strummer was coming back.

When Dempsey said it's Joe Strummer I remember it distinctively. He told me the line-up of the band and I just took the gig without working out the merits, without going through the ins and outs of it.

I remember putting the phone down and running around the flat waving my hands in the air, going yeahhhhhhhhhhhhhh, celebrating.

I had written down the line-up of the band and thought, this is too much, you can't do this on your own. So I phoned Dempsey and told him, so he said, work it out and get somebody you want to work with.

They had a meeting with the band and Mark told Ants that Boo would do it but he needed some help. Ants agreed to it, which was great.

We were in Germany, it was about 7.00 in the morning. Joe and I were having a smoke and drink and on the telly it came up about the Beach Boys playing in town that night.

Joe was going, "The Beach Boys, yeah, let's all go and see the Beach Boys." I just thought yeah, right. OK, Joe you're having a laugh.

At lunchtime all the band and me went to a Japanese restaurant. The only reason they let me go was Ants looked at me and said, "You look more like a band member than a crew member in your 'day off' shirt."

In the restaurant this geezer's only got out the karaoke book. Joe's sitting there tapping his foot as various Mescaleros sang a song. I said to Joe, "A good song to do for karaoke is *We Are The World*." Look, there's seven of us so we can all be somebody. I'll be Michael Jackson and you can be Bruce Springsteen, Joe!

Joe just sat there and Ants said, "You're not really into this Joe, are you?" Joe said, "No."

So The Mescaleros did this rendition of *We Are The World* with Joe sitting there tapping his fingers on the table.

After the meal Joe's come up again with this thing about going to see The Beach Boys. I really thought he was joking. But he was serious.

So a few went to the Stadtpark, Hamburg with Joe where they bought the tickets, Joe was never a big blagmeister and at the gig Joe was apparently dancing away, having the time of his life. When they came back to the bus Joe said, "You're all sacked, you're all sacked. This morning I said we're all going to see The Beach Boys and hardly any of you came."

We were all re-employed the next day!!!

When we were in Australia, I was in my room watching telly and there was this history of The Beach Boys programme on. So I rang Joe's room and said, "What you doing?" He said, "Nothing, why?" I said, "Look there's this programme on telly about The Beach Boys." He said, "I know, I'm watching it!"

When we played Finland Pabs had to fly back to England. I was on the bongos and the set had been altered accordingly. Joe attempted to introduce me a couple of times but I hid as I was tucked away right at the back. A couple of songs later Joe signalled that he was having some problems with his guitar strap and as I came to the front of the stage to help, he grabbed my arm and declared "Ladies and Gentlemen, Rufus on the bongos."

Joe put a lot of faith in me to do things and I took that seriously. I used to say, "That's what the guvner wants" and some people would say, "Oh, that's stupid, that is." I used to say it's not about what we want to do ultimately!

One night Joe said he wanted some flight cases on the stage for him to stand on so people at the back could see him. As we were doing it comments were passed about "This is stupid." I just said shut up and do it. I know it's stupid, I know it's one of the worst ideas I've ever heard.

But in retrospect it was sheer brilliance. I'll never meet another artist who thinks that way and does a similar thing except Dave Grohl. It's only the mavericks, your people who are of the people and were formerly of the people. Who used to go and watch a lot of gigs, who knows what it's like to shell out £17.00 and stand at the back and can't see anything.

I used to sleep in the studios; I had the lucky straw as I was looking after Pabs so I had the conga bags. I used to get into the conga bags. I lived in the rehearsals for a few weeks. But after the first batch I had to put my foot down – I asked for a hotel.

To be brutally honest we drove ourselves a bit mad because we were doing loads of gear. It was unhealthy.

Before we even got it up and running Joe was a legend. Some people that should have known better wanted it to fail, some people in high places. They were wanting to concentrate on *From Here To Eternity*. Joe said, "Nothing to do with me, leave me out of it."

The first rehearsals were so intense, Ants was running himself into the ground.

Joe had a big thing on loyalty; I felt that loyalty when I got sacked and then brought back. Joe knew what worked for him. Joe was always good reaching back. It's like Barry Myers on the last tours – he got Barry back on the firm because he had lost all of us. He loved to retain his links. Why get to go through all this cautious period with people?

When Joe used to look stage right, I knew what he wanted, what he was feeling. The more time you spend with people the better you know them. If I saw he was a little bit twitchy, I'd leave him alone – something's going on in his head.

When we first went to America we were sponsored by Von Dutch. They had their name all over the posters, the promotional stuff. We were supposed to get a load of clothes out of them but we got fuck all, as ever.

Joe was into Massimo – that black jacket he would always wear was Massimo. Everything with Joe was low-key, no slogan. Nobody could pin their name to him.

As usual the crew get a bit funny with support bands. Nobody was prepared to look after them and give them a good run at it, but I went out of my way to look after Little Mothers, because I knew who the dad was and he had played with Joe, so that's how they got the slot.

I went out of my way to look after them because these kids were performing with "the guvner" before I even met him. That was also indicative of what he was like and what the vibe was like. Joe was into connections with the past. Joe never consciously forgot anybody or anything. He always had a lot on his mind; he was one of those people that were always thinking about something.

We stopped at a truckstop on the way to Boston from Toronto, Martin was there, Scott was there and Pabs was there. I went out the back to use the phone. I kept peeking around to check people were still there. I popped my head round again and no one was there.

I thought perhaps they had grabbed their food and got back on the bus. So I finished my conversation, strolled out … no bus!

Now this was the fourth time in six months that I was left behind, What used to peeve me about when they used to leave me behind (I think this is why Pabs laughed when you and him chatted about it)... now look at this; there's like 16 or 17 of us on that bus, how many fuckin' black people are there on this bus? How many black people? There was one black geezer on the bus! And they still manage to leave me behind. They never left Smiley, they didn't leave Pabs, didn't leave Gordon.

So I'm left behind. I've got no cash, they're about an hour from the border so I've got to think quick. If they get to the border and sail through, it will be a case of they get to Boston and I'm not there. The crux of it was, they thought I was in my bunk. I had my mobile but it wasn't triband (it didn't work in Canada or America). I tried to reverse calls to Gary Robinson's mobile, but you can't. I rang BT who I had an account with but they couldn't help (when I got home I cancelled my account with them). So in the end I had to reverse a call to a mate of mine in Birmingham – God knows what time of the day it was in England! I said, "Listen, you've got to ring this number for me." I explained the situation – he thought I was having a laugh. I said, "Listen you've got to ring him."

In the meantime, thank God for Pablo because the satellites came round again and he's online with the world again. He apparently has said: "Where's Boo, where's Boo?" Everyone else has said, "Errrrrrr, I don't know."

Pabs raised the alarm and they checked my bunk. My mate had rung Gary and he said, "I know, I know." So they had to turn around and come back and get me.

In the meantime I'm sitting there feeling uncomfortable. It was a real redneck place.

After they picked me up we then got a pull at the border. Normally one of my jobs was to do an "idiot check" – get rid of all the roaches, clear everything up. Those guys used to leave everything just lying around all over the place. They couldn't look after themselves.

We got pulled in Marseilles once. I had to tie stuff up in my hair I had a mouth full of hash. I was only saved because Ants fell out the bus and he took the focus.

When I watched those DVDs you gave me the other night, especially The Who tour, I'll admit to you, it was probably right for it to have ended.

When I saw Joe and the band again in Brixton 2001, I went down to the dressing-rooms. Joe's girls were great and we sat there chatting. I went and sat over with Joe in the corner. I just felt awkward, awkward, awkward. You could have cut the air with a knife. It wasn't like the old days. After everything that we had been through.

One good thing that came out of that night was the picture John Hatch took of you and me which still hangs up in my flat. Every time I look at that picture there's a little bit of hurt in my eyes because I do have a thing about that night. I had more love upstairs than in the dressing-rooms.

Joe didn't like confrontation. I had a couple of run-ins with various people and Joe would always come to me and say, "You're a man. It's down to you, Rasta."

He came to me about Smiley once, saying people want to get rid of Smiley. I said, "You can't do that." Joe said, "Why not?" "Because you once told me The Clash was never the same after they sacked Topper."

He loved that because he realised I had listened to what he had told me in the past. I'd remind him of the wisdom he had given to me. Smiley had just had the baby, plus the Robbie thing. You just can't do that to my man Smiley. Has he ever let you down at the last minute?

I'm not going to knock Mescaleros Mark 2 or whatever because it's all good, but certain decisions were made that people had to and have to live by. One of the worst aspects of it was I had a job that everybody wanted and that's not a nice position to be in. People were going behind your back; I had one of the most sought-after positions in the music business, Joe's tech.

People were even going to Justin asking him to put a word in.

"No offence Boo!" **What? For fucks sake!**

Even Gary used to say to me, "You think you're irreplaceable. I've got people calling me up every week volunteering their services."

It didn't just go for me, it went for Justin, all of us on the crew. We won't be bought. That's what Joe was like, that's what Pabs was like. There is so much good to talk about today. To a slight degree it haunts me, 'cause you can't correct it. It's all happened.

The books going to be great for me because I can see everybody else's take on stuff that happened.

I was a big man before I went to work for Joe and I'm a bigger man now. I'd still walk that extra mile for all of them. I wouldn't change any of it though I might have got his guitar 30 seconds earlier at Wembley!

Richard Flack

Meeting Joe & The Mescaleros – Making Rock Art

I first met Joe and Pablo whilst I was working for a studio called Battery in Willesden. Pabs and Joe came in to do a remix of a Josh Wink single with Bez from the Mondays.

Pablo was producing the track and I was his engineer for the day. It was a pretty mad session, lots of partying and people dropping by. Joe played guitar on it then Bez and Joe sang on it. It turned out to be a bit of a mental track but unfortunately was a bit too leftfield for Mr Wink and never saw the light of day – literally; I ended up clearing up at about eight in the morning!

As I was told, a few months later Joe bumped into Ant in the Groucho Club and they decided to go into a studio and try some ideas out.

Joe must have remembered the session he did at Battery, liked the studio or the vibe or whatever and booked the studio. That's when I met Ant for the first time. I thought he was the producer and was also going to be engineering. When I told him I was going to be his assistant for the session he said, "No, no, no, you're not my assistant you're my engineer!" I said, "OK that's cool; I'm your engineer."

Initially I think they booked the studio for four or five days to see if anything would happen. Three months later they left and *Rock Art* was finished.

It was pretty hard work – we pretty much slept at the studio. Joe slept in a little overdub booth for the most part. He lived down in Somerset and only went back at weekends. Ant slept where he dropped – I'm not sure he actually had a home at the time. I had a girlfriend so I did go home occasionally!

It was the first time I'd seen and been involved with a record being conceived, written, recorded, mixed and mastered in one hit. In fact *Willesden To Cricklewood* was written, recorded and mixed in one night! Ant started sodding around with a piano riff after we came back from the pub about 5pm. Joe said, "I like that, keep on going with that for a bit." He then disappeared for a few hours to write some lyrics. By about five or six o'clock that morning it was finished and we'd put a mix down – that's what's on the record. It's my favourite track on the record and it was played at Joe's funeral – that really choked me up. Joe was probably pissing himself, though, because it's actually about walking from the studio in Willesden to Cricklewood to score puff!

Most of the tracks for *Rock Art* were written in the studio by Joe and Ant although Joe did bring a few ideas up from Somerset on an old 16-track. These turned into *X-Ray Style*, *Road To Rock 'n' Roll* and *Forbidden City*.

Joe had written and recorded *Yalla Yalla* and *Diggin' The New* already with

Richard Norris (the Grid). We took the original recordings and reworked them.

There was also a track called *Sandpaper Blues*, which I think Dave Stewart did with Gary Dyson. This was a track which had already been recorded. I didn't have anything to do with it at all.

Steve Jones came in and played on a track called *Ocean of Dreams*, which never made it to the record. It was a good track, actually, but Joe never sang on it. I just don't think he ever got inspired to sing on it.

When most people make an album, they'll choose maybe 14 or 16 songs to record. Then what happens is over the period of the recording the album a couple will fall by the wayside. They'll end up with finishing 14 and then they'll pick ten or 12 to put on a record. The tracks that are left over are usually picked as B-sides or extra tracks. Every track we started made it on the record apart from that one. Ants started it, Steve Jones played on it, but then it fell by the wayside and never got finished.

After the recording was done all the tracks had to be mixed. Joe had worked with Bill Price before on the Clash records so Bill was asked to come in to do the mixes. Bill set up in studio 4 at Battery to start mixing as I finished off any bits and pieces of the recording upstairs in studio 2. As I'd finish each one the tapes would then go downstairs to Bill.

After about three days it became apparent there was a bit of a problem. For whatever reason I don't know why, it wasn't really sounding as we'd imagined it would. I'm not quite sure how it happened but I think Bill was told he didn't have to come back.

After a bit of a discussion on what to do I think Ant said something like, "Fuck it, how hard can it be. We'll do it!"

So without ever mixing a record, between us Ant and I finished up mixing the *Rock Art* album.

Unfortunately by this stage Ant was in the death throes of his smack addiction and was taking a lot of gear. He had made the decision to go into rehab after we finished doing the record, so this was his last two weeks of trying to get as much gear into his body as he possibly could.

This considered, all the mixes got finished and didn't come out at all bad! Joe came in towards the end and, bar a few changes, OKd the mixes and *Rock Art* was finished.

Initially Joe had wanted me to come on tour with them and do the front-of-house sound as at the time he said he considered me to be the seventh Mescalero. He tried really very hard to talk me into coming on tour with them.

To be honest I think he used the term seventh Mescalero in an effort to emotionally blackmail me into saying yes (Joe could be very persuasive!) but I had to turn it down. I would have loved to have gone, but I didn't really think I could have done the job justice. Studio engineers and live sound engineers are two very different jobs. There's so much more you've got to deal with at once, doing live sound, and to be honest I didn't want to make a hash of it. Joe (and Ant) had been cool in basically letting me cut my teeth on their record but in live sound you can't re-record something later; you've got to get it right at the time. I think that's when Ant got Justin involved.

I went to Sheffield to see the first gig. To be honest it was a bit rough round the edges, but it was so cool seeing Joe and the boys playing live for the first time, it didn't matter. It was a great gig because it was the first and nothing went wrong!

Afterwards everyone piled back to the band's hotel. I didn't have anywhere to kip so I had to share a bed with Smiley. As I remember it, he wasn't very happy about it at all. I think he thought I was joking; I had to really talk him into it!

The night before Glastonbury, Scott and Ant and myself had stayed up all night doing a remix of *Tony Adams*. (This track later formed the basis for *Cool 'n' Out* on *Global A Go-Go*.) The rest of the band were already there, so we had to drive down (still slightly spannered) and got down there about 7am.

When we banged on the tour bus, I think Pabs was already up playing with Titus who was running round like a lunatic.

Ant immediately had to go off to some bog to do the gear that he'd smuggled in up his arse! (The rehab hadn't worked)

I then left them to find some mates of mine; I eventually found them after a couple of hours.

The next time I saw the boys was when they were onstage. Whilst they were onstage Joe dedicated a track to me. He said, "This one's for Richard Flack" and, in a slightly menacing way, "We ain't finished yet." In other words, you'd better come back, you're not getting away from us that easy!

It was a great gig, I really enjoyed it. It's so cool seeing songs being performed live that you've just been working on only a few weeks before.

The original line-up had a real raw energy about them, they had real attitude. Slats was and is just great on everything. Smiley's a very powerful drummer (if a little too generous with the fills!). Scott's a wicked bass player and Ants, whilst his guitar playing wasn't always technically correct, always had the right attitude.

Global A Go-Go: By the time it came to make another record, Ant was no longer in the band. I think Joe decided that we would all make it with no one particularly in charge, a sort of musical co-operative. As it turned out, however, Slats and Scotty turned out to be the driving force behind the recordings with myself at the wheel, so to speak. Joe, however, you could say was the back-seat driver who always got his way in the end! Real socialist politics in action!

Originally Joe had the idea that there would be no drums on the record, just percussion. I think he wanted to make a much folkier record. As it happened, drums did make it on the record but he did get his folk! Another one of his ideas was to not tell any musician what to play, just let them play whatever the hell they wanted and we'd edit it afterwards. This resulted in some really cool tracks. For instance, one day when Pablo walked in through the door, we said we've got a track we want you to play on. When he put his headphones on all he got was a click track! This didn't faze him at all, he just decided what tempo it should be and proceeded to build up this cool percussion track. This is what became *Gamma Ray*.

Joe was mates with Roger Daltrey and asked him to guest-vocal on the title track – *Global A Go-Go*.

I think Roger thought it was going to be a duet, and thought he was going to be singing a lot more than he actually did. What he did was great! He did one line of lead and he did some background to Joe. I think it was cool like that, otherwise it would have been "featuring Roger Daltrey" and taking too much away from Joe & The Mescaleros. It was basically, that's it Roger, that's all you've got to do!

I remember when we were making the album, just down the corridor to the studio, he had this little overdub booth which never got used much. Joe set up camp in there; bits of paper everywhere plus his sleeping bag. He'd either sleep in there or just used to go in there with his dictaphone or "tractorphone" as Joe would call it because it used to make a noise like a tractor. You could only just about hear what had been recorded on it over the noise of the actual machine.

Joe would make sure the door was slightly ajar to the studio and the door was slightly ajar to his room so he could keep an ear out and hear what was going on.

If we were doing overdubs, programming or editing or background vocals, he would always be listening to what we were doing. Occasionally he'd pop in and go, "Yeah, great." Occasionally he'd go, "No, you fools what are you doing? No, stop that immediately!"

I'm sure when Roger was doing the vocals, Joe was skulking around just outside the door, listening.

The first single from *Global* was *Johnny Appleseed*. The video was shot just off Goldhawk Road and on the roof of Townhouse studios where we were all working at the time. I was pressganged (by the ever-persuasive Joe) into shaking a banana and generally dancing around like a loon, or rather doing an impersonation of someone dancing around like a loon.

Minstrel Boy: Joe was asked by Hans Zimmer to record a version of *Minstrel Boy* for the end-credit sequence on the Ridley Scott movie *Black Hawk Down*. We re-recorded it more in a band feel back at Battery. After a lot of conversations with "Zimmer's people" we were asked to go over to LA to finish off the track.

This was maybe Joe's greatest test as a singer. The melody of *Minstrel Boy* is very dynamic and the key the track was recorded in was very high, probably too high for Joe's range. We didn't have time to re-record it so Joe sang on it as it was. He found it very difficult, but didn't give up. It took us nearly two days of doing vocals for Joe to finally nail it. I'm not sure Joe's voice had been up there before and, if it had, not since he was a lot younger!

All we had to do now was mix it. We had only a day and a half before we were due to get our flight home and it was going to be tight. We stayed up all that night and finished into the afternoon of the second day. Everyone else went back to the hotel before going to the airport. I stayed on at the studio to finish up and got a cab straight to the airport with minutes to spare! We'd been booked into the Chateau Marmont hotel for four days but I think I'd only spent one night in my bed!

Streetcore: Unfortunately I didn't have much to do with this album. I just did a bit of programming towards the end.

When *Global A Go-Go* was made we all decided that it was fair to credit Joe, Scott, Martin and myself with the production, since it was us that had spent most of the time in the studio actually making the thing. When it came round to making this record, Scott and Martin came to me and said, "We're going to make another record, but me and Martin are going to produce it! We just want you to engineer."

This didn't sit well with me at all as I didn't like the idea of not being so involved. I thought it over for a couple of weeks. I really wanted to do Joe's third record as I'd been so much a part of the other two (Joe had really made me feel like that seventh Mescalero!) but I knew that I couldn't have given 100%. I went to see the band at rehearsals at the Depot and spoke to Joe about it afterwards. He said he really wanted me to be involved in it, but you've got to do what makes you feel good. Joe was really cool, he understood how I felt about it and consequently I declined. That was the last time I spoke to Joe.

In a sort of cruel twist I did end up doing some work on Streetcore. Joe had gone before he had sung on some of the tracks. Someone had fortunately recorded a few rehearsals, so I was asked to put Joe's vocals from these recordings onto the studio recording backing tracks, which of course I was honoured to do.

I think I worked on four of the new tracks and on *Silver and Gold*, which was a song that was originally recorded during the *Global A Go-Go* sessions. Although I think it got re-recorded and they just kept Joe's original vocal.

Joe was such a great man – it sounds a bit corny but it really was quite a life-changing experience meeting him and knowing him a little bit. Because of him I've met some great and wonderfully talented people. Joe had a very special eye for people. He had this uncanny way of being able to suss people out. To know what their vibe was, know what their strengths and weaknesses were. How to let them use themselves in a way that was productive.

When we made the first record, Joe used to sleep in the studio and go back to Luce at the weekend. So for long periods of time he used to sleep on the floor. When the cleaner used to come round at 8.00 in the morning, we were still working. He used to say, "It's all right, we'll clean up" and he used to tip them anyway!

He would talk to and treat people equally from the Nigerian cleaners (who most people ignored) to, I dunno, Roger Daltrey! Joe treated everyone the same.

Consequently the people that were around Joe were very talented, very warm, just good people basically. Joe attracted that warmth. You could get lost in it sometimes, it was very addictive. When we were making the first record especially. That first record was very special to me because, for the most part, it was really just Joe, Ant and myself in the studio.

Everyone used to come in, do some playing or just to hang out and visit. People used to come and go all the time, but late at nights it was just the three of us. You kinda get locked away in this "cabin mentality". When you work at night the phone doesn't ring and you can just get into what you're doing. When the sun came up it was time to go to bed.

Sometimes a bit too engrossing, though. My girlfriend, who I was living with at the time, left me whilst I was working on this first record because I never came home!

We used to collapse in the studio, sleep until midday, get up, go down the pub for a few pints and then start work again. It was infectious. When my girlfriend left me, it took me two days to realise. She phoned me up and said do you realise I've moved out? I have very happy memories of making those two records. I may have lost my girlfriend but what I've learnt from meeting and working with such talented and warm individuals will stay with me forever. I have to thank Joe for giving me that opportunity. I do miss him.

Gary Robinson

I was initially filling in for "The Grifter", Chris Griffiths. He had asked me to cover a couple of gigs and I ended up jumping in his grave ... actually I was more pushed than jumped. For some reason Joe thought I was "all right" so I got the gig.

If my memory serves me correctly, I think the first show I worked on was the Olympia in Dublin, which is still one of my favourite moments. After the show, I had to go to the dressing room and let Joe and the boys know that the crowd were going nowhere and the promoter was panicking. They just didn't want to leave. I went out to the front of house to let the sound engineer know they were coming back on. The curtains were down and then I heard the first few chords of London Calling with the curtains coming back up. The crowd went mental. It was just one of them moments.

We then did the Limelight in Belfast, where Joe nearly collapsed in the heat. In fact he did collapse in the heat. I remember him falling though the fire escape doors and falling into a heap on the path outside. It was fucking hot in there.

After that we played at Munich. I remember Joe was tired. I suppose in terms of Joe's pride, he was supporting The Offspring, it should have been the other way round really. The reason why The Offspring probably fuckin' exist is because of Joe and The Clash.

That day was pretty unpleasant and you could tell that it was going to be a lairy crowd, a kick-off crowd. I always used to refer to them as a kick-off crowd; you'd go out there and you could just smell it. I can imagine for Joe it being a bit soul-destroying really. Half the kids there probably didn't know who he was even though half the crowd were wearing Anarchy fashion wear ... for fuck's sake.

This poor kid, probably thinking he was being right on and power to the people, started shouting, "Anarchy! Anarchy!" Joe stopped the song and fronted this bloke out. He was like "What the fuck do you know about Anarchy?" This lad had 5,000 people pointing and laughing at him. It was a classic Joe moment.

After the gig it sort of kicked off as well. On the way out the coach was being kicked and punched. I mean, why the fuck would you want to punch a bus; that's gonna hurt, right?

During the British tour, I had a bad case of glandular fever and was in a bad way. I tried to ride it out but couldn't walk by the time we got to the Astoria. I had to take a few days off. They got this guy in who used to tour-manage The Clash years ago to cover the London shows and I joined them again in Norwich – twinned with Seattle apparently.

The UK tour was interesting, especially Manchester, when I think I managed to find two square inches on the bus to sleep that night. Shit, there must have been 40 people on that bus going up to Glasgow – an array of colourful characters. Oh man, Glasgow. I got off the coach that morning to find the driver pulling out the landline and saying he was going home. It was either that or call the police to come and search the bus. With that in mind, I had to get everyone up, including Joe, at 7.30am to get them off the bus as the driver had had enough. Let's just say myself and Joe had an interesting, and somewhat loud conversation that morning which resulted in Ants intervening. Colin McWilliams, the promoter from DF Concerts, found all of this highly amusing. A few days later someone came up to me and said "I heard about you in Glasgow and Shaun Ryder pulling a gun on the bus driver." It's amazing how a story can get so diluted.

After that was the American tour which was quite a tough time for Joe. I don't think anybody enjoyed that tour. It was fuckin' hard work. Joe didn't settle in and didn't really want to be there. He was getting asked to do all sorts of silly things by Hellcat in terms of interviews, of which some were really a waste of time. Myself and Joe used to have to travel for fuckin' miles in the back of a cab to do these interviews to find some geeky kid in a Slipknot T-shirt and a dictaphone

We were only three days into the tour and I've never seen 13 or 14 grown men go so fuckin' loopy in such a short space of time. Ants was just way out, he was just a liability. The minute he walked off the coach you were wondering whether he was going to come back alive. There was a lot of shit going on in terms of rock 'n' roll excesses.

Normal for Joe was boring and he had a point really because they did play brilliantly on that tour, each night crowds were up for it. It's not how well you technically play, it's how angry you play, especially with Joe.

On the American tour we did one show in the midwest where the security were absolute fuckin' animals. The crowd were a real redneck crowd, turning up in tractors and wearing straw hats. When we turned up at the gig we thought there was no way we were going to fill this place; it was in the middle of nowhere.

The venue had not provided a crowd barrier for front-of-stage and I tried to tell the management that it was going to get pretty lairy and I strongly recommended a barrier. They didn't want to know, so I was like, "OK, fair enough, I tried to warn you". Joe was saying, "Don't worry about it, Gal, it'll be cool."

So the gig kicks off and within the second song the place was going mental. I have never seen anything like it. It was mad. The bouncers were grabbing me by the scruff of the neck every time I questioned their somewhat neanderthal approach to crowd control. One of them was threatening to kill me and all that carry-on. Joe was in his element; it did kinda create something for the rest of the tour though.

For many reasons, I had to fire Boo at the end of the British tour; I was made to kinda feel the bad guy. At the time Boo was a liability, he was more rock 'n' roll than the band. I've never disliked Boo, I do like him, but at that particular time he was a pain in the arse ... and he knows it. He probably thought I was a cunt as well, but at the end of the day I had a job to do. As much as Joe wanted chaos, I needed the crew to be solid because we had to carry the chaos at the end of the day. If we were all anarchic, nothing would ever get done, no gigs would happen, everyone would be having a right old party.

Joe rang me when we were in Portland and said that he was finding it hard and needed familiar people around him. I can understand, I suppose, because Joe was losing the plot, he wasn't happy over there. Joe and Boo got on. I had made a decision I thought was for the best, but because Joe was finding the tour quite difficult he just wanted people around him that he knew. For any guitarist, having your guitar tech around you is really important.

Touring America is fuckin' hard work, going from city to city. It is a tough environment to be in, on the bus for 20 hours of the day. So what should have been a really good tour ended up being a bit negative. Plus you've got 14 egos on a bus and you add a concoction of rock 'n' roll behaviour with those egos – it's soon going to be somewhat unruly. I had knocked all excesses on the head because I wanted to take my job a little bit more seriously. It had become important to me because I had a family to look after. I wanted to come back with a salary as opposed to spunking it all on silly behaviour, but in America I started to indulge myself again ... which made it a bit easier actually.

It was never straightforward with The Mescaleros; my main concern was keeping the band and the crew tight. I still have a lot of fond memories of Joe, the band and the crew – Joe "Colombo" Campbell, Justin "The Lobster" Grealy, "Wee" Gordon White, Des "Evlis" Hill and the "Boo".

When we were in San Francisco Ants had said to me "he was going to lose it!" I knew exactly what he meant because he had been on the wagon and he was about to come off big-time. San Francisco is the heroin capital of America. A couple of occasions I found him in a bit of a mess.

Anaheim was probably the closest to *Spinal Tap* I will ever experience. As soon as I got there, I thought, I gotta get out this fuckin' place! It was so "chicken in a basket". They started to put these seats in and I said to the promoter, "What yer doin'?" They said, "We're making room for the diners". I said, "The fuckin' diners?!, Do you know who Joe Strummer is? I'm not being condescending or fucking patronising but do you know who he is? They said, "Yeah, man."

They just didn't see it. So I had to get myself out for a walk and I spotted this coffee house on the other side of the freeway. By the time I had my coffee and crossed over the mile of road between the café and the venue, the gig was getting near doors. At that point I saw the front of the venue for the first time. I couldn't believe my eyes. They had red-carpeted the walk from the gates to the front doors, they had crossing lights driving into the sky, massive bloody pillars. It was just fuckin' ridiculous. There was nothing else around except for this really tacky-looking venue. It was like Oscar night.

Some guy, I think the venue owner or manager, was saying, "Yeah, man I know about these rock guys, we're going to fuckin' rock this joint tonight man, we goin' to do this shit, man. We do rock; we've done rock since '72." He didn't have a fuckin' clue what he was talking about. I knew what Joe was up for and this certainly wasn't it. I think they even wanted an interval as well! We came to a compromise where they served the "chicken in a basket" before the band came on. Fuckin' Anaheim!

During the whole tour we met a whole host of interesting people. When we were in LA Robbie Coltrane turned up. Boo came upstairs and said, "Gary, Robbie Coltrane's downstairs and he can't get in." I went downstairs and sure enough there was this big guy standing there, full of humility, and sure enough, it was Robbie Coltrane. He was out there filming and he asked, "I want to come and see Joe if that's OK." What a nice bloke.

I lost it that night in LA. We were all completely exhausted and the dressing room had become swamped with all these plastic LA-ers. Even Joe had had enough. I asked this woman her name and when she told me I said, "You've just made that up, right? And everything about you is made up."

So I stood up and shouted, "All you fuckin' false plastic LA-ers get out of this fuckin' dressing room now!" They were all going, "I'm an actress, I'm going to be famous." I said, "No you're fuckin' not, now get out of this dressing room!" Every time I see Joe Campbell, he still ribs me for it.

Eventually I realised on that tour the idea was it was supposed to be a chaotic tour, it wasn't supposed to be organised, so I started to relax a bit more. Joining the party massive made it a bit more enjoyable.

When I was working with Joe I saw every single side of his personality, warts and all, and if you still really like a guy after that then he is worth knowing.

I think that tour would have broken most bands. They would have said, that's it, never again. Everyone had a lot of respect for Joe and at the end of the day we didn't want to let him down. It was a fuckin' tough tour and if it had been anybody else apart from Joe I would have just fucked off home.

With Joe, I respected him completely. You knew Joe was fundamentally a good bloke. He did try very hard to please everyone. Joe loved meeting up in the bar for a drink with the crew. In that environment Joe was just the Don at being social. In a bar Joe would hold court, people loved him. He was interesting as well as being very funny. He had a great sense of humour and was very dry. In America it would be hilarious. He would be full of irony and people just weren't getting it.

Looking back now, at this point in time, I would say I enjoyed the American tour because of the experience, but at the time I fuckin' hated it. I had done

America before but this was different. I could not wait to get home. I will never in my life experience anything like it again.

After that we did Barcelona, which was great, followed by Milan and then the Montmartre in Paris. The Paris show was an ideal end to a few very difficult months. Europe was a bit of a breeze. That show was the turning point for The Mescaleros in a very positive way. It was just a great night. Joe's driver Roger came over from Somerset. He turned up at the end of the show because he had got pulled on the way over. Luce's friends and family were there, it was just great. The whole night was electric.

Before Japan and Australia I had pretty much decided that I was wasn't going to do it but Joe just had a way of turning it around. When I was younger Joe was someone I respected and here I was working with him, which was a bit of an honour really.

I think towards the latter part of his career Joe found people he liked and really respected. He definitely found that within The Mescaleros and the surrounding entourage.

I wasn't going to do Japan, I had decided that was it for me; I wasn't going to do any more. I had done America, happy I had seen it through, but felt a bit disillusioned about tour managing and was ready to hang up my boots. Montmartre was so great that I thought it would be good to finish on a high. I thought that was it.

I rang Joe and said I really didn't think I could do Japan and Australia and Joe's response was typical: "Well if you're not doing it, Gal, I ain't doing it."... back at yer.

I think he meant it. I honestly think that he meant it, because Joe was kinda disillusioned after America as well. Joe always wanted people around him that he liked and trusted. At the end of the day I was the one that was going to be around Joe more on a day-to-day basis than most. I could be completely wrong but I think at that particular time, if anybody would have turned round and said they weren't doing Japan and Australia, Joe probably would have said the same thing.

So when we went out to Japan I was out there reluctantly at the beginning. My level of hospitality was probably at zero level. I was doing the tour for Joe and no one else. Band, crew, you, promoter, anybody would have been in the same category.

When I went out my head was all over the place. When I was finally getting back to the hotel, I was emailing and faxing Australia and New Zealand, making sure they had all our freight requirements and our hotels and flights were booked. A lot of this job is looking in advance and when you get back to the hotel, you are still working whilst everyone else is on a jolly.

Joe could be quite volatile, but he was full of humility. One particular time in Tokyo, a situation occurred in the dressing room. Joe started ranting (I think you were there) and I said "Look, Joe, no way, you've crossed the line. I'll do whatever I can for anybody but...." The next day he rang me in my room: "Gal, Gal, me and Luce have just been out shopping – can you come up to my room, we've got something to show yer."

They gave me a CD player (which I've still got). That was Joe's way of saying, "Look, sorry about last night, I pissed you off and I'm sorry". How can you not like someone like that? The way that Joe used to apologise was quite unique really.

Through that particular time Ants was going through a difficult time and I used to keep an eye out for him on tour. Every time I've seen Ants since it's always been a real pleasure to see him. I'm really glad he came out the other side. It was going to go one of two ways – he was either going to kill himself or come good. When I saw him at Joe's funeral he had thankfully come out the other side and it was a pleasure to see him. Ants was one of those guys that you just couldn't help but like, as much as a pain in the arse he used to be. He knows he could be a pain in the arse. Mind you, anyone who manages to call me, "Here's to you" for a whole fuckin' year commands respect.

As with the other guys as well. Smiley's ... Smiley. He's a top lad. I think that might be his downfall really because everyone says "Smiley's Smiley." It's actually very complimentary because you always know where you are with Smiley, there's no hidden agenda, he's not going to try and pull the wool over your eyes or get one over on you.

Pablo was always a logistical nightmare because he was a well sought-after guy; every band wanted him to make a noise for them.

When I was working with Joe, Pabs was always juggling his commitments with Moby. Doing this interview has kinda brought back a load of great memories actually. I haven't thought about Pablo for a long time, but thinking about him now and how funny he was ... if Pablo was up for some surrealism then that was right up my street. Pabs just wanted a bit of insanity. Anything kinda normal and straightforward was not his bag really. He had a great sense of humour, completely off the wall. Yeah, Pablo man, fuckin' hell!

Scott and Martin for me were just like Morecambe and Wise, a comedy duo. They just bounced off each other. Two of them in company was almost like you can't have one without the other. Mind you, there were times when I saw their relationship go a bit Terry and June.

It was great to be involved in something that was quite integral; everyone just wanted to rock basically. After the run of shows I worked on, the vibe started becoming a bit wishy-washy apparently. When we were touring, it was full-on.

All these new bands think they've toured. They haven't fucking toured at all. They think they've done hard tours and they think they've done all this rock 'n' roll behaviour. They haven't seen anything. They're just kids.

If you've toured with Joe and the associated entourage you go to hell and back fuckin' ten times over. You find yourself along the way and pass yourself on the way back.

You experienced more on tour with Joe in a year than most people would experience in a lifetime.

When I worked with Joe we went through all the UK, America, Europe and Japan and at times I felt that I wanted to turn it in. Then we went to Australia and Australia just blew my mind.

It was almost like Joe's reasons for making me see America through; wanting me to see Japan through was for us to get to Australia, because when we got there my relationship with Joe changed completely and he just became an even more fuckin' amazing bloke to be around. The whole band, the whole crew just changed – it's the most enjoyable tour I have ever been involved with. The Australian tour (the Big Day Out or the Big Day Off as they call it) was just fantastic.

Everyone was on a high, it was sunny, Joe was on top form. He was great to be around. I was so glad it ended on a high ... it needed to.

The Australian tour was necessary to kinda regroup and appreciate what it was all about. Joe and myself would often sit in the bar and chew the fat. We were all travelling together, the Chilli Peppers, Primal Scream ... Mani was on top form ... Foo Fighters, Chemical Brothers, Beth Orton, and we all stayed in the same hotels and took over the bar after the shows. The Big Day Out seems to take the whole of Australia and New Zealand over.

That tour just paled everything into insignificance. In a weird way it was almost as if Joe had planned it that way. The total chaos, arguing, people getting pulled in different directions and then at the last minute, throw in Australia. I really enjoyed that tour.

Ben Gooder

I went to a friend of mine, James's, house in Chelsea for a dinner party and there was Joe Strummer. I couldn't believe it. I spent the whole evening asking a thousand questions about him, what happened to everyone in the band and the good old days. He was very modest and tolerant of my endless enthusiasm and curiosity.

At one point this girl leaned over and was feeling a bit pissed off that she had been ignored. I asked if she realised who this was and Joe said, "No, I'm nobody. I just played rhythm guitar in a band 20 years ago." I said, "This is only Joe Strummer from The Clash." She replied, "Oh never heard of them".

He told me he had got a new band together etc.

A week or so later I went down to Portsmouth to the Wedgewood Rooms where they were playing one of their first gigs. It was great, though Joe was a bit unfit, he had to lie down at the end of it he was so knackered. A lot of people were there – Damien Hirst, Keith Allen. I went down with one of the Boomtown Rats.

After that I went to see them when they were recording the first album at the Battery.

One day in the pub Joe said, "When are you doing the video then?" I said, "The video for what?" He said, "The video for the single." I said, "Are you serious?" Joe said, "You've been filming us, why not? Don't want anything special. ou've got the video camera!"

I was totally thrilled; Joe said speak to Simon Moran.

I said to Simon Moran, "Joe's asked me to do the video". He said, "That's good, how much do you need?" I said, "Twenty grand." He went, "Ten." I went, "Done."

Joe wanted a kinda fly-on-the-wall-type documentary-style video, bits of them on the road... Troubadours. So that's what I did.

I went round with an old 60mm film camera and my video camera and shot backstage, onstage, side of stage, soundchecks, parties, hotels. I grabbed bits of footage from the Elysée-Montmartre gig, the New York gig.

After that gig Joe was sitting in the corner listening intently on his busy box, listening to this weird music and said, "Oh it's something Mick sent me." He was really listening intently.

The after-show party, everyone was there – Matt Dillon, Joey Ramone etc. All there in honour of this guy who had been away for so long. I remember Joey Ramone was so quiet, so thrilled to be there, he was clearly so fond of Joe.

I remember when Joey Ramone died; Joe listened to every Ramones album and single, the complete Ramones works as a tribute to Joey Ramone.

Joe was very accommodating, very generous and very open. He didn't judge me, and he let me do whatever I wanted.

Joe loved America. I remember sitting in this breakfast place in Manhattan and Joe looking at these trucks, road vehicles – he loved those bits of Americana.

It was very hard keeping it altogether, because you'd be up all night with him – he wouldn't let you go to bed. Of course the next day you'd have to work and Joe would be in bed until lunchtime, whenever. There was no quarter given in regards to the normal human needs of neither sleep nor time.

I filmed the band shots by the Flatiron Building on Broadway just off Times Square.

When this was filmed it was raining and we had about 20 minutes to shoot it. It was mad, me squatting down in gutters trying to get interesting angles. We were on the streets totally illegally with no permission, right under the noses of the cops. We just told them, yeah it's all fine, we've got permission from so and so. We got away with it.

We were also filming in the Lower East Side; you know sometimes you see things that seem like strange coincidences. I remember seeing a big Clash graffiti; I saw a shop called Jimmy Jazz shoes. Everything seemed to be Clash images in New York.

It was very hard to get any time with Joe. He didn't really want to do anything special for the video; he wanted it to be completely natural. He didn't want anything set up.

But it was difficult; I had lots of footage of him sitting around exhausted after gigs and gig footage, but nothing to really pull it all together.

I had this idea about Joe being a kind of travelling troubadour, absorbing influences from what he sees around him, a man of the street, a man of the people.

So I wanted to put him on the street, so it was in fact a bit of a set-up, but Joe went along with it and gave me an hour or two. Bob Gruen came down; he was shooting pics of me directing Joe.

All Joe wanted to do was carry his box, wear a pair of shades and amble along.

The shots of Joe with the headphones on singing his vocal part to the song were filmed in the main studios at the Battery. It was about as close as you could get to Joe and his working methods as was possible.

Having done all this we weren't sure whether it was going to work or not. It wasn't until we got back and saw what the lab had processed that we breathed a sigh of relief that we had actually filmed something.

It was shot in colour but we graded it. The films were actually bits of short ends, bits of reject stock, and it was a mixture of bits and pieces from film stocks. None of them matched. I took it into a grading suite and gave it a rough, gritty, desaturated look, which gave it a kind of consistency. It gave it an old 70s look.

I put everything together, edited it for the *Yalla Yalla* track. I had everything done.

Joe wanted to see it, so he called in Damien Hirst, Keith Allen and various other people to kind of OK it. I got the third degree. They all had their own ideas. Actually Damien Hirst started to ring me up with various ideas I should put in the video, usually at 3.00 in the morning – he'd ring me up in some over-refreshed state.

I found myself going down to some place in Devon, called Magic Mortimer's Music Water Wheel or something like that, some old Victorian thing that Damien had seen.

I went all the way down there and it was just ridiculous. So that was a total waste of time!

I did Glastonbury where Joe smashed up a BBC camera; I spoke to the head of the O/B unit who was in charge of the whole thing, to see if I could have some of their footage. He was hopping mad and told me I didn't ever have a chance of getting hold of any of their footage... Ever!

It was such a great time being on the road with such a legend, such a star. Joe would let you film in his face anywhere, any time – he didn't care. The only time was just before a gig, when he'd go "that's enough" and grab a couple of minutes' quiet in a corner of the room. He'd just focus his mind, remember what he was doing and get psyched up.

There was always a lot going on internally, a lot going on inside, I felt with Joe – he had so many ideas.

He was so obsessed with music. I remember chatting to him about the Rolling Stones. He loved them, which I never really expected. He was a big Stones fan.

After I finished the edit, I never got paid, couldn't get a penny out of anybody. Tried numerous times contacting Simon Moran, nothing. So I had only one option – I wrote a letter to Joe in the form of I rewrote the lyrics to Yalla Yalla... *So long Simon Moran, let's forget you didn't pay, not in my time, nor my sons' and daughters' time.*

I got a letter back by return from Joe with a cheque – he loved it. So humour worked where threats didn't.

We became very good friends. I continued going to gigs. I actually tried to get the *Tony Adams* video together as well; I approached Tony Adams (the player) – he agreed to be in it. He actually said he would love to be in it, he was a fan of The Clash.

But for some reason the dates never worked out. I could never get them together at the same time. In the usual chaotic way, it just got forgotten about.

I also loved The Mescaleros – they were a great bunch. I was at the time writing a script for a film about a drummer and Pablo was very helpful, giving me advice etc. Scott lent me some video footage.

I found Joe's tolerance and generosity trafficked its way throughout the band. I was always made to feel part of the family. The only difficulty I had was containing Antony Genn's creative ideas.

I went to see The Mescaleros play Wembley Arena supporting The Who. I went backstage during The Who set and Joe said, "Come on, let's go back to the hotel." He then said, "Carry this" and got a big case of beer. We walked across the back of the stage whilst The Who was on, carrying a case of beer. We got out to the compound where the trucks etc. were and this roadie-looking bloke with long hair and a lived-in face, came up to me and said, "Can I have one of them?"

I said, "Sure." So he opened the beer and suddenly said to me, "You know, I was mistaken for Roger Daltrey once, Max's Kansas City 1976. I thought, that's strange, and as I looked closer, he wasn't a roadie, it was Robert Plant. So I was standing in a car park, sharing a beer with Robert Plant and Joe's going, "Come on, come on."

He was actually like a father to the band, they all looked up to him. He was carrying an enormous burden especially during the first album, the first tour, because so much of it was about Joe Strummer from The Clash and he was so interested in creating something new, moving forward, and there was always a dilemma thing about being who he was, a legend, and wanting to be part of a music collective that was new.

There was an age gap between the band and Joe and he was always very careful to spread the acclaim.

I actually think it was more like it was during the 101ers days – it was more of a collective spirit. He was reacting against the gang mentality of The Clash, the ego in-fighting that had gone on.

He was much more at peace with himself and prepared to take other people's contributions, regarding the whole thing as an egalitarian process. Joe seemed at times almost a reluctant leader/figure head.

Nikola Acin

Joe Strummer appeared up on the stage impeccably dressed in black motorcycle boots, black jeans, red shirt and bolo tie, battle-weary Telecaster on his hip, gunslinger-style. This was 1990, Joe's first solo tour ever. It had been five years since the final shows of the post-Mick Jones version of The Clash and most of the Paris audience, like me, had never seen Joe live. From the front row, the crowd seemed white-hot, packed in the Elysée-Montmartre, a decrepit pre-war boxing hall located in Pigalle, the town's historic red light district.

Approaching the microphone, Joe took a few seconds to absorb the rapturous cheers coming from the frenzied crowd and calmly said, "good rocking tonight in the city of lights."

I was 16 years old and I came out of that show with a feeling I_ve never felt since, something that forced me to realise that I had to have a rock 'n ' roll band of my own and that I'd open for Joe Strummer one day.

Not long after the tour promoting his first solo album *Earthquake Weather*, Joe had stepped up to replace Shane McGowan in the Pogues for their 1991 shows. They stopped in Paris for two nights at the Elysée-Montmartre in November and although I_ll never know if Joe had any say in the choice of the venue, I suspect he did. The place, located midway between Place Pigalle and the Barbès-Rochechouart axis, has never been very fancy, clean or safe, with a PA just as unpredictable as its security staff. But it has soul. That's why Joe never played anywhere else in town.

With my two good friends the Levy twins, dedicated record collectors who shared identical looks and a passionate approach to buying vinyl, we'd come up for an autograph that afternoon and Joe, not particularly in a good mood, inadvertently destroyed the glass door of the venue's entrance by swinging sharply into it his huge traveling bag full of God knows what. A fierce-looking bouncer arriving on the scene immediately grabbed the person closest to the door and lifted me off the ground, threatening to do some serious damage. Joe and Joey Cashman, the Pogues' road manager, calmly walked down the stairs to see the damage done and ordered off the bouncer, who dropped me to the ground with no ceremony. Joe looked at the wide array of broken glass and smirked "rock 'n ' roll". We shook hands, he asked if I was okay and that was it. We were friends. He immediately put us up on the list for the post-show celebrations and after a failed attempt the first night, Joe made sure we made it backstage the next one. A crowd of sweaty people made it a bit rough to talk and it was soon clear that there wasn't going to be any real occasion to hang out, so we went for our autographs. This time, we'd brought the good stuff, the original Clash 45s we'd carefully protected in our backpacks so they wouldn't get crushed by the crowd and started saying our goodbyes and thanks. Joe whispered, "wait here," took his pencil and a piece of yellow paper, quickly wrote a few worrds, grabbed me by the hand, slipped the paper in and said "go out and read this". Working our way out, I unfolded the note: "Hotel Mercure, Place De Clichy, En Le Bar In 1 Hour."

So we met him up at his hotel where a selected group of friends were rubbing elbows at the bar, including Helno, the superb singer of Les Négresses Vertes who died soon afterwards. Someone had brought a tape of Gene Vincent to play on the bar's stereo, which caused a cheer from Joe. We talked a bit and he said casually that I should come to the show at Brixton Academy, being that it was going to be their traditional Christmas show and all that.

I did, showing up the same way, on the afternoon of the gig. Joe gave me my first glass of brandy that night after the show and, upon learning it had been my birthday not long before, proceeded to show me one of England's apparently oldest traditions, ordering me to drop my jacket and let him grab me by the feet while another accomplice was busy taking my shoulders. I soon was horizontally positioned and, dreading some obscure British college esoteric habit involving buggery, tried to talk my way out or at least find out what the future might hold. It turned out to be simply a series of what is apparently known as "the bumps", each of the 18 more perilous than the other.

It took a few years, but Joe finally returned to play live Paris in 1999 with the Mescaleros, in June, for their fifth show, and a crucial one for the brand new band. Joe knew what a vital burst of energy a crowd that loves you can bring to a band and how important this was for the Mescaleros.

Rock 'n ' roll is nothing if it isn't chemistry and Joe knew this more than any man. He also knew he could count on Paris to provoke exactly that. The show left no doubt on the subject: the band worked and played hard and Joe had shown once again that these painfully mediocre 90s during which he had laid low hadn_t finished him off along with most of his contemporaries.

Quite the opposite. This was a man ready to embrace his time and his position as an elder, wiser man, whose view of the world was still fresh and enthusiastic, still full of vibrant energy. With Joe, Pockets, Pablo, Scott and Martin, we went for drinks around the neighbourhood, closing up the night at seven in the morning at the Jack Bar, an after-hours hole in the wall where the local characters, drunken sleepwalkers, transvestites and party animals would stop for late night libations and delicious food.

That morning, after taking out the trash at the Jack Bar, The Mescaleros drove me home on the tour bus, Joe shouting in my ear something about how nights like these were fuel for the next show. "What are you gonna do if you're on tour, stay in your hotel room and watch CNN? No, you want to smell the town, feel what's going on and meet people. It gives us something to sing about, you know." He went on about how I had to come on the tour with them, "all you need is cream for your hair."

The next show was 7 December 1999, the final hurrah of a world tour which had started in June and confirmed his healthy appetite for making music.

The answering machine kicked in on Monday in the early afternoon with a voice that sounded like a tiger waking up. "Hey babe," said Joe, "it's your old friend Giuseppe here. Dinner at eight tonight. Meet me at the hotel." Joe's regulars, his closest friends in town, would then gather up for nightly excursions with no precise destination. FJ Ossang and his mysterious partner and muse Elvire would suddenly appear, shouting out loud quotes of Lautréamont and other French surrealist poetry from memory while Joe kept poking me for a quicker translation. Ossang, often accompanied by the actor and former boxer Stéphane Ferrara, had directed *Docteur Chance*, Joe's last film role. Maybe his best, if only for the magnificent scene that shows him leaping on a table to the sound of the Stooges' *1969*, screaming out "les gonades!" with his face contorted in joyful pain.

The two of them would regale us with weird and colourful anecdotes from their epic shooting in Yquique, a small frontier town in the Chilean mountains, which resulted not only in the film but also in Ossang's fascinating book, *Les 59 Jours*. Ossang's grandiosely decadent personality was often balanced out by the reassuring presence of Richard Schroeder, one of Joe's dearest friends, who had taken him in during his little disappearing act of 1982, and had since become a respected photographer. All kinds of people would appear when Joe was in Paris, people who are never seen out on the town, sitting in the overcrowded cafés where a film goddess like Béatrice Dalle would be next to some fans who had followed the movement, all treated equally by Joe who had time for everyone, rolling smokes and never parting with his precious sharpie pen, for use on any occasion.

That Wednesday my girlfriend Lou had taken us to an artists' squat located in the north of Paris, rue de la Grange Aux Belles, a typical art-boho thing where the wine was cheap and a group of people passed around acoustic guitars and an upright bass. Pablo Cook was with us, joining the band on impromptu percussion using wooden chairs while Joe had sent me to score weed. Gradually, people started respectfully walking up to him to ask him if he was who they thought he was. Incredulity quickly gave way to complete awe. One guy with a face that looked like he had been punched pretty hard a few times that very afternoon came back with a huge painting that he gave to Joe. Joe hauled the huge canvas all around town for the rest of the night, cursing the guy for not being a miniature artist.

The next night was a complete contrast: a friendly acquaintance named Eric Dahan had invited on the fly to join him at the Man Ray, one the poshest spots in town, right off the Champs-Elysées, for a special charity night in the honour of the cause of the Dalai Lama. We were taken to the only empty table of the evening, smack down in the centre of the place, table to table next to some of the country's biggest stars, while atrocious portraits of Richard Gere and Cindy Crawford painted by a former model turned buddhist with a brush were being auctioned off for vast sums of money. As Eric kept the smokes rolled and the white wine did the rest, our table started getting crowded with people who wanted to know where all the laughs were coming from. Lou had joined us by this time and we were hungry, and we were soon out to find some food. We walked a good while along the Champs-Elysées, all lit up with Christmas lights, and Joe was absolutely thrilled at Paris. I can exactly picture Joe now, taking great big rapid steps in black boots and jeans, short black ted-style coat with his huge tobacco-brown scarf (which he lost that night) wrapped around his throat for protection, his body decidedly pointed forward.

"You_ve got a great town, you know," he told us repeatedly. The gig was still a few nights away but that night Joe took on his old problem with addressing foreign crowds by inventing an international lingo of his own, nicknamed Esperantique and whose vocabulary answered to a single rule: only if it sounds good.

And then came the show. By this time, I_d been part of a rocking little outfit called the Hellboys for a handful of years, recorded a few things, and when it had been announced that Joe was coming back in December, I'd decided to gather up my courage and offer him our services as the opening act.

"You got it," was all he'd replied.

That was his gift for me, something I'd promised myself almost ten years before and that he made happen. I don't remember much of it except my mother being there and yelling out my name from the crowd but what I do remember is that my heart had never pounded so fast and so hard in my chest for the entire solid half-hour of our set.

Joe and The Mescaleros were phenomenal that night, apart from a complete failure at making himself understood in Esperantique, which drew a complete blank from the audience and a few perplexed stares from the band. At some point the entire crowd took over the backing vocals for *Bankrobber*, Joe guiding them slowly through with his hand pressed hard over his ear, every soul in the hall holding on to the moment. The band had become a tight, pugnacious unit, showing a cool confidence in the strength of The Mescaleros' material, which by now had been absorbed and embraced by the major portion of the crowd.

We all came down afterwards to his hotel's lobby on the Place de la République where he took the time to talk to each one of the guys in the Hellboys, Abdul, Adan and Christophe, and made it clear that he'd watched us play all the way through, passing on comments, compliments and drinks, all of them generous.

Joe came over to Paris during 2001 for interviews to promote *Global A Go-Go*, one evening ending up at a gay eighties night called London Calling with Robert Lopez, a Mexican-American Elvis impersonator going by the stage name of El Vez. There was also the time when we went for dinner with the photographer Anton Corbijn, whom Joe had done a shoot with that afternoon. Corbijn had reserved him and Lucinda a room in a small but beautiful circular hotel on the Left Bank, famous for having been Oscar Wilde's *pension* of choice in Paris. We must have walked all around the Latin Quarter three or four times before returning for a nightcap, polishing off a bottle of brandy that he'd got as a present earlier. At their room, I got to play a bit on Joe's magnificent ancient acoustic guitar and we listened to Brian Setzer's new record *Ignition*. I learned about what Joe called "the hipsters's mistake", which he voiced as "never go out with Joe Strummer without a pair of shades, cos you'_ll still be up when the fucking sun rises."

Which is when I crept out and as he went to shut the door, he said something about having had a great night. "One for the books," that's what he said.

We opened for Joe and the Mescaleros in their new version again at the end of that year. We were joined by our producer Yarol Poupaud on keyboards and managed to raise a few cheers from the crowd. The new Mescaleros brought the best out of the magnificent songs from *Global A Go-Go* for two hours of loud, generous and multi-flavoured rock 'n ' roll, swapping instruments and looking smart, particularly Martin Slattery in his superb *Blow-Up*-period Jeff Beck-style cream two-piece suit. Joe's entire crew of friends from Manchester had made the trip, a party-hungry mob of intense characters who quickly invaded our dressing room, before departing for more celebrations.

At some point he asked me if I thought he should play some other venue than the Elysée-Montmartre, maybe a bit more upscale. My opinion mirrored his: not a chance.

There was some talk about adding a Paris date to the "Bringing It All Back Home Tour" in 2002, but the title itself suggested that this was going to stay a strictly insular affair.

'Next year for sure,' that was one of the last things I heard him say over the phone.

Joe never came back to Paris.

I realise now that although I was there as a witness only for a few years, I could see that the love affair between Joe and Paris was for good and had started long before my time, when the shows played here by The Clash had become the stuff of legends, reported by some spectacular photos, fervent press reports and poor tape recordings. It is an indisputable fact that, Joe, like Mick with BAD, never played a half-hearted show in this town, and have never been greeted with less than absolute mayhem at each of their visits.

Because once you're in our hearts, you're there for life and we'll expect nothing but your best when you come out here. I'm sure there's people elsewhere in the world that feel the same way but I can only testify for my own neck of the woods and there's no doubt in my mind that this town loved Joe with a devotion and a dedication that its citizens reserve exclusively for people of true value. Say what you want about the French, they've got one thing, they recognise a hero when he comes around. Because we knew that Joe Strummer was for real, a dignified human being and a great artist in a world of lifeless zombies and shameless imposters. And we know how important and rare people like him are, because in the end, it shows that all this stuff, all this nonsense, all this pop music and rock 'n ' roll business that we try to find some meaning out of, comes down to people like Joe finding in it the only place where their voice can be heard. And by the simple act of writing and singing songs, making this world a little less miserable to live in.

That's what Joe Strummer was about.

Over Land and Sea

This part of the book has been written using diary notes and a bloody good memory.

Introduction

1 May 1977: Guildford Civic Hall: The first time I saw The Clash on the *White Riot* tour – can't really recollect much about that evening in the heart of Surrey, just that what I witnessed that night didn't so much change my life but was the start of a journey which over the course of the next 25 years would bring great adventures, make great friends, nearly cost me my marriage and business, take me to numerous countries, get me in all sorts of aggro, but above all have one hell of a good life.

Throughout the late 70s and early 80s, I saw The Clash approximately 40 times, including the Anti-Nazi Rally at Vicky Park where The Clash played an electric, 12-song set in front of a crowd reported to be 80,000+, and all five nights at The Lyceum.

I had fortunately met Joe on a couple of occasions. The first time was at The Dammed farewell concert (first of many) at The Rainbow in '78 – made a bit of a nuisance of myself, but despite my somewhat drunken stupor Joe was very patient. Mick seemed to be on a different planet and actually appeared to be intrigued by my stupidity.

The second time was at an Iggy Pop concert at The Lyceum – *Gates of The West* EP had just been released and Joe asked me what I thought of it. Nervously remembering what I had been like when we previously met, I struggled to find a constructive sentence and just blurted out "shit" – again, I had messed up.

When the band split, I, like many others thought that was it, finished, but with Clash II (or whatever, still to this day it's a source of debate by those on Satch's forum) I had many a great night watching Joe, Paul and three new heroes, the highlight being Arthur Scargill's Xmas party at Brixton Academy.

In the late 80s caught Joe and his Latino Rockabilly War on British tours and at the Amnesty International bash at the Bowl Milton Keynes. Never actually saw Joe with The Pogues.

In March 1993, I was down at the studios with my sister's husband Simon Hanson. He was putting together the finishing touches on his single, *Passion*, which two months later under the name Gat Décor would enter the British charts at Number 28. It was rave, not really my scene, but he was family!

It was during my time at the studios that I picked up a copy of the NUM's handbook. Flicking through, I came across Joe Strummer in the members' section, address, fax/phone number, the lot.

My daughter had just passed her first classical guitar exam, and what better excuse to write to Joe asking if it would be OK if I posted a copy of the recently released Clash guitar book for him to sign? I had originally written about seven foolscap pages, but luckily my wife had pointed out that after a couple of pages he would be thoroughly bored, so I trimmed it down to eight lines.

Joe kindly replied, stating of course that would be fine. In the short letter accompanying the book I asked if he would be kind enough to also send a signed pic for my younger daughter.

The book came back a week or so later signed, "To Amée" with an attached letter, stating, "Believe it or not, cannot find a pic of myself anywhere, so have drawn Ellie a front seat view" – and in the book was an A4-size, signed self-portrait.

Well, over the next couple of years, despite wanting to write every week, I kept the letters to a minimum, approximately every four/five months. Joe always replied and put on one, "If you're ever passing, pop in." Two months later, in 1995, I did with my girls – he wasn't in!

I met instead a man known as "Pockets" who for reasons known only to him was very offhand, and the last I saw of him was cycling at a distinct speed on his pushbike into the Hampshire countryside – leaving my daughters and I somewhat confused and disappointed.

1999

The Mescaleros... summer 1999

In early June 1999 my business associate and good friend Neil Lewington came into work one morning and wouldn't stop talking about the PC he had purchased the previous weekend. Having no interest in computers, I found this line of conversation totally boring and despite my attempts to change the subject over the next few days, he didn't stop going on about what his computer could do.

Totally sick of the topic, I said almost as a challenge. "OK, if your computer's so bloody brilliant, look up Joe Strummer, look up The Clash." The following day he came in with a wad of paper he had printed off his computer. A couple of pages in particular caught my eye, they were titled Casbah Club, and on it were some dates of a band called Joe Strummer & The Mescaleros.

The British dates had passed, but coming up were dates in Amsterdam and Paris. I immediately got on the phone with my credit card, booked the tickets, would have to collect on the door as not enough time to risk the post, booked the ferry and a couple of days later my eldest daughter and I were driving from Calais to Amsterdam.

We arrived at Amsterdam round about lunchtime, sorted out the hotel and arrived at RAI Parkhal collected our tickets and walked into a large hall, checked the times – Joe was due on about 4.00. Not wanting to miss out we decided to watch the band before Luscious Jackson, all-girl American rock band who were really good.

Then, for the first time in ten years, my hero appeared onstage with a band comprising five fellas – I had no idea who they were, remember thinking they really look young, the drummer seemed to be continually smiling.

I've said it before – only those dads fortunate enough to have taken their children to see Joe will fully understand – it was one of the greatest moments of being a parent to share *White Man In Hammersmith Palais*, *London Calling* with your kids live – your hero onstage and them singing and dancing with you.

They played some songs I had never heard before – first impression, catchy tunes. Forty minutes later it's over.

We returned to the hotel absolutely delighted, that was it for me, but after some deliberation we returned to the hall later in the evening – my daughter wanted to see Blur and Alanis Morrisette: crap.

The following morning, on attempting to leave Amsterdam, I wrongly decided to follow a German coach – surely they must know the way to the motorway?

It was a costly mistake. The coach ended up in a cul-de-sac with me right up behind it. Suddenly its reversing lights appeared and, before I could think, it reversed into me, shunting me back. I got out, saw my pride and joy caved in at the front and looked up to see a window full of kids giggling.

As the large female coach driver approached me, the steam coming out of the engine was only matched by the steam coming out of my ears. Her lack of English and my total lack of German made it even worse.

Then through the steam I could see a large middle-aged blonde figure, strutting her way towards us… it was the English teacher. In totally Germanic coldness she said, "Vy you cry over zee spilt milk? In Germany, Mercedes Benz are two a penny."

Well, that was it, the little Englander in me came out in full flow… "two world wars and one world cup" was the mildest of my many expletives. My daughter later said I had looked like an impression of Freddie Starr, goose-stepping up and down, sieg-heiling, the lot.

To cap it all, a passing Dutch policeman had overseen the exchange of insurance documents and suggested calling a nearby tow-truck company to tow my car away.

"I can't, I can't" is all I can remember saying as I drove my smashed-front-end pride and joy at a considerably reduced speed out of Amsterdam en route for Paris.

We entered Paris some three hours later than planned, driving along the Boulevard Rochechouart with passing people looking across at what seemed to be an impression of Chitty Chitty Bang Bang.

We arrived at the Montmartre ticket office just as the doors were opening. Outside we met a really nice fella who had travelled up from Italy. Having overcome the main obstacle in getting there, surely nothing more could go wrong?

"Zere is no ticket in the name of Davie," was the reply at attempting to collect from the ticket office… "Shit… no, no, no, listen, I paid for them by credit card, please."

"Sorry" was the reply. At that point a large security gorilla with a ponytail came across and gestured we move outside. "Please hear me out, if you think I came all the way over here on a wing and a prayer…" At that point he grabbed my daughter's arm tightly and pulled her towards the door. "Oi, you cunt!" I shouted as I ran up to confront him. My 14-year-old daughter was crying, "No, no Dad." At that point a well-dressed lady coming down the stairs shouted out. The gorilla stood to attention – she was the owner/manageress. I fully explained my story; she kindly put us on the guest list.

As we walked upstairs I asked Amée if she was OK and explained that I most probably would have got my face filled in, but it wouldn't have mattered one iota because if a dad can't stick up for his kids, then that is an even harder thing to live with than a few missing teeth and a black eye.

As the boys came on at 9.00 we hugged each other, we had made it.

After a great show, we drove straight back to Calais. Looking across at my daughter fast asleep, I said to her: "We're going again – this is rock 'n' roll." I had caught the bug again.

Over the next couple of days I went out and got myself a computer, found the Casbah Club site and waited expectantly for further dates... Dublin and Belfast appeared set for July.

I booked the tickets and the flights, only to find out a week later these had been put back to the end of August.

In the meantime US dates came up; Japan – too far, could never go there. So I waited patiently for the celtic dates. Whilst waiting I had sent a couple of emails out to Casbah Club – had struck up a distant friendship with one Jason Stebner. I had also sent a couple of emails out to a certain Sukwoon and a Mr Satch. Had been impressed by their sites, they even had copies of The Mescaleros live... the stumbling-block was they would only swap. Couldn't work that one out because what happens if you have nothing to swap?

I sent a couple of emails to them explaining my position and waited somewhat expectantly but alas to no avail. Every day I checked my inbox – nothing. Oh well!

In an exchange of emails with Jolly Jason, I explained that I had not received any replies and he suggested I try contacting a certain Italian called Giuseppe. This turned out to be my lucky link and the start of a friendship that still exists strongly today. Within a week the Paris CD had arrived. I now had The Mescaleros in my house, in my car.

On the morning of 24 August I took the first flight out of Luton to Belfast, travelled by train to Dublin and arrived at approx 16:00. Walking from Connolly station to the hotel, I thought I'd better do a recce re: the venue. Walking down the side of the venue, a dingy side street... as I walked by, the door opened. A familiar figure walked out accompanied by a Rastafarian. I froze, mouth wide open catching flies. "All right," was the only thing that came out.

"Yeah," was the reply. Seeing me standing there gawping, they turned away only to stop a split-second later, turned back and said, "Are you here for tonight?"

"Erm, yes," I replied hesitantly, "I've got to pick my ticket up, but the box office isn't open yet."

"Better come in here and wait, then." So the three of us went in through the stage door.

"Take a seat. Want a beer?"

Bloody hell, the adrenalin was pumping, my leg was shaking and when I put pressure on it the other one started.

"Where yer from?" Joe asked in between sorting things out with what I later found out to be the tour manager.

"Er, London... well it's actually Northampton now, we moved out several years ago."

As the rasta kindly offered me a bottle of beer, I noticed mentioning Northampton had caught his attention. Perhaps it was because of the Roadmender, the club where Joe and The Latino Rockabilly War had played. Perhaps it was me just imagining it had caught his attention.

As the tour manager called to Joe that the soundcheck was about to start, I plucked up all my courage and blurted out, "You've moved from Mattingley?" Joe turned back, stared, nodded his head in agreement and disappeared.

The show that night was brilliant, plus I had met my hero for a third time – hadn't ballsed it up, I reassured myself as I kept re-running the five-minute meeting over and over again through my head.

The following morning I caught the train to Belfast, walked the two miles to the hotel, dropped my stuff off and went walkabout.

When visiting cities I do like to have a stroll, have a coffee or beer, a bite to eat etc. That afternoon I walked for what seemed miles. I could feel my heel blistering against my new shoes. As I stopped to check my blisters I looked up. All around me were terraced houses with murals ablaze with IRA emblems and anti-British slogans. Tricolour flags everywhere.

So here I was in the middle of a nationalist stronghold area with a T-shirt and belt buckle which read: "British by birth, English by the grace of God."

Fuck! How do you take a T-shirt off and walk bare-chested down the street without drawing attention? I tried to unbuckle my belt and stop my trousers from falling down at the same time. The glances from passersby were, to say the least, weird. Hopefully they were thinking I was a weirdo and would keep a safe distance.

I struggled to put my T-shirt on inside out, all the time conscious of my trousers slipping down. I smiled pathetically as I shoved the belt down my trouser leg, my legs moving so fast, but desperately trying not to be seen as running. At that point an RUC Land Rover turned the corner... oh God, they'll arrest me for indecent exposure or something, I kept walking past the vehicle and on for about a quarter of a mile until I saw a Union Flag emblazoned on a side of a terraced house about 100 yards ahead. Luck had shone on me yet again.

I found my way some 20 minutes later back to the Holiday Inn, totally exhausted, covered in sweat now. As I was about to enter the hotel a strange smiling face said to me, "Have you got a light, please?" I looked up somewhat nervously as I got my lighter out of my pocket. Was I imagining things or was that Joe's drummer and percussionist? Had I completely flipped???

As the smiling one said "thanks," I asked somewhat doubtfully, "Are you with Joe Strummer?"

"We sure are," was the confident reply. "Why? Are you coming to watch us tonight?"

"Yeah, yeah, I saw you last night in Dublin and in Amsterdam and in Paris."

"Really, that's great, are you doing the British tour?"

"Yeah, yeah," I repeated like a stuck record.

"OK, I tell you what, the last date is in Glasgow, we'll put you on the guestlist," the drummer said. Before I could get my mind round to thinking how would they know who I was, how could I give them my name etc, "We gotta go, the taxi's here – soundcheck."

I entered my room, threw the shirt and belt on the bed, had a shower – it was like the scene in the film *The Long Good Friday* where Bob Hoskins showers and the water washes away all emotions and evil. Bloody hell, what a day and I hadn't even got to the venue yet.

I got to the Limelight club at approx 6.30, sat in the adjacent bar, had a nice pint of Guinness, my mind still concentrating on the day's events in between watching Sky Sports on the television above the bar.

As I sat there a figure stood next to me and in a distinctive Brummy accent said, "Who's playing tonight?" in reference to the television. As I turned to look, it was the rasta from Dublin, Joe's guitar tech. "All right mate?" he said

"Yeah, yeah. You?"

"Not too bad," he replied, as I insisted on returning the drink from yesterday.

The venue was so hot, it was so unbearable, that Joe insisted the fire exits be opened for fresh air. The manager was getting quite anxious as this let the full sound of the Marshall speakers into the surrounding streets, which in turn would lead to a passing RUC patrol being called. The manager shut the doors, Joe insisted they be opened, and when the set finished The Mescaleros were exhausted.

I have never seen so much sweat. The crowd wanted more. Joe opened the fire doors again. The whole band stood in the street having a smoke, drink etc – they really couldn't do an encore. The crowd were going crazy for more. A few years later I learnt that the manager had said, if you don't go back and play an encore they'll wreck the place, literally. So, to avoid a riot Joe and the boys played a great two-song encore and the crowd was happy.

The Clash had released *From Here To Eternity* and I was chuffed to find my story had been printed on the gatefold, though they had added, "To cut a long story short!"

I later learnt Pat Gilbert was given the job of sifting through the hundreds of submissions, sorted out the chaff from the wheat and Mick and Paul selected the final ones.

Pat Gilbert distinctly remembered mine nearly four years on: "How could I forget it, Ant? It was so bloody long!"

British tour: October 1999 / USA tour: November 1999

18 October: On my own I make my way to Nottingham, the opening date of a nine-date British tour. A good night – I bump into Joe and his tour manager before the show. The meeting was brief:
"Are you liking the shows?"
"Yeah, yeah, very much so," was my usual boring reply.
"Good," Joe said as the tour manager ushered him away.
A little spring in my step followed – I hadn't ballsed up, had I? – as I reran the conversation thro my head again and again.

19th, Leeds Town and Country Club: again on my own, but another good night.

21st: first of two nights at the London Astoria. Met up with a few mates. The place was heaving, good night, Joe even jumps into the crowd to have an altercation with someone who has pissed him off! The massed choir of the audience during *Safe European Home* had been the highlight.

22nd: Second night at Astoria, go with Janet's brother Alex, great night again, the place was heaving.

23rd: Norwich UEA. As it's a Saturday, take Amée. Small venue. Standing by the bar waiting patiently to be served, a tap on the shoulder makes me turn round, a friendly face with a distinctive Brummy accent says, "Come to the side of the stage, the beer's free." By now the rastaman is known as Andy; we accept his kind offer. I thank him very much and proceed to leave the backstage area with our beers when both my daughter and I are stopped by security. "Can't take the bottles out there!" Why me?
"Erm, OK. Look, we'll just put them down here." So much for a free beer!!
At that point Andy says look, the band are due on any minute – stay here. As the band goes onstage, Joe passes us, winks and says "all right?"
"Yeah, Yeah," my daughter and I say in stereo.
We finish off our drinks and disappear into the audience, not wanting to outstay our welcome.

After the show, we were about to leave when Andy called out to us. He asked if we were going to Wolverhampton. I said I had a ticket. He asked if Amée would like to be on the guestlist. I was honoured, but declined as it would be unfair to the youngest one,
"Don't worry, I'll put both of them on the guestlist."

25th: Cardiff Uni, the longest drive yet. Taffies go mental up the front!
By this time I'm sending pics and reports to Jason at Casbah Club. Arriving home at ungodly hours sitting on my computer sending emails, the following day getting one-hour development on the pics for his site.
Really enjoying doing it, even had a couple of nice emails via Jason from people glad to be kept up to date. My new friend Giuseppe has sent me another tape. Everything is hunky dory.

26th: Wolverhampton Civic Hall. A proud father oversees his two daughters collect their guest tickets. They have to go through a different entrance than me, an ordinary punter! We excitedly look at their passes: after-show on an SJM Concerts sticker.

A great show, though I get slightly protective, as the girls are desperate to be up the front in the mosh pit. I stand as a one-man protective shield, getting battered.

The door to the after-show is well signposted. We queue up with about 30 others; we are standing there for about 15 mins when Andy walks by, says come with me and takes us straight into the dressing rooms.

The three of us sit in the corner, trying to keep out the way. As we are sitting there a rather attractive lady with a Welsh accent comes across. "Have you seen a black CD case?" We stand up to have a look. "No, I'm sorry" is my pathetic reply.

As I look to the girls I notice they are staring with their mouths wide open. "God knows, what's a-matter with you two? Don't start misbehaving."

"But, but dad..."

"Just sit down and behave."

"But, but—"

"But what?" I impatiently reply.

"Dad, that's Cerys Mathews."

"Who?"

"Cerys, Cerys Mathews, Catatonia," they excitedly reply.

"Never heard of them, now just sit down... er, evening Joe."

"Evening, and who are these two?" Joe replied with that devilish grin.

"Er, erm, my daughters Amée and Ellie."

He shakes their hands and enquires, "Are they good kids?"

"Yeah, yeah... erm, I don't know what's come over them but they were having a funny half hour about that lady over there, now they're having a funny half hour right now."

Something in my head is telling me, "shut up your babbling, you're talking crap." Paranoia sets in.

"They seem to think they know her."

"Dads, hey?" Joe replies to the girls as they nod their heads, smiling. I'm feeling totally out on a limb on this one...

"That's Cerys Mathews, Catatonia, ain't it girls?" They nod their heads in unison.

"Who?" I ask still feeling somewhat out of it.

"Perhaps this will jog your dad's memory," as he begins to sing a song which the girls join in.

"You've got me on that one," I confess.

"It's *Roadrage*," I'm informed by both Joe and my daughters.

"Ah, yeah, right." I try to join in, knowing full well Joe and the girls are not fooled for one minute.

He sits down on the floor in front of the girls for over 40 minutes. The subject varies, but one thing that makes me spring to attention is when Joe asks Amée... "How's your guitar playing?"

WHAT? Rewind, rewind... did he just say what I thought he said? I've lost it. I'm hallucinating. He can't know who we are, who I am, surely not. I'm nobody – we're nobody.

Joe told us how he had visited Newport the previous day, how it had changed since he was there. It was great Joe just sitting in front of us chatting. I plucked up the courage to ask if he would kindly sign a shirt I had bought the girls. Joe called all the band across: "Come and meet my friends," he said to them. "Sign the shirt for the girls."

We get introduced: "This is Smiley."

"Hi!" (please don't remember me from Belfast).

"This is Pabs." (oh my God he'll remember me).

"This is Martin Slattery." (never met him, he won't think I'm a dick).

"Hey where's Ant? Cerys, where's Ant? These girls want their shirt signed."

A rather dazed-looking fella takes the shirt, signs "Ant x" and goes back to sleep.

"Where's Scott?"

"No, no, that's fine." God, am I making a pain of myself or what?

I've still got one more favour to ask: "Joe, please would you sign this *Yalla Yalla* CD, it's for a fella in the States called Jason, he runs a great site all about you and The Mescaleros, The Clash, it's super. I've started doing some reports for him and a few pics."

He gladly signs it, adding he has very little knowledge of computers, but has heard that there are several sites. And makes a note of the Casbah club address: "I'll get someone to show me."

Afterwards, as my daughters and I head for the NCP, I couldn't help feeling how the evening had gone so quick – and wow, I hadn't ballsed up again.

Arriving home I spent about two hours searching for flights to the US. I've never been before. Jan and the girls have never been, it's got to be the four of us. KLM to Los Angeles £199.00 ea, fly out on the 4th, return on the 9th, booked. I immediately book Anaheim, book two hotels at Anaheim and Hollywood and fall into bed at 5.00. I excitedly wake my wife up... "We're going to America!"

28 October, Manchester Academy. I hate Manchester, I hate Mancs... it's a London thing, mainly football-related.

The bash is a good one. I'm stone cold sober as I'm driving. Clicking away with my camera, just before the end of the show, I'm trying to take shots when this prat starts jumping up and down in front of me, deliberately. Every time I raise it he jumps. I lower the camera to my side, when all of a sudden the camera is pulled; luckily I've wrapped the strapping around my wrist. That's it. "Come on then!" As I charge towards him a gap appears, he steps back, job done... I wrongly assume. All of a sudden I've got three of them on me. I feel the thuds in the back of my head as I am vainly attempting to punch and kick thin air. All of a sudden I feel I am being dragged away, the side door opens and two gorillas throw me face first onto the concrete outside and slam the door behind me.

So I'm cut, bruised, The Mescaleros are coming on for an encore, I'm outside, my heroes about to play *Bankrobber.*

I feel that Glasgow is too far to drive – after all, I'm on my way to LA IN A FEW DAYS!!!!!

5 November, Anaheim: Me and the family have had a great day out at Disney. Fantastic!

I leave them at the hotel at about 6.30 and drive down to the Sun Theatre, collect my ticket at dead on 7.00 as the box office opens and sit on a bench in the open space directly outside.

Pablo and Martin come out after soundcheck and politely nod in my direction. Pablo then ventures nearer, asking, "Haven't I seen you somewhere before?" When I explain exactly where and when, he is astounded: "What, you've come all this way, to see us?"

"Yeah, yeah."

"Fuckin' hell, that's great. Martin, this guy has come all the way from London to see us. Listen, wait there, just wait there!"

Five minutes later Pabs comes back with a working pass. "This is for you, as a thank-you from the band. Wait for me after the show, if the security try to throw you out show them this, they'll leave you alone."

I walk into the venue as it opens. It's quite big, but I can't understand why there are tables near the front, with seats. Still, take a seat quite a while before they're on.

"Would you like the menu sir?"

"Pardon?"

"The menu, for your dinner." He's having a laugh.

"You're winding me up, right?"

"No sir, these tables are for people wishing to eat and watch the band." This must be cabaret, I must be in the wrong part, but Pabs gave me a pass. I vacate the area quickly and head for the bar; I later learn that this date will go down in Mescaleros history as the "chicken in a basket" gig.

I decide to stand in the mosh pit – fatal, for as the band come on, it's full of kids, skinheads. I'm nearly 40, my shins take a good hiding. It's all good fun, no malice, just that I'm too old. A few songs in, Joe winks in my direction. I instinctively look behind me, thinking who's he winking at? He does it again, this time nodding in my direction; again I look around. Someone's not paying attention and he's trying to acknowledge them.

Another good night musicwise though the venue is crap. I hang around by the side of the stage as instructed by Pabs afterwards and, as pre-warned, security approach me. I dig deep inside my pocket to get my working pass,

which I've carefully preserved. Just as the security guy is about to question why I have got a pass and not even taken the sticker off, Pabs appears...
"Come on, let's go backstage for a drink."

We enter the dressing rooms. Joe and Luce are sitting together and Pabs says, "This is the guy I told you about, who's flown over from England to see us."

Joe says, "Yeah, I was acknowledging you, did you see me?"

"Yeah, yeah... I did, yeah." Christ, it was me... oh shit... and I was turning around... cringe!!!

"Hey Pabs, have we got any laminates left? Give Anthony one. Are you seeing any more shows whilst you're over here?"

"Erm, yeah, er Hollywood."

"Are you on your own?" Joe enquires.

"Er no, erm, the wife and girls are back at the hotel."

"Have you taken them to Disney?" Joe continues.

"Yeah, yeah... we went today."

"It's great, ain't it? I've taken my girls there, we love it."

Pabs asks me if I want a drink and encourages me to take a seat before the dressing room doors open and place gets crammed.

As Pabs and I are sitting there chatting, people start coming in, a few nice pleasantries are exchanged before this weird-looking fella in a bastard chequered jacket says to Pabs, "I love you guys, I love you guys." Pabs politely accepts the compliments when all of a sudden this fella comes out with one of the most outlandish suggestions I have ever heard:

"Do you want to fuck my wife?" as he points to a scatty bitch to his right!

Oh shit, this must be a groupie thing, like you read about in the *Sunday People*. Shit, what do I do? Do I disappear?

At which point Pabs shot up like a bolt of lightning.

"I'm fucking married with two kids... now fuck off."

Ahah, I know what to do... "He's married with two kids, now piss off." Pabs looked across to me... "We told him, didn't we?"

Yes, Pabs, you most certainly did. Big respect to the Pabs.

The coach and all the entourage were about to leave. Just as everyone was about to board the coach Pabs introduced me to a rather large gentleman with a strong Yorkshire accent. "This is Tim" – he crushed my hand whilst shaking it, said "all right" and shot off.

Pabs said, "See yer tomorrow" and got on the bus... This is rock 'n' roll.

Arriving back at the hotel room, I immediately woke Jan and the girls, with my laminate around my neck like some army dogtag. As I was midway through re-enacting the night's events I noticed all three were asleep... they must be tired!

6 November, Hollywood: Now, when I booked the hotel, I noticed "House of Blues, Sunset Boulevard". Book hotel, Sunset Boulevard – simple. No one

told me Sunset Boulevard was 14 miles long; it isn't like the English high street.

I left the family again in the hotel room; we had had a crap day. Hollywood's shit, tacky crap. They were getting cheesed off, outside looked rough – not like Anaheim, where they could walk about in the evening. This spot we were in was dog-rough.

The next four miles to the House of Blues, I'm offered everything from snidey watches to full-blown sex and those that aren't trying to flog me things are hurling abuse at me. Have I put too much hair gel on tonight or something?

I get to the venue and decide to give my ticket away to a fan outside who was calling out for tickets. Why not pass on my good fortune?

Quietly confident with my laminate tucked inside my jacket, I queued up. First mistake – those with laminates who queue up in an orderly fashion are either very naive or of dodgy character. Guess what the security had me down as?

The situation was made worse by the fact that additional passes had been issued to those with laminates and I didn't have one. So here I was ticketless, with a laminate that this particular venue didn't honour.

I found the fan that I had given my ticket to and, to my horror, he wasn't a fan – he was a bloody tout. So I had to buy the ticket back for $40.

Once I got inside, straight to the bar – "pint please." Have a deserved gulp of beer, light a cigarette... "No smoking in here," I'm told in no uncertain terms... and I hate *Manchester*?

The show was good – no cameras allowed, I learnt when I got it out ready to take pics.

I went backstage after – they let me in on the laminate. Pabs came over and took me over to where he was sitting, next to Smiley. We had a good chat; the conversation came round to football and fishing.

Both were absolutely super with me. Joe popped over to check if I was OK! It just seemed such a shame that I was only doing the two shows.

Pabs explained that he was looking forward to Vegas tomorrow.

"Why don't you come?"

"I can't, it's too far."

"It's only 400-odd miles... each way. You'd love Vegas. Your wife and girls would love Vegas," Pabs suggested.

I had told him that we were really disappointed with Hollywood...

"Nah, Vegas is super, you gotta come."

"I don't know any hotels, I don't know..." I said, somewhat unsure.

"The Monte Carlo Hotel – your wife will love it, trust me. And when you're there, take the kids next door and go on New York, New York's Manhattan Express. Look, here's 20 bucks, tell the girls it's Pab's treat... they'll love it."

As I enter the hotel room, her indoors has got the hump big-time. "I'm not staying here one more night – the place is a madhouse."

"I know, and tomorrow we're going to Las Vegas," I coolly reply.
"What?"
"Las Vegas. The Mescaleros are playing there tomorrow and we're going." (It had better be as good as you said, Pabs.)

7 November, Las Vegas: A long drive through Death Valley and a slight altercation at the petrol station – I kicked the pump in frustration because no matter what I did the pump didn't work, and an announcement came out over a loudspeaker, "Do not kick my pump." Talk about big brother...

I hadn't needed to fill the car up before and apparently, as it was the last petrol station before Death Valley, to stop people filling up and driving off into the unknown, you had to pre-pay. Great! How much do you put in? So after two trips back to the cashier, $17 filled it up. That's about £11 to fill a 4.3 litre V8 motor up. God bless America!

We arrived at the Monte Carlo. Pabs was spot-on – they loved it. It was class (and as it was a Sunday night only $80 for all of us).

I took the girls on the New York, New York ride. Janet insisted that if they go on, I had to go on – "please Dad, go on, you told us it was Pablo's treat." I won't go into graphic details because it still brings me out in a cold sweat just thinking about it. Needless to say, as I was going round upside down, the air was blue with expletives directly aimed at Pablo.

I headed off to the Hard Rock on foot. Jan and the girls were more than happy to go off shopping along the Strip – perfect!

I arrived at the venue, had a couple of beers, popped across to see Andy, who had just arrived from England. We exchanged big hugs. I could feel it in my bones, this was going to be a night I would not forget in a hurry.

It was a quite sparse crowd; you could stand approx 6ft from the front and have space. Lovely for an old fella like me – peaceful. The band came on and several songs in this nutty woman was throwing herself about like a loony, people were pushing her off. Joe had had a dig at her earlier, referring to her as "the mouthy broad" but she was game and was flying around. Just as *Safe European Home* was coming to an end she tripped and fell in front of me... poor cow, knickers showing, tits hanging out... what a state. Oh, sod it. It's someone's daughter... "Come here my dear," as I stretched out my hand to lift her up. "Come on."

As she climbed to her feet, she threw this punch that missed my nose by about an inch.

"Bleedin' cow!" I shouted as her shoes started flying into my shins. A gap appeared in the crowd, my hands in front of me frantically trying to block the punches. I looked nervously up at the stage. Scott was in hysterics, Joe was singing and laughing. What could I do? I couldn't hit her so I was just backing off, ducking and weaving the punches.

As the song finished Joe shouted out over the mike:
"Hey babe, you're on vacation, we don't want you to end up in hospital."

Laughing, he said, "You've got your laminate, come to the side of the stage," and pointed. As I walked away, she shouted out to Joe to get his clothes off. At that point two burly security guards carried her off, still fighting. I was only trying to help!

Right, OK, erm Joe pointed that way, so off I went through some doors. Where do I go now? Try these doors through here – try these doors. It was an office, must walk through the office to the side of the stage.

Bit strange, but Joe had pointed. As I went into the office, I could see a man sat at the desk, he immediately appeared to press a button. "What are you doing in here?" he shouted and before I could answer two security guards came in and pinned me on the desk.

Trying to explain oneself with your face squashed against a desk is not easy. After much shouting, mainly by them, I managed to explain the story, as I reached inside my jacket to get my laminate out, which caused all sorts of mayhem! After five minutes of rerunning through the complete story I was told, "Fuckin' get out of here you schmuck," or words to that effect.

I left attempting to brush myself down and regain my composure. I decided to just go back in the hall, stand in front of Scott and Martin and take some pictures.

I had taken no fewer than three shots when I felt the back of my collar being grabbed and I was frog-marched out. "No photos" – my face was shoved in the direction of the sign.

I reached inside my jacket, took the laminate out, and said defiantly, "Please, just leave me alone."

"Why didn't you tell us?" was the reply

"URGHHHHHHHHHH you didn't give me a chance to."

I re-entered the hall for what must be the umpteenth time, looked nervously over my shoulder every time the flash went and as soon as the show had finished rushed backstage to grab a beer. As I entered, I could hear the laughing and cheering. It was good banter – after all if it had happened to anyone else I would have thought it was hysterical.

I had carried the girls' *Rock Art* T-shirt around with me for three nights in the hope of Scott completing the signatures, and lo and behold, he came up to me and said, "I've been informed I've got to sign your girls' shirt" – completion!

The big Yorkshireman slapped me on the back, nearly knocking my false teeth out, and introduced me to two fellow Yorkshiremen who had flown in just for the night: "Thought you lot would have a thing or two in common."

They were decent fellas. Had a chat and a beer. One was called Nyle – nice fellas, doubt if I'll ever see them again, though!

As I left, I passed the bus; I heard a loud banging on the darkened windows and a Brummy accent I had grown to love hearing. Andy and I hugged each other as true friends; he tried not to laugh too much about my fracas. What a night!!!!

I was walking along back to the hotel. It was approx 1.30am. As I was walking my head was still back at the venue, still dreaming about three great nights, how everyone had been so kind, how lucky I was, when all of a sudden three Hispanics stepped out of a building site and proceeded to walk around me singing some sort of rap song.

"The motherfucker's going to die tonight."

"Give us $10, give us $20," they added.

My head was spinning. I was turning my head so quickly, trying to keep an eye on all three at once as they walked circular-like around me. I couldn't get my wallet out as it had everything – all our money, my credit cards, my travellers' cheques and my passport. They'd want the lot. My body was pumping, at every orifice things were going clang, bang, my legs were giving way. I felt a slight release of urine – fuck, fuck.

I could see the lights from the strip about half a mile away. My heart felt like it was ready to explode... my temples were throbbing.

I know, I'll smack that one right in the kisser and then run like fuck! No, my legs wouldn't make it. Besides, these bastards had never heard of Queensbury rules and they've most probably got knives or shooters. I'd seen too many episodes of *Kojak* – fuck... fuckkkkkkk.

"Give us your money, motherfucker."

Without thinking and definitely with no planning I shouted out as loud as I could, "*I am a citizen of Her Majesty the Queen, I am a guest in your country, I am a BRITISH subject.*"

Surely someone must hear me. The odd car sped past; nothing.

"*How dare you stop a member of Her Majesty's Commonwealth.*"

Any old crap that came into my head. They started to look at each other. "*I am a guest in your country.*" A big gob landed right on my jacket; that's cool. I breathed deeply.

"The motherfucker's lucky tonight... the motherfucker's lucky tonight..." The rap tune faded as they disappeared into the darkened building site. I lit a fag, my legs seemed rooted and they weighed a ton. It was the calves – they were jelly.

It took what seemed eternity to reach the hotel. I had a coffee and another cigarette. Perhaps Mancs weren't so bad.

On returning to Blighty, I set about updating Casbah Club with a short review and some pics. Jason had received his CD and was over the moon. He also said a couple who had been at Vegas (they came from Salt Lake City) had been in touch. Would I like their email? A lady called Tami.

A week or so later Giuseppe had kept his word – the Las Vegas CD had arrived. I must have played that bit where Joe talks to me over and over again. Sad!

For the next two weeks I closely followed the tour from afar. By all accounts Boston was outstanding. *White Riot* was played for the first time.

2 December, Barcelona: I had booked my flight to Barcelona. Easyjet, out of Luton.

I arrived in the centre of Barcelona, had a shitty cup of coffee, bought a map and proceeded to the venue called Zeleste.

I eventually found it, in an industrial part of the city, very grey and drab. On the front doors was a large sign which read: Joe Strummer & The Mescaleros. Spanish, Spanish, Spanish lingo? I tried several times to attract passers-bye with my non-existent Spanish. "Excusimoi Juan, please, vous read me le signo, gracias."

After several failed attempts, this really nice fella, who spoke great English, informed me that the venue had been changed to the Bikini Club, more to the city centre.

All this had messed up any chance of visiting Nou Camp, home of the legendary Barcelona FC, but never mind, I found the venue, found a hotel close by, dumped my stuff, showered and headed off.

Above the club was a library, which had a bar and a veranda where you could sit, have a beer or two and watch the world go by as the sun set – idyllic.

Oh Christ, there's that great lump from Yorkshire! Oh God, and he's seen me.

"Hi." I ain't shaking hands with him. "All right?" he said broadly as he found his way up to where I was. Better buy him a beer as I nervously ran my tongue over my false teeth. After about five minutes I relaxed – he was OK. He told me how the remainder of the tour had gone stateside, how he had "enjoyed" life on the bus during that tour. He was all right. Timmy Tim, I like you!

He explained the reason for the change of venue had been that the promoter had basically bottled it because advance ticket sales had not been good and switched to a smaller venue. "You watch... it will be heaving in there tonight."

I decided to accept his offer of going downstairs. Just as we entered the venue, the band were just finishing soundcheck. Pabs and Smiley joined us at the bar. I had printed off several copies of Casbah Club to give to the band. I couldn't believe it as all six sat in the dressing room, reading different pages; they really liked it, the facts and figures, the lot.

The show was heaving, full house and more!! The show was top-drawer, will always stand out as special because of the nine-minute version of *Straight to Hell*. Joe adlibbed, Smiley just kept the drum beat ticking over whilst the crowd clapped in tune.

After the show, I joined Smiley, Pablo, Martin and Gordon (Scott and Martin's guitar tech) in an adjacent hall where an eight-man cover band were playing. It was all right, foot-tapping. Martin was not so much into the music, more into how well the instruments were being played.

The coach left at about 1.30 bound for Milan. I had decided to give that one a miss but come Monday would be Paris-bound.

7 December, Paris: Catching a midday ferry from Dover to Calais, with the English Channel at its worst, Amée and I arrived in Paris at about 7.00-ish. This was the last date of '99, the last date on my America, Canada and Europe AAA. As we arrived outside the Elysée-Montmartre the first thing I saw was that gorilla with the ponytail. OK!

I deliberately headed directly for him, not showing any ticket he put his large arm right into my chest and sneered, "ticket." I reached inside my jacket, pulled out my laminate, shoved it right underneath his nose and sneered, "**I'm with the fucking band.**"

As we stood watching the support band The Hellboys, Smiley and my new mate Tim approached for a chat. Smiles asked me a question. The noise was so loud and after several attempts he said let's go backstage and gestured to us. As we went backstage, sitting on a chair outside the dressing room was Joe: "Hey, Anthony."

"Hi, Number One."

He seemed a bit keyed up and asked Amée, "Are you hungry? Would you like a coke, crisps?" Then added, "Is she all right, has she got a pass?"

"Don't worry Joe, I've got mine."

"No, no, she must have her own pass."

"It's OK. Honestly, Joe."

"No, get her a pass," Joe said quite abruptly as he summoned the tour manager. "Get her a pass, these are my friends."

God! I knew the tour manager didn't like me and I had always kept my distance. Now he was going to hate me. "It's fine, Joe, please, it's OK!"

"It's not fuckin' OK, get her a fuckin' pass."

The tour manager came back two or three minutes later, complete with All Access sticker. Joe said, "Give it to me," as he beckoned my daughter closer and stuck it inside her jacket. Joe whispered to her, "Don't lose it, people try to nick them and I want to see you afterwards."

"Thanks, thanks," we both somewhat nervously replied.

I decided to make a sharp exit, as they were due on in about ten mins. "Have a good one," I said as we left.

"Don't worry, we will," was Joe's confident reply.

That night Paris rocked. In conversation, trips down memory lane, and in interviews I have done with various Mescaleros since, Paris December 1999 always gets mentioned – four encores, *White Riot* twice.

I remember writing in a review for Casbah Club afterwards, "If you haven't got the bootleg, contact Dom and get it." I still stick by that sentence today; they were awesome. I got through two rolls of film and got what I consider to be my best shot – all six of them, arms round each other, onstage after the final encore.

The crush to get backstage was frightening. Anyone and everyone was trying to get past. Amée and I got split up in the crazy scenes. I desperately tried to literally fight my way to her. Getting desperate, I tried once more. I started to panic – she was only 14.

I needn't have bothered. I looked again only to see her safely behind the crash barrier standing next to Smiley. She cockily undid her jacket and flashed her AAA sticker at me!

Happy she was safe, I went back to the stage. The crowd were being pushed out of the venue via any exit possible. I saw Andy and the rest of the crew onstage dismantling the equipment. I jumped up to say goodbye to a true friend; we gave each other a big hug and he said, "I was talking about you to Joe the other night. I asked him, what's the crack with Anthony? I said, he's a good guy and all that, but why have you asked me to look after him?"

Andy then did a Joe impression but with Brummy overtones:

"Even in the wilderness years he used to write to me." Andy then added that Joe had come back about a minute later with: "He was the only cunt who did."

The Casbah Club was always my favourite, but recently a new site had emerged, Road to Rock 'n' Roll – not a bad site. I had exchanged emails with Celia – she had seen Joe at Glastonbury in the summer and got hooked.

Giuseppe emailed to say he had got backstage at Milano and Joe had asked him if he could get a copy of The Sex Pistols at the Nashville for him. I think Giuseppe was overwhelmed with honour.

Well, the year had been beyond my dreams. I was still basically travelling on my own, but had met many good people along the way. No further dates were planned – that is, not in England or Europe for the foreseeable future. Japan and Australia had been announced but that was out of the question – too far!

2000

"How much to fly into Osaka and out of Tokyo?"

"How much? OK! I'll take it."

She'll kill me, I whispered under my breath as the lady started to take my details. It was 2 January. I'd toyed with the idea all over Xmas and New Year. I just had to go.

"How would you like to pay, Mr Davie?"

"Ah, this is where I need a little favour. Can I pay £300 on my American Express which goes straight to my business address and £299 on my MasterCard, which the monthly invoice goes to my home address? I'm not being fraudulent or nothing, it's just that when the wife finds out I'm going I'm as good as dead. It will help me if I can hold up the bill and say, look, it was so cheap – only cost £299. Oh, and could you send the tickets to my business address?"

The days ticked by. I couldn't pluck up the courage to tell her. The only one I told had been Giuseppe and with his poor English I doubt if he knew what I was on about. I just had to tell someone.

The days were running out – time goes so quick when you don't want it to. I was putting it off every day. Tommy tomorrow.

Then out of the blue a package arrives on my doormat!

"Any mail for me?" I shout from the bathroom. No reply.

"Anything for me?" I repeat. As I look over the top of the stairs my wife is holding this package.

"Who's that for?"

"Joe Strummer," was the reply.

"Yeah, right?"

"No, Joe Strummer c/o 22 Kirby Close – and there's a note on the bottom," she adds as I reach the bottom of the stairs.

"Let's have a look."

"Anthony please you give tapes to my friend Joe when you see him in Japan regards Giuseppe." Bloody Italian is my thought as I nervously giggle towards my wife.

I don't like doing my dirty washing in public, so won't go into the finer details. Suffice to say the rabbit was good company in the garage for the following nights. I actually asked Jason to put on his site, tongue in cheek, about my plight and could any contract killer reading this help me. He sent me quite an abrupt email back saying he thought I was taking this a little too far and wouldn't put it up because there are some very weird people about. Jason, I was joking!

Osaka, 16 January; Tokyo, 17/18 January: Flying out from Heathrow to

Osaka via Hong Kong, Cathay Pacific were doing a special offer, one-night free stopover in Hong Kong – lovely jubbly.

After a terrific night in Hong Kong, I continued my journey to Osaka.

Arriving at customs in Japan is different to say the least, especially a man travelling on his own. My luggage is thoroughly searched; I am then taken aside and interviewed!

"Why you come to Japan?"

"Erm, to see The Mescaleros."

"The who?"

"No, no, not The Who! (No sense of humour.) The Mescaleros... Joe Strummer... er, The Clash."

I then attempt air guitar: a complete blank look is all I get.

"Er, music, wok 'n' woll – sorry!'

They begrudgingly stamp my passport.

Now I am a typical Englishman abroad, I know that. Don't make any attempt to speak the lingo, expect everyone to speak English. But have you tried understanding the Osaka subway map. It's all in Japanese! After jumping on and off so many trains I eventually reach Zepp Osaka. It's about 4.00 in the afternoon. I can see quite a bit of activity at the main door – shit, I haven't got a ticket or anything. I dig deep through my bag. Old faithful is there, the laminate from the last tour. Putting it around my neck I decide to bluff my way and with a quick flash I'm in, easy. All of a sudden I'm stopped.

"Please, we escort you to dressing room."

"No, no mate... er I'm fine."

"No, it is our honour." Oh God! It's made even worse he's a chatterbox, desperate to try out his English.

"What instrument you play?"

"I don't play any instrument," is my bland reply. It fell on deaf ears.

"You drummer?"

"No, I'm not the drummer."

"I know, you play guitar?"

"Yeah, whatever! Listen, my old mate I need a leak."

"Eh?"

"Erm, a Jimmy, a piss." I put my hand to my flies to demonstrate.

"Oh yes, no worry, toilets in dressing room and dressing room very near."

I was getting flustered; I like to be in the background. I would hate to just waltz in. Just as we walk along the corridor the dressing room door opens and Joe walks out. The Japanese fella continued to babble something. I was doing OK until Joe said, "Anthony, what are you doing here?" Did he mean, what the fuck are you doing here? I wanted the ground to open up; I'll kill that over helpful little...

"Hey guys, Anthony's here, come in, come in."

I got a lovely greeting from Smiley. He kindly takes my bag – he seemed to know whenever I was getting edgy. Such a cool character, our Smiles, always made me feel completely at ease. The rest of the band welcomed me in. Pabs gave me a lovely welcome.

Joe asked me a favour: "Did you buy any Benson & Hedges?"

"Yeah, yeah, I've got 600," I replied somewhat puzzled.

"Could you give a couple of packets to the promoter, Massa? He loves B & H."

"Yeah, yeah, no probs," I enthusiastically stated.

"Have you got a hotel booked?" Joe enquired.

"Er... No."

"Listen, we're going back to the hotel for a couple of hours. Feel free to jump in the minibus and stay at the hotel we're at."

On the way to the hotel I give Joe his package from Giuseppe. "Ah, Giuseppe, I met him in Milan – he's the king bootlegger, told me he was a good friend of yours." *Was* being the operative word, I thought, still shuddering at the memory of that plate flying across the kitchen at me, but as I said I don't like doing my dirty washing in public!

After giving the promoter 200 Benson – I felt tight opening up a box to take 20 out – he was genuinely delighted. I had got a friend for life.

"I pay your hotel bill," he says. What a result, this place was pukka as well, what a saving.

"Then you pay me, we get block booking discount."

Champion!

Meet at 7.30 in the foyer is the order of the day. I get downstairs ten minutes early. Ants and Smiley are already there. They tell me all the tips about being on tour – never use the phone in the room, so bloody expensive, plus we have to pay for it ourselves if we do! Get a phonecard. Never drink from the minibar – too expensive – always free beer at the venue.

The minibus arrives. The tour manager gives me a working pass. He definitely doesn't like me. But so what?

As we pull up outside there is a large crowd waiting by the stage door. It suddenly hits me, there's only me and the band in the bus. I get off last deliberately. I still got a couple of pats on the back.

The show is good. Being 6ft 2in I can stand anywhere and see! You basically can do anything, I sit right by the crash barrier stageside taking my pics and no one disturbs me. Pure bliss. Even the crowd surfers as they come over the top and are escorted back, carefully avoid me so as not to knock me – such politeness.

The tickets in conversion to the pound are over £40. This is one hell of an expensive country. After the show, I meet up with Andy. Always great to see him. Pabs invites me to the after-show dinner, checks with the promoter who is proudly showing everyone his B & H. "Of course, he can come." I was waiting for the punchline!! It didn't come!

The whole band (except Smiley) plus Joe, Luce, Eliza, Andy and I are taken by the promoter and his wife for a meal. It's Japanese, never had it before. Scott and Martin are the experts and try to help me as much as possible, though I detect Scott's got a great sense of humour. But even he nearly falls off his chair when I mistakenly start to drink the finger wash water when it is put in front of us! I was so thirsty.

As we get back to the hotel about a dozen fans are waiting outside for autographs and pictures. Joe has so much patience and would gladly stand there all night adhering to every wish until Andy puts his arm around Joe to lead him inside the hotel.

I get in the lift with Joe, Luce and Eliza. We get out on the same floor, "Goodnight Anthony."

"Er, yeah, goodnight."

Is this Disneyworld I'm in or something? Never-never land?

I was told the previous night to meet in the foyer 9.00 sharp, travel up with us to Tokyo. At 8.30 I'm down there, bag packed, showered, shaved, the lot. Gary, the tour manager, comes across. "Listen, I'd prefer it if you didn't travel with us – nothing personal, you'd be better off travelling on your own."

What can you say? Nothing except OK!

I felt a bit low, not so much that I wasn't travelling with the band – that was not in my original plans anyway – it's just that he said it with such a wide grin. It's that time in Paris, I knew it, with the pass for Amée. I trudge off to find the station. Ah well!

I arrive in Tokyo. What a place – fantastic! The subway maps are in English. I make my way to Tokyo Capitol Hotel. The promoter had told me that was where the band were staying and I could stay as well, same deal. I go to the reception, take my room. It's about 4.00; soundcheck's at 5.30. I must eat – haven't really eaten anything of any substance since Hong Kong. Struggled with the Japanese last night and couldn't face that again. During my walkabout, it was as though I saw a mirage – McDonalds or, as in Japanese, McaDonaldo.

As you walk to the counter, it's "Hi." As they bow I gladly return the "Hi," and I raise my hand, somewhat taken aback by such politeness in a McDonalds.

After three Filet-o-fish it's off to find the Akasaka Blitz. It's a monstrosity of a building and as I get to the front Andy and the boys are unloading the equipment. I give a helping hand but seem to get in the way more than helping. I bump into Gary: "Ah, you made it OK then?" he says, seemingly disappointed. "Suppose you want a working pass?"

"Er yes… that would be very kind of you," I sheepishly reply.

He is starting to get me down. I know I'm a walking disaster, but I have always attempted to be polite, keep myself to myself and desperately not make a pain of myself. Oh well, perhaps it's me. I wander past the dressing rooms to get a cup of coffee from the vending machine. I get a call from Martin: "Anthony, Scott wants you."

I walk in. "Anthony, would you video tonight's show for me… here's my camera and tripod. I've had a word with Justin, you can film from the sound desk – is that all right?"

"Yeah, yeah, no probs."

Christ! I've never used one of these before, what do I do? I can't have a beer, especially with my bladder I can't leave the camera. Fifteen minutes before they're due on, I trundle across to the sound desk, set the tripod up. "You haven't got any idea how these work, have you?" The Lobster shakes his head. "Sorry mate." Oh God!

As the music starts I make the decision – just point and shoot. The band come onstage, pan, pan, all I can think of is *Top of the Pops* and how they film it. As the show gets under way. I'm panning, scanning. After three or four numbers I'm getting the hang of this. Then all of a sudden – the cap, the cap, I've left the bloody cap on.

I desperately feel for the cap. All I can see through the lens are my fingers. Phew; I took the cap off after all. Shit! Now the film's been messed up with my fingers in it.

The actual show I have no memory of – pure concentration. So much so, when it's over my head is throbbing. I dismantle the camera and tripod and carry it back to the dressing room. It's etiquette to let the band unwind before entering – give them five or ten minutes – but this bloody thing weighs a ton.

I knock on the door, nervously pop my head round.

"Sorry to disturb you, can I just drop this off please?"

"Anthony, come in, pull up a chair, grab a beer," Joe kindly says.

To quote my hero Ronnie Barker, "It's been a funny old day," I think as I sit there with just Joe, Luce and the band sipping champagne. But what a great end to the day. I'm in total peace until Scott says come on Ant, let's have a look at your filming. Oh God, those bloody fingers.

The following day, I decide to visit downtown Tokyo – do a bit of shopping, visit numerous record shops in the hope of picking up a Japanese copy of The Clash, The Mescaleros... nothing. They are identical to the ones I can buy at Woolworths.

Approaching the hotel I bump into Joe coming out. We exchange pleasantries. He asks me for a bit of help with the local map everyone's been using, provided by the hotel – it's crap. Everything seems back to front. I point him in the right direction; he's going walkabout.

About 6 o'clock I make my way down to Akasaka. As I walk in, the first person I bump into is the dreaded tour manager. He brushes past, totally ignoring me, just as I'm halfway through saying "Hi yer..."

I grab a coffee and take a seat as far along the corridor as is possible. At this point I'm regretting coming; rejection can be hard to handle.

I think back to when I was just 16. I had completed two weeks at Portsmouth FC. I had trained hard, was never late, and did everything I could to the very best of my ability. Ian St John was the first team manager; Ray

Crawford, an England International from the 60s, was the youth coach. On the last day we were sat down in the changing rooms at Fratton Park. Four names were read out; they were asked to stand outside. Are they the selected? Are they the rejected?? So your mind goes into overdrive. Mr Crawford then says to us remaining, as the door closes, "I'm sorry, we won't be asking you to stay" – and that's it.

That's rejection because I wasn't good enough; it actually came easier than I thought. I had my father to thank for that. When he was scouting for my team, Crystal Palace, he took me down to the ground and into the offices. Arnie Warren, later to find fame with El Tel in Barcelona, was sitting there and after their conversation Arnie turned to my father: "Is this your boy? Would he like to come training with the youth team? He's a big lad! Is he any good?"

Training with my team, wearing the Palace shirt? A teenager's imagination is so quick and wonderful. "No thanks, Arnie, he ain't good enough" – and the conversation just changes. All those hopes and dreams...

As I stop daydreaming, I realise that was South London in 1975; this is Tokyo in 2000. I am brought down to earth by a tap on the shoulder and a yell of "Oi!" It's my mate Gary (not). "Come into the dressing room... now."

I'm gonna smack him one right in the kisser, I don't give a shit. I'll knock his bleedin' lights out. The aggression is building in me. I'm gonna hit him so hard. As I walk through the dressing room door a loud cheer rings out – the roadcrew are cheering and guess who's standing there with a big grin? As he places the laminate's cord over my head: "They were done this morning, we thought we'd wind you up – funny weren't it?" (Bloody hysterical.) As he lays it on my neck: "Inner sanctum now" and puts his arm around me.

I honestly didn't know whether to laugh or cry. I could feel my bottom lip quivering and immediately bit it. I then ask if I could take a pic of them all for posterity – and of course the Casbah Club.

It's 8.00; the band are due on and are only just entering the dressing room. There's been a bit of a cock-up – they forgot there was no support band tonight, so it was starting earlier, and it's one mad rush. Smiley reached into his bag and hands me his camera. "Take a few pics for us, Ant." Pabs leans across and hands me his as well so the three cameras and me take up position. It's a great gig. Joe had apologised to the audience for being late, they loved him and I've done my job with Smiles' and Pabs' cameras plus taken quite a few decent shots of my own.

Back in the dressing room, I'm having a beer and sharing a spliff with Martin and Scott, giggling – even more so when this Japanese guy walks into the dressing rooms, looking somewhat lost. He is dressed like Rambo and he has in his hands a pile of white paper cards; he approaches Scott: "You drummer?"

Scott smiles and says, "No, that's Smiley." Rambo scribbles something down on one of the cards.

"You Antony Genn?" Again Scott smiles and points to Ant, now asleep on a couch. The scribbling of notes continues.

"You Martin Slarrey?" "No. That's Martin there."

"Ahhhhh, so who you?'

"I'm Scott."

"So you not drummer then?" To which Scott replies, somewhat frustrated, "No."

"So Smiley guitar?" asks Rambo who is by now also somewhat confused.

"No, Smiley's the drummer..." and so it continued.

In amongst all this bedlam I could see Joe walking out of the dressing room. I'd put it off for the previous two nights but I must do it now. I had been carrying around in my jacket, up my jumper, down my sleeve, numerous items that several people had sent me to ask if I could get Joe's signature.

I had a Clash book, *From Here To Eternity* CD, a *Yalla Yalla* CD, three pics and two Mescaleros T-shirts, both of which had been signed by everyone except Joe. It was now or never. I can't let people down.

As I walk into the corridor, Joe is sitting at a table. Thinking this is the right time I walk straight up and say, "Sorry Joe, but could you possibly sign these for a few punters around the world?" As I turn to look round there's queue of about 80 fans and I've pushed in!

A security fella tugs my arm and with what most probably is his only English word says "No No No."

"I'm so sorry, it was a complete accident, sorry Joe, so sorry." I attempt to pick up the items unsigned and leave, wishing the ground would open up and swallow me.

Joe calmly says, "Stay, don't worry. You're always worrying, never worry," and starts to pick up the first of the items to sign. As he comes to the last item, the *From Here To Eternity* CD, Joe casually mentions, "I've heard you have a story in here?"

"Er yeah, it's... er, here" as I nervously flick through the gatefold.

Joe reads it. "Does your mother still hate us?"

"No not at all."

"That's good."

With everything signed I return to the dressing room. I pass the queue. If looks could kill!

Once I get back inside the dressing room, the band are starting to leave. Pabs and Smiles recommend I jump in the bus with them as it's going back to the hotel first. Gary calls out to ask me my room number as there is a last-night party. "We're looking to leave at about 11.30... just under an hour's time. I'll call your room when we're all ready to leave."

"Yeah... smashing."

Once back in the room, I throw the autographed items on the bed – feel great I'd got them for various people, glad to not have to carry them about any more. Had a shower, put on a clean shirt and sat on the bed waiting for the call.

I'd sat on that bed for nearly an hour and a half. It was now gone 12.30am – nothing! Oh well, it hasn't been a bad few days, I thought to myself as I stood there in my undies folding my trousers up. All of a sudden the phone rang – it was Gary. "Listen mate, so sorry, we're at the restaurant, are you coming? Please come. I'm so sorry."

"That's fine, I'll be there – where is it?" I struggled to hold the phone between my shoulder and neck as I rushed to put my clothes back on. "Listen Ant, get a taxi, we'll pay. I'll fax details to the hotel now, just hand it to a taxi driver."

"Yeah, great... see you in a bit." As soon as I put the phone down, I legged it to the lift, "Come on, come on," encouraging the lift.

As I got to the ground floor I went straight up to the reception. "There should be a fax for me, please." He went away, flicked through several faxes and came back empty-handed, "Sorry, Mr Horse, there is no fax for you." For some reason, both the day and night reception had called me Mr Horse – God knows why? But I had never corrected them; it didn't seem important.

"Listen, my name's not bloody Mr Horse, it's Anthony Davie, now is there a fax for me?" Again he flicked through the faxes and this time came back with one in his hand. "There is one for a Mr Davie, but you're Mr Horse."

"Don't worry about it." I snatched it from his hands and went straight to the taxi rank at the front of the hotel.

Twenty minutes later, I walked into the restaurant to a big cheer. Everyone was sitting on the floor. I was approached by a waiter to step outside – apparently I hadn't taken my shoes off and put a pair of flip flops on!

I sat between Andy and Justin the soundman, had a few beers, attempted some of the food, looked around the very long table. The security fella who had told me "no, no, no" when I mistakenly pushed in the queue earlier was there. You don't smile a lot, I thought as I nodded in his direction.

Gary was telling Smiley about "his great wind-up". It was really good to be there.

As I was talking to Andy, a Japanese fella, somewhat the worse for wear drinkwise, shuffled his body between us. Andy politely said "hello" and his first words in replying were, "You nigger" – and laughed!

I was shocked, in disbelief, questioning myself – did he just say what I thought he said?

He said it again: "You nigger, you black nigger." I looked at Andy; he just smiled politely. I could see by his face that this hurt him.

"You fuckin' nigger," and so it went on for what was only a short while but seemed ages. "You fuckin nigger, yes?" That was it! "Listen you cunt, he's my mate, and don't you dare call him a nigger." He just laughed. I tightened the grip on his neck.

"I'll wipe that stupid grin off your face" as I showed him my fist, "that man is my friend... now fuck off!" I pushed him away.

The aggression in my face must have shown. Smiley shouted across from the other side, "You all right?"

I raised my hand. "Yeah, fine thanks, Smiles."

It had been very upsetting to witness at first hand such ignorance that was racism. It stunk. Andy said, "Thanks mate, I didn't want to start a scene. I'm like you, always in trouble, and with Luce and Eliza here it wouldn't have gone down very well."

"Don't worry about thanking me, you're my mate, that's what friends are for. He was a total wanker."

We did giggle when Andy said, "it does look funny two fellas sat on the floor having a row!"

After the restaurant, we all headed off to a nearby bar. As we were standing around waiting to be served, we were discussing what we were going to have: "I fancy a Coke actually," "Yeah so do I," "I'll just have a small beer," etc etc. So Gordon thought he'd be clever and get what seemed a cheap round in – five cokes and a small beer. It worked out at over £40; later when I left Gordon was still arguing the toss.

They had all decided it was time to move on to a nightclub. I opted not to; it was nearly 3.00am. Outside I gave Andy a big hug. We punched each other on the arm – "See you soon... yeah?" Smiles was standing next to him – again, big hug – "Enjoy Australia – wish I was coming." "Will do, take care, I'll give you a bell when I get back."

And so I trudged off into the night. Decided to take a long walk back to the hotel – had a lot to re-run through my head because this time tomorrow, I'll be back in the real world.

Let's set the record straight right:

In Osaka, I was just fuckin' delirious, let's just say there were one or two problems that morning!

When Anthony was left at the hotel on the last night, it was genuine forgetfulness, seriously! I remember getting to this Japanese restaurant, sitting there just thinking fuckin' hell I'm knackered. Then thinking "shit! I've left Anthony behind." Smiley and myself sorted out calling him up and faxing him directions. It's strange how Anthony saw me, because I had quite a fondness for him, I saw him as a friendly face.

When I used to see Anthony, in a weird way it used to be quite comforting. The only way that I can describe it is that in a situation of chaos and being away from home you tend to vent your frustrations on the ones that reflect normality.

I was quite fond of him. I thought he was a lovely bloke.

– Gary Robinson, Tour Manager, 1999

Now my life has never been simple. Even jobwise it confused many. I had been at the Post Office for 18 years; I worked at Mount Pleasant sorting office in central London, the second biggest office in the world after Chicago. It was great, 4,500 men and women.

Since 1995 I had been on an experimental new shift, Saturday 09:13–20:00 and Sundays 10:00–22:00. That was it, two days a week. As soon as it had been confirmed I was on that shift, I had bought a franchise – leather furniture; we were subcontractors for large furniture retailers, insurance companies etc to inspect and rectify furniture. It had been quite successful. I had my own business premises, employed three people.

I had stuck with the Post Office because there had been strong rumours of large-scale redundancy. I didn't want to miss out. It had been knackering working seven days a week for basically 48 weeks a year.

I had kept my nose clean, never took much time off for a few years, etc. But since following The Mescaleros all that had gone out the window. It had got to the point that I didn't even phone in sick, never filled out any self-certificated sick notes anything. No one had said anything either!!

I thought I had found a loophole until one day in February I was pulled into the office and a large-scale printout of my sick record was unveiled in front of me.

"OK Davie, no bullshit – let's start with the weekend 15/16 January. You are down as unauthorised absence; can I ask where you were?"

"Sure, 15th Hong Kong, er 16th Osaka." There was a deadly silence. "Don't try and be funny. I'll try again. Where were you?"

"Hong Kong and Osaka."

"Look, I'm trying to help you. You are in serious trouble. Are you trying to hide a personal problem? Do you want to discuss it?"

I remained tight-lipped.

"Davie, I notice from your history in the past you had quite a bad sick record: three hernia operations, two broken arms plus a lot of time off where you state your wife was having serious mental problems."

(Arghhhhh, that was one of my previous excuses.)

"Look, what is discussed within these four walls is totally in confidence."

"Yeah, I can't pretend any more, she's back to her old ways. I'm to the point where I'm scared to leave her alone."

At that point he put his hand on mine and said how hard it must be for me. "Why do you try to hide it with these strange stories? You have got a very vivid imagination."

So, that was it: in Post Office records my wife is fully certified radio rental and I'm a poor, suppressed struggling husband who lives in cloud cuckoo land!

British/Irish tour May 2000

1 May, Dublin: I had started to be in regular email contact with Celia. She had gone to the Poetry Olympics, wangled her way backstage and had a great time.

We had both stated we were going to Dublin and we would attempt to meet up. I had arrived at the Olympia Theatre for the soundcheck. Tim gave me a nice greeting. He had a young fella with him called Joe. We had a few words, watched the soundcheck and after I walked over to the stage, saw Andy, saw Smiles who introduced me to the new tour manager, Neil Mather. In some ways I was disappointed that Gary had gone.

Smiley and I decided to go for a couple of beers in Temple Bar. As we walked out the stage door a couple of ladies approached Smiley for his autograph. It was the northern accent of one of them that made me say, "Are you Celia?" It was; we shook hands, had a quick chat. I said to her to meet me after the show and I would take her backstage. She was delighted.

As I returned backstage before the show, Joe asked me if I knew what the setlist was from last year, as he didn't want to repeat the same opening numbers. And could I find out via the internet? I was given the use of a laptop. I looked at it, not even knowing what buttons to press. "Ermmm, it will take me a few minutes... er www. Er... oh God, what's Celia's website address?"

At home I just press favourites, then click. After much deliberating, I went to search. I could feel sweat on my top lip... aha, found it. Now, er... I felt under intense pressure, with Neil and Joe standing behind me. Ahah, gigs, setlists roll down: Dublin 1999, nothing. "Sorry Joe, it's not listed." I felt terribly disappointed. I had been asked to help and couldn't come up with the goods. Joe showed a certain interest in Celia's site, but...

The roadcrew had changed greatly, new faces – all that friendship had been lost.

I bumped into Nyle and his mate Seymour. I felt pleased to see them – such nice fellas. The show was a good one.

Celia met me after the show as planned. As I took her past the security a couple asked me if I could let Smiley know they were here. The dressing room was the usual madhouse. I asked Ant if he knew where Smiley was. "In the shower, I think," as he pointed to the door shut with the lights on. I waited patiently, thinking I can't do anything until I've given Smiley the message about his friends. Twenty minutes later I'm still waiting, thinking he's taking his time. My bladder was starting to concern me.

Five minutes later as I made my way to the loo, there was Smiley and his friends! "Thanks for letting me know, Ant'. I could see the friends looking at me slightly disappointed... but, but... I've been waiting for you outside the shower room... I was told you were in there. I went back, the door was still shut, the light was still on, I turned the handle, opened it... empty. I had been waiting outside an empty shower room. This was not my day. I felt a bit despondent.

Celia was chatting with Pablo's wife Laura; she was OK. I said one or two goodbyes and shot off early. As I walked the cobbled streets of Temple Bar back to the hotel, I decided to call it a day. I think I had been so looking forward to this tour that it had not been the same.

I missed Sheffield, Newcastle and Liverpool, much to my wife's surprise... "Are you all right?" The only reason I decided to go to Brixton was Andy had kindly offered to put the girls on the guestlist whilst we were at Dublin and they were so greatly looking forward to it.

6 May, Brixton Academy: I had purchased two tickets for my business associate Neil and me. We walked to the side door where the girls had to pick up their guest tickets. As we approached the door I heard someone shouting my name. I looked round – couldn't see anyone – "up here mate." Smiley was leaning out of the dressing room window. "Wait there... I'm coming down." We gave each other a hug.

"Where yer been? Everyone's been asking after you."

"Well er... I've been busy... that's it, I've been busy... haven't we Neil?"

"Look, have you got after-show passes?" Smiley enquired.

"No, we were... er going to shoot straight after." I was now starting to get in a fluster.

"Look, I've got you four, come back after, it'll be good to see yer." Just then Martin and Scott were returning from their meal.

"Anthony, where you been man? You coming backstage afterwards?"

"Yeah, see you later." I nervously replied.

As we walked back up to the main entrance, Neil said to me "I thought you said..."

"Yeah, yeah, I know what I said."

What a prat I am – and I'd missed three shows.

I love Brixton Academy, one 'cause it's near to where we all came from, it's South London's main venue, plus with the steep slope, no matter where you stand you always get a good view. The place was packed – over 4,000. It was a great show. As I stood up the front in my usual position right of stage, Smiley raised his stick and nodded to me just before *I Fought The Law*.

Backstage again was heaving, I said hi to all the faces but shot off early. It was good to be back.

The last Monday in June, my mobile went – it was Smiley.

"Are you coming to Italy on Friday?"

I had thought about it, but hadn't made my mind up.

"We're flying out from Stansted on Friday morning with Ryanair."

"Course I will."

That evening when I got home, "I'm going to Venice on Friday!"

"You're not," was the curt reply. "You said the other month you weren't going again."

"Yeah, but... I told you I was being a prat, you know what I'm like."

"Why should you go gallivanting off all over the place and we're stuck here?"

I was getting read the riot act. I think it had been building up for a while; now I was getting the full throttle, "Cow," I thought to myself. Despite several attempts at massive creeping, she refused to give in. For a reason that still haunts me to this day, I accepted it, but can remember thinking at the time: never again will I not go just because you say so.

17 August, Leicester: The V2000 warm-up bash. Met up with Nyle and his lovely lady Clare, had a beer with Smiles beforehand. It was so hot it was unbearable. To get to the khazi was literally a fight – it was very uncomfortable.

In the end I sat outside with Tim, desperate for the breeze. It was the least enjoyable gig I have been to. Rumours were that the V2000 would be Ant's last show. I was never close to Ant; he always acknowledged me but that was it. However, it wouldn't be the same without him. I felt quite sad about Ant's departure, he was very talented. I left early that night.

Celia's site had grown in stature. The Casbah Club was falling by the wayside. I think Jason was struggling to find the time that is needed to put into running a site.

27 October, 100 Club: Like Leicester, the place was packed to the rafters and the heat was terrible. As the band came on, Ant had been replaced by Joe's old friend Tymon Dogg. What, no Scott? I later found out Scott had nervous exhaustion and had been replaced by Martin's friend Jimmy Hogarth. The scene was chaotic – it was too packed.

Folk Riot had replaced *White Riot*. Had a drink with Nyle – we both thought it was OK! But it was only a warm-up for the forthcoming Who tour.

I was never a Who fan and only got tickets for the first Birmingham show. I hated seeing my heroes playing second fiddle, plus being sat up in row Z somewhere, it seemed 90% of the audience were still at the bar when The Mescaleros were on. I left halfway through The Who – just wasn't my cup of tea.

Celia's site had been given "Official Status". I was so proud for her, she deserved it – the site was great, though I didn't like the message board. Some people got very nasty towards various Mescaleros. I couldn't sit there and read the crap they put up. I shot one or two messages back – it was shit.

The politics got on my tits; this is rock 'n' roll, not bloody politics.

In the end even Pabs got fed up with it.

It's only the minority that put crap up, the vast majority just want to read news, swap views on their favourite band and share experiences.

2001

Farewell Smiles

It was the new year 2001. Thought I'd give my old mate Smiles a ring, see how he was, catch up on the gossip, see how the new album's progressing. He seemed a bit unsure. He had done the last night at Wembley Arena and everyone had said they'd be in touch in a few weeks. It was now mid-January and he hadn't heard a thing. He had turned down offers of other work because he thought he would be in the studios.

So now he had nothing. He said he would give it another week and then would ring Joe. He emailed me about ten days later, he had rung Joe; he was no longer a Mescalero.

I felt very sad; Smiley was my friend as well as my hero.

I had a weekend in Norway, thanks to The Mescaleros!! They had planned to play Bergen festival, so I booked the flights and hotel for Jan and I. When it was cancelled we couldn't get a refund, so we still went.

I had kept in close touch with Smiley. He had turned his attention to forming his own band with long-time friend Johnny Wilks called one*iota.

In the meantime he had no work. I offered him some work at my place. He gladly accepted and we spent a couple of weeks together stripping furniture, reminiscing... even though it was great to work together, I still felt very sad; this was one of my heroes.

His first one*iota concert was at a dingy club in Charing Cross Road on 4 June. I hadn't seen him for a few weeks and when Janet and I entered the venue he gave us a lovely welcome and big hugs.

I didn't really know what to expect from his band. I knew I'd be biased because it was Smiley, but I really loved the music.

New Faces

16 July, HMV London: A list of instore gigs had been announced on RTRNR. I got my wristbands and had arranged to meet up with Celia and my mate Shirley (his real name is Brian – just that he had long blond hair!).

It was a shambles, the queue stretched round the block; they were holding the queue back, only letting in about six at a time to buy the new album. We were still outside, a couple of people were walking up and down the queue pulling the luvvies and the darlings out to jump the queue, you could hear that the band had just come on. In all total honesty, I was hoping that I'd be pulled out. I must be honest, I had followed them half way round the world, struck up a bit of a relationship etc, but at the end of the day, I reminded myself, I was only a punter.

The one I did feel very sorry for was Celia; she ran the official site – she was part of the set-up. By the time we got in we had missed the first two numbers and were stuck right at the back behind a stanchion. Couldn't see a bloody thing. As I stood there with my wife and girls, I turned around and Celia had gone.

I had made the usual mistake of agreeing to get several *Johnny Appleseed* 7in singles autographed for people in Japan, Italy and America. The queue for this was over an hour long and we were stuck at the back. As we approached Joe, Martin and Scott, Joe turned to them and said "Hey guys, look who it is!" He said hi to the girls and was somewhat confused when Amée asked for her single to be autographed to Giovanni. I said this is my wife, er, Anna. He looked at me in a strange manner as he signed "To Anna". The youngest one was having none of it: "To Ellie please!" I think that confused him even more because he knew that was her name!

I knew no one from the roadcrew. Andy had not been retained! Pablo was away with Moby... it all seemed surreal.

To cap a piss-poor evening off, when we got back to my pride and joy, the side window was smashed and my CD player had been half-inched. Great!

I had planned on going to Leeds the next day, it was just turn up at this one, but the previous day's events had put the dampeners on it, so I phoned Nyle and said I'll be giving it a miss.

About a month or so later I was very much privileged to go and see Help! at a small venue near King's Cross. This was a band comprising Antony Genn, Pablo Cook, Martin Slattery and Simon Stafford as well as an unknown drummer and a very attractive female singer, Becky Byrne.

They were really good, music was super and it was great to see Ants and Pabs onstage again. Also there was Scott and one Jarvis Cocker who was the DJ for the evening. All the boys were very chatty. Had a long chat with Pabs and his wife Laura, he had decided it was time to move on Mescaleros-wise for good. I'll miss Pabs; he is such a friendly person. That's three of my heroes gone!!

The tragic events of 11 September had sent the RTRNR message board into overdrive. The hatred that was being put up was terrible. Celia had gone AWOL – the actual site hadn't changed since mid-July. The whole scene was becoming a shambles. Celia pulled the plug and wiped the board on what was a brief return.

With the site basically no more, Celia came in for a fair bit of stick, mainly from those who knew Jack-shit. I now would like to put in print: Celia, you did a great job, under circumstances which few to this day could ever contemplate. I am proud to have called you my friend.

The band had spent the whole of October on the road in America, had just done a short Japanese tour and in November would tour Britain/Ireland. In the month leading up to the British tour the emails and text messages were quite frantic as to who's going to what gigs, who's flying in where, who's meeting up where etc.

15 November, Brighton: Having said all the above, I ended up at Brighton on my own. Wreckless Eric was supporting. I for the life of me couldn't understand why he ad-libbed for about five/six minutes through a song totally slagging off America. I just could not see the point of slagging off a country that has nothing to do with you on a cold and wet November evening in Brighton of all places!

The following day I picked Giuseppe up from Stansted Airport.

17 November, Manchester: With Giuseppe navigating we had got lost in Manchester city centre.

"My mate, I ask people where we are yes?"

"No."

"But mate in Italy when you…"

"I don't care what they do in Italy, I'm not giving some Manc the satisfaction of sending me completely in the wrong direction. Now read that map."

I had been hard on him, it had been a long drive up, the traffic had been heavy, the breakdown in language had caused a strain... plus I hate Manchester. The only light relief I had was when Giuseppe produced a pen and paper and asked me for nice sentences when meeting someone.

"Your face is liker the back of a bus. What does this mean? You say, I say when meeting a woman 'any port in a storm', yes? You are my brother, Ant!"

Eventually we found the Academy. I had arranged to meet Nyle and Tim but on sitting down for a drink Giuseppe had just spread these enormous batteries, tape recorder, wires, the lot, all over the table in the main bar which attracted the attention of every Tom, Dick and Manc.

"Hello my name is Giuseppe. I am from Italy." Arghhhhhh!

After the show, I decided we would just shoot off.

"We not see my friend Joe?"

"No, we not see your friend Joe."

Glasgow was never on the cards – too far.

20 November, Birmingham: Tim had rung me to see where I had got to at Manchester. He said he had a working pass for me for Birmingham. I asked him a favour; I had felt guilty about Giuseppe. I had been a bit hard on him – could he sort out an after-show pass for him, please?

We all met up. This was more like it, a good crowd of us. Tim had introduced us to a friend who had just flown in from New York, one Johnny Hatch. He was one of those people you took a shine to immediately. I gave Giuseppe his after-show pass.

The show was not bad. Afterwards we took Giuseppe backstage. He was totally in his element – had his picture taken with Joe about five times and every other fan that had their picture taken with Joe that night somehow also had Giuseppe in the picture as well!

Martin came up and had a chat. "Listen, Anthony, what's happened to the site, man?"

"I don't really know," I replied.

Martin added, "I know Smiley and Pabs used to be like cuddly bears to the fans, which was great, but we really need a site. Why don't you run the site?"

"No, it's not really my cup of tea, Martin."

"You should think about it, do it," Martin seemed to insist.

"I don't really think so," was my final say on the matter.

21 November, Dublin: We flew out from Luton Airport. We had persuaded Giuseppe to leave behind his bootlegging gear, as it actually resembled bomb-making equipment. Met up with Nyle and Johnny Hatch. I must take some responsibility for what was to be an interesting evening. As I hadn't been able to have a drink for three of the previous concerts, I pushed that we start the drinking early and hard. We all got stuck into the Guinness; Giuseppe had joined in after we said "cheers."

"In Italy we say salutei." OK then, salutei. As the rounds followed we tried to persuade him that there was no need for salutei before every round. Giuseppe only stopped when he fell off the bar stool on the sixth round.

Tymon walked in with another person whose face looked familiar: Pockets?

The show was great, the place rocked – even danced to a few numbers myself. *Johnny Appleseed* is such a great number to dance to.

The after-show was held in the back bar. I had another chat with Martin; again the question of running the site had come up and he kindly gave me his laminate with the comment, "You usually have one!"

The tour manager had changed again. I now avoided them like the plague. Martin introduced me to Luke, who was great. I think he was aware I was pally with Smiley; he asked after him. Luke was so polite and kind, plus he ain't half a great drummer.

As I sat there chatting I could see Giuseppe looking over at Joe and Shane McGowan, who were sitting down having a beer and a chat. What happened next was a mixture of too much beer and Giuseppe's over-excitement at seeing his two heroes in front of him. Giuseppe attempted to give Shane an Italian-style welcome, a kiss on the cheek from behind. Instead it appeared as if he was trying to mount him, whether he slipped or what I will never know, but the celtic expletives that came from Mr McGowan were those of a man in distress. Joe got up and attempted to pull Giuseppe off him. I shrunk down in the corner – he wasn't with me!

Deciding to make an early exit and retire back to the hotel, on the way out I saw a face I hadn't seen before – this short, stocky fella in a long black coat

He said "all right?" Arghhhhhhh, he was a Manc!

As we were leaving Dublin we passed our hand luggage through the x-ray machines. A security guard called Giuseppe back,

"Ant my mate, what he say?"

The security guard was trying to explain to Giuseppe that the nail clippers in his luggage weren't allowed on the plane.

"Errrrr, it's your – God, what's Italian for nail clippers?" I mimed trimming my nails. "They are not allowed in your hand luggage."

"Not in my hand?" Giuseppe asked, somewhat puzzled.

"No hand luggage, er hando bago."

"Listen my old mate," I addressed the security guard. "Any chance of you detaining him under some anti-terrorist law for 48 hours? I'm sure he will confess to something and I know he has a Brigade Rose T-shirt with Red Army Faction on it. I've seen it in his house." The security guard had a grin as wide as the Iffy; he apologised for not being able to assist, but still wanted to know what to do with the clippers.

Showing signs of growing concern and complete bewilderment Giuseppe kept repeating "What he say?" as I instructed the security man "just bin 'em, mate."

"What he say, Ant, my bro?"

"Nothing, just get on the plane will yer."

24 November, Bristol: I took my daughters; Tim had put them on the guestlist.

The girls and I sat up stairs in the gods with a terrific view.

I introduced my girls to Johnny Hatch. He really is a diamond. After the show we went backstage. The short chubby Manc was there checking passes, directing people. Who the fuck does he think he is?

25 November, Brixton: I love Brixton Academy, it's South London's finest venue, just down the road to where me and my family were brought up. It was my manor. Tim had put Janet and the girls on the guestlist. As my turn came to approach the ticket office, I confidently asked for three tickets in the name of Anthony: nothing on the list.

Anthony Davie: Nope.

Davie, A: Nope.

Ant? : "Sorry, nothing under A or D."

Feeling slightly let down I pulled my laminate out and said they're with me anyway, and walked in.

The show was great. Don Letts was filming and Hellcat were recording.

Backstage after the show, it was a great surprise to see Andy. The big hugs of true friendship returned after too long an absence. Also there were Smiley and his lovely wife Lisa. Ant was there too, what a great night. Also in the bar was Mick Jones.

As we were leaving, I passed Tim and Joe at the bar and said goodnight. Tim said, "Did your wife and girls get their tickets all right?"

"Ermm, actually no, though don't worry, I had my laminate."

"What name did you ask for?" Tim further enquired.

"I tried every permutation of Anthony and Davie."

"No, they were under your nickname."

"What nickname?" I asked inquisitively.

"Internet Anthony," Joe replied. "Internet Anthony," he repeated, this time moving his fingers in the air in a musical fashion – "sounds like a tune."

Somewhat bewildered, I left the building. Internet Anthony?

The following day after I said farewell to Giuseppe, thinking I had been a bit impatient with him – after all he had been a great source of entertainment – I thought about what Martin had said re: running a site, I had very little knowledge of computers and hardly deserved the nickname. Internet Anthony!

27 November, Paris: My favourite venue of them all, Elysée-Montmartre. Amée and I had seen both previous shows, they had been great, so this time the four of us went. Yet again it was another good Paris show.

After a chat with both Martin and Luce, who was very keen for a site, they had been given SJM's details. Upon contacting them they too were keen for a site to take over from RTRNR. There was only one snag. They said, "You're not going to have a message board, are you?" Apparently SJM weren't keen on the site having one, which was great, especially as I'd be attacking anyone who slagged members of the band off.

Apparently Strummerville was long gone, as the fella who ran it just didn't have the time to regularly keep it up to date.

So it was now decided who was going to runs Joe's site. Internet Anthony… ugh!

I had noticed that there were also plans afoot by others to start new sites up. RTRNR had left a vacuum that many were eager to fill.

I had pressured Rob, who had agreed to help, to start ASAP. He was somewhat slow in responding but I was desperate not to miss out. So one weekend I spent 48 hours basically non-stop and built a site from scratch on a Lycos tripod.

Now to those with even a limited knowledge of computers this might not seem a great deal, you might even be thinking so what, but to someone like myself who often used to get the kids out of bed late at night to help me after I had done something wrong – "You've just got to press this button, dad," they said, still half asleep – this was a major mind-blowing adventure.

So I had done it. Rob, feeling a bit guilty about taking his time helping build the site, gave it a plug on the message board.

I can still remember exactly what the first reply to the message was: "It has all the design of a colour-blind mathematician" – Dave, London.

Rob, again knowing I had been disappointed at the response, immediately set about over Xmas and New Year designing a proper site. Mine might not have been terribly good, but as I have been reminded since, it had been the first of a new batch up, plus I had the bonus of calling on Smiley to give some quotes.

The other sites were the work of Tami and Lavonne; they looked really good and had put my effort to shame.

I had sent a floppy disk to Joe and Luce, but unknown to me this was no good as they were on Apple. I then sent a complete colour print-out of every page by registered post to them.

I received basically the same response, mainly about the pictures, that Joe had received from Johnny Cash about his song *Road To Rock 'n' Roll*: "What is this, boy?"

No one had told me that pictures which look good-quality on a site can look shit when printed!

2002

I was kindly offered a monthly income in the region of £100 which, though it was generous, I declined. I just thought it was not the done thing to take money for something I loved and was honoured to do.

Initially the info was quite forthcoming from SJM. However after a while this dried up – it was as if the initial honeymoon period was over and I was basically left to chase the info myself. This was in fact a problem Celia had found too.

After a few false starts re: new tour dates in South America, I finally got confirmation of five nights in Brooklyn, which was great. However, I was told to keep it under wraps, OK?

This became quite frustrating, as other sites had already got the venue, dates etc and I was told to keep it under wraps.

I had been in contact off and on with Tami since Las Vegas 1999. She was a true sport, especially a couple of times deliberately holding back on something she had found out so as to give me the privilege of announcing it. I know it was due to SJM contractual agreements with promoters etc. But this did prove to be very frustrating, trying to explain what's the point of keeping it under wraps on the band's site when everybody knows anyway?

The only advantage I got was to book flights, hotels etc quite in advance.

I had been told there was no way I was going by "her indoors" who was putting her foot down. Business had slacked off six months previously, my franchise contract was up for renewal after five years and I had decided not to renew it and try my luck on my own. This had proved very difficult, as business had declined quite drastically. Also my decision to resign from the Post Office was now coming home to haunt me. That additional wage was sorely missed. So we remortgaged, times were hard and now I wanted to bugger off to New York for a week. I think the situation was made worse by the fact that Janet had always longed to visit New York herself.

The emails again were quite frantic. Nyle was going, Johnny Hatch would be there and Tim was going.

I decided, sod it, I'm not missing out on this. I borrowed a couple of hundred quid from my mum. Gave Nyle the cash to get my ticket. Again it was déjà vu. When do I tell her?

This job was made easier for me. Nyle rang up and when I wasn't in got a bit too chatty with Janet: "So Ant's off to New York with us next month."

"Is he now?"

When I walked through that front door later that evening the Japan aggro two years previous paled into insignificance. The only thing that was better this time was I didn't have to sleep in the garage with the rabbit. He had died!

Nyle texted me that evening knowing he had dropped me in it. I knew he didn't mean it. He wasn't to know – "Don't worry!"

Five nights in Brooklyn: And so on 1 April in the early hours of the morning I headed for Heathrow. I had to make my own way, no chance of a lift. Plus I had, ringing in my ears, "If you go, don't bother coming back."

I had been in contact with a fella called Kev. He said he had been on the last tour, and I'd know him. Couldn't think until we got to the bar the other side of check-in. It was him, that Manc in the long black coat!

"How are yer, all right?" he greeted me with a bear-like hug.

I stood rigid – bloody Mancs. We had a couple of beers at 9.00 in the morning, chatted about recent tours, Giuseppe in Dublin etc.

We met Nyle as we landed at JFK. He had just flown in from Hawaii where he had been on holiday and we took the famous yellow taxi to Brooklyn. We had just missed the soundcheck and went for a beer at Water 66.

The show was good. I had the usual tap on the shoulder bit about photography, but was not in a Mister Nice Guy mood – the AAA was out in a flash, followed by "Now fuck off."

The after-show was the usual madhouse. Firstly you've got to make sure you get your mates backstage, pointing out to the security, "He's with me." I was getting a bit cheesed off; perhaps I was tired from the flight.

I was meeting and being introduced to all different people, Beat Surrender, Washington Bullet etc. Lovely people, but it always baffled me – must be an American thing – but if your name's Harry, Susan or whatever, why not call yourself that, instead of using strange names? Perhaps it's me showing my age!

Johnny Hatch was his usual lovely self. Met Tami and her partner Shaggy (I know his real name is Shoghi, but from that moment on he was to be known by the English crew as Shaggy).

The place was heaving; Mick Jones and Bob Gruen were there.

The drink was flowing after we all went next door to the Water 66, had a good chat with Scott and Martin. Later I was introduced to a fella called Graham who seemed a bit quiet.

The following morning we toured NYC – Empire State, Times Square – it was great but really we were just passing time until the bash in the evening. Again it was a good show and again a good backstage after-show.

The only slight hiccup came when I was bursting for a pee, rushed to the dressing room loos just beating Luce, only to find when I entered the loo there was piss everywhere, all over the seat – some people...

Thinking that Luce would think it was me, I ended up completely cleaning the toilet!

Manchester Kev collapsed through overconsumption of alcohol and drugs. Graham was very kind; whilst everyone else just left him in the corner, Graham turned him on his side, cleared his airways, laid a jacket under his head etc. Just as I was thinking humanity still exists, Graham gave him an almighty boot in the side and had a go at him for getting himself into that state. Kev was completely abliss, but I liked that Graham giving old Manc a kick.

Kev's oppo Plank was completely different, very quiet, kept himself to himself.

Wednesday was rest night. I decided to retire early and, with teabags I had brought from England (you soon get sick of coffee), sat in bed with my cuppa and fags, watched baseball on the telly and generally had an early night. The rest went off to CBGBs. I must be getting old.

Time Out magazine had a full-page advert for Joe and at the bottom it had *www.strummersite.com* – wow, that's our site.

Thursday, it was getting harder to waste time during the day – we tried the Staten Island ferry, got to Staten Island: so boring... and came back. All we really wanted was for the shows to come round as quickly as possible. We visited Yankee Stadium, but despite Graham's brave efforts, they wouldn't let us in.

Thursday night's show was the best so far. We decided we should do some videoing, so we shot from side of stage, facing the crowd. It was hard work, again no drinking, plus Nyle's camcorder weighs a ton. We got some great footage. We met up with Johnnytheglove and his brother Nick who also had flown over from England. The initial introduction got off to a bad start; Johnnytheglove was very aggressive in suggesting to me that when I had originally set up the site I had put "we even went as far North as Leeds" – was this a dig at him?

Johnnytheglove and Nick are today good friends of mine, but I think he might have psychopathic tendencies because, as I tried to explain, how could I have a dig at him if I didn't know him at the time when I wrote that? But he wouldn't have it. Things got a bit tense (English abroad!) until Nyle's intervention, saying the fact that he came from Leeds may have influenced my writing. The fact was up until that date I had seen Joe in 14 countries, but had honestly only ever gone as far north as Leeds in England.

I was getting more and more touchy, was missing the girls and Janet. I tried to forget the fact that I was in deep shit when I got home. It seemed strange that I was here with all my mates, watching my heroes, and yet I wanted to be at home.

Friday night came and went; we videoed the whole show again. Basically as I couldn't drink before the show so as to avoid running with the camcorder to the loo, by the time the show's over everyone else is very merry and I'm stone cold sober. Left early on my own to return to the hotel.

Saturday: went on my own on a train journey to Brewster – only chose that place because it was the name of a good friend of mine, Selwyn Brewster. What a one-horse town, nothing there. Waited an hour and got the first train back.

Later that day I plucked up the courage to ring home; it seemed all right, but made me miss home even more. Went to the show, videoed all again and left as soon as the last song had finished.

Couldn't wait for the flight home. We arrived at Heathrow 6.30 Monday morning, exactly a week after I had left. Said goodbye to the boys and got the coach back to Northampton.

8 June, the Fleadh: I had been eager to meet up with everyone again, especially after NY. Life indoors had improved. I was told that if I hadn't rung when I did then the locks would have been changed and even the garage would have been a no-no.

We had arranged to meet up in a pub along the Holloway Road. What a turnout – two Italians, Ferruccio and Ricardo, Australians, Yorkshiremen, Mancs, Lancs, you name it, they were there. We had a good session and all the Brits had been quite generous getting rounds in for our mates from overseas. They were so impressed at our generosity.

Upon entering the beer tents in Finsbury Park, they were eager to start buying us drinks. They were twice as expensive as in the pub. Sorry boys, we knew all along!

I popped into the VIP section, had a chat with Scott, and met up with Johnny Green and his family. I was getting somewhat the worse for wear drinkwise and spotted "Nigel" out of EastEnders (for those outside Britain, it's the top soap programme here). He was very patient with my somewhat idiotic questions, explaining that Dot Cotton was not a real person!

Afterwards we popped back. I honestly can't remember much, apart from congratulating Martin on the birth of his daughter and somehow getting hold of a pic that we would put up on the site. I wandered off back to Graham's car, collapsed on the pavement and was woken up with a boot in the side and a blurred image of Graham trying to help me into the car. Graham, I always meant to tell you this: you're a star.

The early part of July the band were stateside. Graham went – I had sorted him out with tickets/laminate on the proviso that he reported back after every show, setlist etc. I didn't hear a dickie bird – somewhat frustrated, as it would have been nice to put reports/setlists up as they happen. God only knows what he was up to out there!

The planned show at Shepherd's Bush Empire had been booked on the presumption that the site, through the mailing list and being on the news section, would boost sales. Actual advertising was kept to a minimum.

A lot of friends had said they were coming over. Giuseppe had rung me the day it was announced and proudly informed me he was coming!

I had had a brainwave. Smiley and his band One*iota were looking for one London date. I suggested they play the night before the Shepherd's Bush gig and get Giuseppe's Clash tribute band RadioBrixton to support, guessing a lot of people going to Shepherd's Bush would be in town the night before.

What a night! Smiley suggested that RadioBrixton headline. I was going to sponsor it, obviously gambling on getting my money back, let alone making a profit. But a promoter wormed his way in, thinking this would be a killing. However, even though over a hundred people showed up, this was way down on everyone's expectations. It seemed that the majority of people coming into London were arriving on the day of Joe's gig. So thankfully that promoter saved me.

Manc Kev was compere and gave RadioBrixton a super welcome and they played a great setlist. All the regular boys were there. The absolute highlight was when Smiley joined them onstage and drummed on *I Fought The Law*. I have never seen such happy men as Giuseppe and his band – they were over the moon, they had just played with a Mescaleros drummer: Joe's drummer.

The kisses I got afterwards from all of them were actually quite nice, Giuseppe had sussed out that I had asked Smiley if he would do it.

11 July, Shepherd's Bush Empire: Again, a big meet beforehand all over the pub basically next door to The Empire. Mark Gibson-White (a major contributor to Marcus Gray's *Last Gang In Town*) joined us and special guest was Fivestring, who had flown in from Vienna.

It really is great to meet up and put a face to a name you have only emailed or seen on a message board. They are never how you imagine them to be. Tymon came and joined us for a beer. I think one or two on our table were somewhat taken aback. One of the Italians said to me, "Anthony, look other people are saying is that Tymon Dogg?"

"Yeah, good isn't it?" was my reply.

I had arranged to put the boys on the guestlist on condition that they help dish out some flyers advertising the band's tour dates and the site before the show.

It was nearly a full house, so the site must work. It was a good show. We made Giuseppe's day by taking him to the side of the stage where he was not only impressed with a great view of the band but also seemed to be somewhat shocked watching Manchester Kev dance.

For those never fortunate enough to see Manchester Kev dance, you haven't missed much, he can't! Well that's not quite the truth, I'm sure there is some long-lost tribe in the Amazon who do a similar dance!

As we had so many to get backstage, I had to stand with the security saying, "him, er him" etc. I'm not really the right person to do it. Despite getting laminates etc, I still remember how much it meant to me my first time, so anyone saying, "Please could you get us backstage?" ended up with me telling the security, "Er, them as well." Everyone said "thanks." I didn't do it for kicks, just that it is nice to be thanked.

The dressing room was heaving, mainly with Italians, including a new edition, Mauro who runs the great Italian Clash site RadioClash. It was really a great night, all the crew had been there, the show was super and the band was very chatty.

12 July, Manchester: We headed up to Manchester, only to get to Watford Gap services and the Italians said they had left their tickets behind! After much fannying around, they found them in a bag. The thing that does get on one's tits (as much as I love them) is they think it's hysterical. The fact that we were now running late didn't mean a thing.

We got there just in time; it was a good show, got plenty of good shots, though the audience was there mainly to see Ian Brown. We finally met up with Ian Corbridge, a long-time friend of Giuseppe's, nice fella, and Clive from Wigan. The thought of the long drive home with the Italians was starting to wind me up. I was all for shooting off, but relented to their request to see a couple of Paul Weller's numbers.

I again decided against going to Scotland and T In The Park. Sorted Nyle and Graham with passes and by all accounts I missed an awesome display by The Mescaleros.

Towards the end of July, Martin, Scott, Simon and Luke toured with Paul Heaton; I went to see them with Janet (a big Paul Heaton fan) in London. We had a lovely evening out and surprisingly I quite liked the music.

3 August, Cambridge Folk Festival: We had all agreed to meet up in a local pub. Graham and his son Khole had picked me up so I could have a drink. Manc Kev, Plank, Johnnytheglove, his brother Nick etc – everyone was there. The drink flowed, the spliffs were smoked. Manc Kev and Johnnytheglove were having a row (both psychos).

We eventually arrived at the ticket office to collect our AAA. It was a shambles – it seemed it was a total free-for-all, everyone was claiming anything. The people behind the desk weren't used to this and in the end completely gave up.

We had a five-hour wait before the band was on, had completely no interest in any other band and all of us after a chat with Scott and Martin took over the VIP bar.

By the time the band came on we were totally gone. Someone made the mistake of booing The Mescaleros only to find Johnnytheglove in an even more than usual aggressive mood. It was men behaving badly, climbing over fences where all these nice people were sitting having a picnic etc.

Totally exhausted, I sat by the side of the stage and as the band came off followed them back to the dressing-room. The crowd were really hollering for an encore, Joe looked completely knackered; the band automatically went back on, leaving Joe behind, where he stood at the door shouting at me to go and get them back.

For once in my life, I shouted at Joe: "No, you go back on, the crowd want you."

He just shrugged his shoulders and trotted back onstage. They were really great that night.

In September, I arranged to meet the great Pablo Cook for an interview. Pabs is a lovely man and sitting at a pavement café in Islington he gave a great in-depth interview. Like Smiles, I very much missed Pablo being with The Mescaleros.

The end of September had seen the band complete a three-date Japanese tour.

It was whilst the band were in Japan that I received an email that – little did I know at the time – would result in the making of a little bit of history. It was from the FBU asking if it would be possible to get the band to play a gig in support of the firemen.

Apparently, a couple of members of the FBU had been to the Fleadh at Finsbury Park in London in June 2002, had seen Joe Strummer & The Mescaleros onstage and were really impressed. The union had a meeting about what band they could approach to ask to headline. One of the union, called Gardha, said she had seen Joe Strummer play and suggested them.

I received an email from the union asking if we could arrange it. The message was forwarded to Fozzie whilst they were on tour in Japan. Joe read the email and contacted his management to contact the union to say yes.

The union were very grateful to the site and when they rang us up to say thanks, I asked about tickets for the fans.

The allocation of tickets for Strummer fans was vague; after a bit of deliberation I managed to secure 250. I agreed to sell them via the site. I really enjoyed going to work every morning, picking up my mail and dealing with all these people who like me just wanted to see Joe play.

I was neither for nor against the strike. Didn't really give a hoot, it was another date to me.

The last tour

Most of us had given the Opera House a miss. Tickets were very expensive – no doubt we could have got passes etc, but it was Luce's favourite project, the Gorillas, and to get a freebie would have made us feel guilty.

11 November, Edinburgh: In 25 years following Joe, this was my first venture north of the border. Graham, Nyle and I arrived during soundcheck. Fozzie had been true to his word and dished out the laminates.

The place was small. Again, this time out of my own expense, I had decided to plug the site and further dates. I had 5,000 cards printed, exactly the same as the tour poster, including dates, colour etc. We got a nice position and were introduced to Scott's dad, Bob – what a nice man and a proud father.

Graham was booting the show in his usual quiet way when some nutter attacked him!

Anyone who knows Graham will know he is one of the quietest, politest people you could wish to meet. Graham wouldn't even answer him back, let alone row, as he was bootlegging.

The nutter took this as a total blank and went after him. I stood directly in front of him to protect Graham; the next thing, people are stepping in to break it up, including the support band.

Scott's dad gives me a look as if to say, "Why are you causing trouble?"

No one had seen the start of it. Graham couldn't say a word in my defence, because that would bugger his tape up!

After the show, I somewhat sheepishly went backstage, Joe was his usual very friendly self. Called me over, chatting about the site, an email I had from his cousin etc.

Even when Fozzie came across and said there's people waiting to see you, Joe replied, "Tell them I'm doing an interview – I'm having a chat with Internet Anthony."

As much as I felt honoured, I politely made my excuses and departed.

12 November, Newcastle: We sat through the soundcheck, during which Scott ad-libbed a song aimed at us entitled *Three Little Crows*. As the doors opened we were handing out the flyers – really enjoyed it.

A lot of people stopped and chatted, stories from days gone by: one couple told us how they had got married in the afternoon and gone to see The Clash in the evening.

We got Johnnytheglove and his mate Reg in; they had to pay us back by handing out the flyers. It was a sellout.

The Geordie nation are great people; halfway through the set they sang en masse *"there's only one Joe Strummer, one Joe Strummer."* Joe laid down on his side on the stage, hand held to his ear... loving it.

I decided the following morning to give Blackpool a miss – mixture of reasons, hanging around all day waiting, plus the continual lingering worry about my business.

15 November, Acton: I picked Nyle up from Wellingborough station; we headed straight for west London. This was a date that strummersite could be proud of as we had set the ball rolling.

We had to meet several people beforehand, people who had flown in from the States and Japan, to collect their tickets. Plus people from not quite so far who had left getting their tickets to the last moment.

We had arranged to meet Tymon for our now customary pre-bash drink. We were running around like blue-arsed flies. We had to hand over all the cash, bank slips etc to Gardha.

It was a great evening; Joe and the boys were at their best. The encore was a step back in time when Mick Jones took to the stage for *Bankrobber*, *White Riot* and *London's Burning*. Joe and Mick were playing together for the first time in nearly 20 years.

Nyle got totally cheesed off with me with my director's hat on giving instructions to him videoing: "pan, pan, **CLOSE UP**."

Backstage afterwards was a nightmare. I didn't hang around.

Graham, Nyle and I sat up to 4.30 am in my house watching the vid, downloading pics for the site etc. We had an exclusive, right place right time.

The emails and phone calls I received over the next few days were unreal, not only from fans but the music media in general – *Rolling Stone* mag, *NME*, *Mojo* etc. All desperate for pictures and info. Scott later told me I was mad for letting the magazines etc use the pics and not getting any money. The pics used were a mixture of mine, Johnnytheglove's and Graham's. To be perfectly honest, it never even crossed my mind to think about asking! I just felt chuffed the site got a mention.

16 November, Newport: I always felt sorry for Nyle as he usually had to leave halfway through a tour return to work. So Graham and I headed off to South Wales.

Upon entering Newport, we by chance came across the bridge and spotted the venue – lo and behold, there was Scott in front of us, crossing the road. I deliberately swerved the car across the road and went for him, skidding to a halt about a foot from him.

His reaction after the initial shock was of pure aggression but just as he was about to attack me and my car he realised it was me and burst out laughing, though also notifying me "you're a fuckin' nutter."

Before the soundcheck, we met up with Tim and Pockets for a drink and after a few rounds curiosity got the better of me. I asked Pockets to go back several years to that day near Joe's house where he totally blanked me and my girls and shot off on his pushbike. Strangely, he remembered that day very vividly.

"I had unfortunately that morning sacked a young man I had working for me and had just received a threatening phone call from his father saying he was about to come up and do irreparable damage to me and, just as I'm about to make good my escape, you turn up! Sorry Ant, but I wasn't going to hang around."

Now I know why!!

The show was good – had a drink and a chat with a man I had seen previously on many occasions, one Joe Swinford. He is a star. I like him a lot.

The after-show was held upstairs adjacent to the venue. Manchester Kev and the boys carried a fella in a wheelchair up several flights of stairs. He was a big man as well. I love little touches like these, it reassures one that common decency still exists.

The following morning I decided to give Bridgwater a miss. Graham was still going, but I left the B & B and headed home.

19 November, Portsmouth: Took the youngest one. We met up with Johnnytheglove and Nick. Graham never came – he got stuck in a massive traffic jam south of Manchester! It was totally sold out. I love to see the sign on the door, "SOLD OUT." The boys deserve it.

20 November, Hastings: Met Nyle again at Wellingborough station, took Ellie for the second night running. Hastings is a lovely place, but the roads to and from are single-lane, wind-y roads. It is perhaps the least enjoyable drive I have been on.
The Pier: as the band came on the place was barely half full. Wasn't a bad show; Joe and the boys gave their all.
I felt a little disillusioned. Since first seeing The Mescaleros, I had noticed Joe always patted his chest with a clenched fist. I always took this as a sort of gesture from his heart to the audience. I learnt that night it was a sign to the soundman to cut the intro music!
The following day we drove to the steel city, Sheffield, and the Leadmill, home of The Mescaleros' debut gig in June 1999. It was a great show, the place rocked. Nyle bought his "celeb" mate Lee of *Emmerdale* and *Crossroads* fame. Christ, does that man dance.
After-show was at some wine bar a few miles away. Manc Kev was at his happiest; his other heroes Dermot and Fat Neck were amongst the guests.
Joe spent some time explaining to my eldest the goodness and benefits of drinking red wine. I could see her facial expressions as she politely attempted to consume the drink he had bought her.

22 November, Liverpool: The last night of the tour. Again took my eldest, Amée, this time with her boyfriend Chris. I think they were somewhat taken aback by the pre-gig drinking. We had watched soundcheck, the band seemed in a great mood. Before the show we met a hell of a lot of lovely people, some complete strangers, but everyone seemed so friendly. I very rarely thought about using my laminate to gain favour or as power, but when the security refused to let a lady who was several months pregnant sit in the circle upstairs, I had to:
"They're with me, there's spare seats, now, she sits down, OK."
There are times in life when flexing a bit of muscle is a good thing. It's not really power, it's just a nice feeling that you can influence a situation where commonsense has failed.
Before the band came on DJ Scratchy dedicated *Soul Rebel* to the strummersite crew.
Some nights you just have that feeling that it's going to be a good one. I had had similar feelings at Elysée-Montmartre, London Astoria, Dublin etc. It

was just the crowd, the venue, the vibe, whatever! You just knew it was going to be special.

Joe Strummer & The Mescaleros did not disappoint that night. It ranked alongside the best.

The after-show was complete chaos, it was heaving. I think I upset Fozzie, but it was water off a duck's back with me by now, I was a seasoned campaigner at unknowingly upsetting tour managers.

I had my daughter and her boyfriend to get in. When walking in accompanied by four or five fellas with AAA no one says a thing.

However, along the way I met a lovely fella called Jo Campana who had flown over from Italy, then the couple with the pregnant wife plus Tymon's Liverpool family who couldn't get past security, so what could I do? One man (me) with an AAA (the rest had disappeared) and an entourage of a dozen people. I expect he thought I was taking the piss. So be it!!

I introduced Amée to Scott; she had a soft spot for him. He somewhat ruined her dreams by telling her, "God, don't you look like your dad?"

I didn't see what the problem was!

As I was leaving, one of Tymon's relatives grabbed my arm and thanked me. "No problems," was my reply.

Outside we said our usual farewells to the crew: "See you next year."

Rumour was rife that in May they would be supporting Pearl Jam on an American tour. As we all walked back to the hotel, we were all discussing what part of the tour we'd do in May.

I got a bit of stick re: how I would be approaching Janet on the subject!

The saddest day

The month since the tour finished had been quiet. I had had a great evening out with Amée courtesy of Smiley when he was playing with Archive in Oxford supporting Gomez.

Archive had really impressed me that night, they played a really tight set. There had been a bit of trouble in the crowd, resulting in everyone's Mister Nice Guy Smiley aiming his stick and hitting this pissed yob right in the forehead, big respect.

Met up for a drink with the band after, super people. I'll be following them as well in the future.

A couple of weeks later, I met up with Martin, his lovely wife Kirsty and baby Isabella. We went round to Scott's house where Martin was mixing the work they had done recently on the week at Rockfield in Wales.

Some of the new tracks sounded terrific. Scott's dog Maggie put the fear of god up me, which seemed to appeal to Martin's humour. We did a super interview. I love talking with Martin, he is always very forthright, says what he means and means what he says.

Driving home, I thought this will certainly make interesting reading!

It was an ordinary run-of-the-mill Sunday evening. The only difference had been I was on the computer typing up the interview I had done with Martin a few days earlier. It had been a good and lengthy interview and had taken a good three hours to knock into shape and with any luck it would be up on the site the following evening. I sent a few emails out to the boys and one to Joe and Luce, wishing everyone a happy Xmas and successful 2003.

Before retiring to bed, I decided to have one more fag and thought I'd have a quick look at the message boards. Not a thing I usually do, as it must be obvious by now I don't particularly like them. It must have been from typing up Martin's interview, in which he passed comment on the site not having a message board!!

The message I read totally threw me: "Joe died earlier this evening."

My first thought was that it was some sick joke. My immediate reaction was one of anger. Then after ten minutes the anger subsided. I had started to really hope it was some sick joke. Tami emailed me to ask for any clarification. By this time I was on my eighth fag.

I went to bed in a somewhat dazed state. I'm not a religious man by any means, the usual: weddings, christenings etc.

But I'm not ashamed to admit how that night I had prayed that it wasn't true, prayed that it was a sick joke. "Please God…"

I struggled to sleep, waking up what seemed like every ten minutes.

I got up at 6.00, switched the computer on, checked my emails and my worst fears came home. "Ant, ring me immediately, Paula" (Simon Moran's PA).

I rang straight away. "Ant, Joe died yesterday."

The rest of the conversation I never understood then, so could never recall now.

I immediately rang Nyle. After you have given someone bad news it's just a terrible silence.

It was decided to put something very simple on the news page. This also followed with Paula's second email that there would be an official press release. Some people have been critical about that short statement that was put up, which worried me greatly, but the biggest compliment came several days later from DJ Scratchy when he told me "how simplistically beautiful it was."

I sent Tami an email, confirming her worst fears.

It had been a tradition in our household for the past 15 or so years that I took my girls "up West" on Christmas Eve.

Just a dad and his daughters Xmas shopping, finished off by pie, mash and liquor at our favourite pie and mash shop in the East End.

I insisted we still go and so the three of us sat in silence in the traffic jam that is the M1 southbound in the morning.

Martin rang me on my mobile. Timmy Tim rang me too. It was all so surreal. I rang Smiley at his home... he was speechless.

Giuseppe had rung me a couple of times, but the mixture of his poor English and crying had made me short with him. I just didn't want to know and I hated myself. I hadn't cried, why? A feeling of guilt hit me. I'm a great believer in the stiff upper lip, put on a brave face.

Giuseppe rang again this time with a friend who spoke perfect English. I stood in a doorway holding the phone in one hand and pulling my hair with the other, "Giuseppe just wants to say how sad he is and share his sadness with his English bro."

"Please just leave me alone, go away, please" – and with that I hung up and switched the phone off.

We basically turned around as soon as we got there. It had been a bad idea to go.

My girls looked so sad. Joe had always been very kind to them. I had told so many people (most probably bored so many people) with my stories about "my girls and Joe."

As we were driving home Ellie asked if she could turn the radio on. I had deliberately avoided the news but the silence was terrible.

As we sat in the car crawling up Highgate Hill the *Radio London* station announced. "We are now going to speak to Smiley, Joe's former drummer." We listened intently. Smiles has such a lovely, kind voice. He finished the interview with:

"I thought Joe was Captain Scarlet: indestructible."

The tears started to roll down our cheeks as the radio station went straight into *Tony Adams* or, as it was introduced, *The Morning Sun*. It had never been one of my favourites, yet that particular moment it seemed such a beautiful song. The three of us sat there hugging each other, crying. The rain was pelting down on the windscreen as if the whole world was crying with us.

I texted Smiley: "Smiles you're a star, that was beautiful, Ant x."

I have not enjoyed writing this chapter, whilst writing it I had tears in my eyes nearly a year on. But what hurt and upset I felt that day was a mere drop in the ocean compared to the hurt and pain Luce and the girls must have been feeling.

Anyroad (with a cough and a deep breath) upon reaching home, I switched the computer on; the emails were flooding in hundreds running into thousands. I sat down and over the following two days attempted to reply to all.

I sent Giuseppe an email to say how sad I knew he must be.

I avoided the news – just couldn't, even when the youngest one came in to say the site was on CNN.

I had given up with the site, just couldn't get on it. Our own site and I couldn't get on it.

Several of the emails I had received were from television stations: "Please ring us on…" There was no way I could deal with this.

I rang Paula; she gave me a number of a press agent who had been appointed. I rang him to say, "the BBC on so and so number, Sky on this number."

He said he hadn't known "anything like it since U2 played the Astoria."

WHAT? You're comparing the death of Number One with fucking U2 playing the Astoria?

I never rang him again. Fuck it. I'm only a punter. I'll stick with the people I'm happiest being with, fellow punters.

We were given news of the funeral arrangements but were asked not to disclose. It was so hard – people were desperate to know, to pay their respects, and I couldn't tell them.

When the site started, SJM's offer of a monthly wage had been deliberately rejected. It was turned down for two reasons, firstly it was an honour and I loved doing it, secondly it gave a level of independence. If you accept a wage you accept rules. But on this occasion, requests/orders had to be adhered to out of complete respect.

I received an email from Luce, which simply said:

"Ants please ring me."

I had wanted so much to ring, to say how sorry I was. But what could I say, how could I say it? Who was I anyway to ring anyway? Answer: No one!

But with the request to ring I had to. Luce is such a brave lady; she did all the talking. She needed help with the funeral cards.

I received a call from Gardha of the FBU; she was stunned at the news. She asked if the FBU could provide a guard of honour. I couldn't make that decision; it had to be referred to higher authorities. It turned out that Luce was very much in favour and it was arranged.

The service was humanist – no hymns or prayers, but readings from Dick Rude, Keith Allen and Paul Simonon. *White Man In Hammersmith Palais* is better than any hymn, *Willesden To Cricklewood* is such a beautiful song and *Coma Girl* is Joe at his best.

Afterwards we met Gardha, said big thanks and individually thanked the 24 men and women who formed the guard of honour. Big respect to them all.

The wake was held at the Paradise Club. A lot of old faces were there: Timmy Tim, Smiley, Ant, Gary Robinson, Andy Boo, Joe Campbell, the original crew that I had got on so well with.

Everyone's heart went out to Luce; she was so brave under what must have been harrowing circumstances.

Also there was my old schoolmate and ex-Clash security man Slim, suitably dressed in his rockabilly attire.

I had had a lovely chat with Roger (Joe's driver) and his lovely wife Paula. They were really kind people whom I had got to know quite well.

I left after a couple of hours, said goodbye to Tymon, Luke, Simon, Scott and Martin. As I walked back alone to my car, my mind was spinning with thoughts of the last 25 years and especially the last four.It had all very sadly come to an end but I consoled myself with the happy memories that I so fortunately had stored in my mind.

As I sat in my car on the North Circular, stuck in traffic with the rain still teeming down, I also remembered the files I had seen whilst working at New Scotland Yard and the secret I had kept to myself for nearly 25 years: Joe Strummer in 1977/78 must have really frightened the British government because Special Branch had kept tabs on his movements.

Joe, you had put the fear of God up the establishment.

The following evening I saw the year out with Smiley at a venue in Hornchurch, Essex.

Smiles was playing acoustic solo at a massive New Year's Eve party. He played covers of Travis, Oasis etc. He was a firm favourite in this part of metropolitan Essex.

The crowd was a massed choir to songs such as *Why Does It Always Rain On Me* and *Sing* halfway through his set, he played the opening lines to *Bankrobber* and as Smiles, my girls and I alone sang for all we were worth, we could see the tears in each other's eyes.

Smiley finished by announcing to a stunned, silent audience:

"God bless Joe."

Tour History

1999

Joe Strummer & The Mescaleros – line-up unless otherwise stated:

The Band
Joe Strummer: Guitar/Vox
Antony Genn: Guitar/Vox
Martin Slattery: Keys/Guitar/Vox
Smiley: Drums
Pablo Cook: Percussion/Vox
Scott Shields: Bass

The Crew
Mark Dempsey: Tour Manager
Justin Grealy: FOH Sound
Mike Hornby: Monitors
Dave Morris: Lighting Designer
Andy Boo: Guitar Tech
Roger Middlecote: Drums/FX

THE GIGS

05/06/99 Sheffield, Leadmill
6/7 Leadmill Street, Sheffield
Capacity: 900
Support: Seafood, Llama Farmers

06/06/99 Liverpool, Lomax   **SOLD OUT**
34 Cumberland Street, Liverpool
Capacity: 300
Support: None

07/06/99 Glasgow, King Tut's   **SOLD OUT**
272a St. Vincent Street, Glasgow.
Capacity: 300
Support: None

08/06/99 Portsmouth, Wedgewood Rooms   **SOLD OUT**
147b Albert Road, Southsea, Portsmouth
Capacity: 400
Support: None

13/06/99 Amsterdam, Tibetan Freedom Concert
RAI Parkhal
Capacity: 14,000
Also appearing: Luscious Jackson, Ben Harper, Thom Yorke, Garbage, Alanis Morissette, Blur

14/06/99 Paris, Elysée-Montmartre   **SOLD OUT**
72 Bvd de Rochechouart, Paris
Capacity: 1,400
Support: Cox

16/06/99 Brussels, Botanique
Salle de l'Orangerie, Rue Royale 236, Brussels
Capacity: 600
Support: None

17/06/99 Hamburg, Markthalle
Klosterwall 9-21, Hamburg
Capacity: 1,200
Support: None

19/06/99 Sweden, Hultsfredfestivalen
Basebovagen, Hultsfred, nr Vimmerby, Sweden
Capacity: 25,000
Also appearing: Helgan Varligt, The Hellacopters and Suede

20/06/99 Finland, Provinnsirock Festival
Tornava Festival Park, Seinjoki, Finland
Capacity: 20,000
Also appearing: Supperheads, Ne Luumact
*Andy Boo appeared on percussion in Pablo Cook's absence

26/06/99 Glastonbury Festival   **SOLD OUT**
Capacity: 100,000
Also appearing: Manic Street Preachers, Underworld, REM, Blondie

29/06/99 Washington, Nightclub 9:30   **SOLD OUT**
815 V Street, NW, Washington
Capacity: 1,200
Support: The Delta 72's

30/06/99 New York, Irving Plaza   **SOLD OUT**
17 Irving Place, New York
Capacity: 1,000
Support: The Slackers

02/07/99 Chicago, The Metro   **SOLD OUT**
3730 North Clark St, Chicago
Capacity: 1,100
Support: John Langford's Leeds Original Death Rocker

06/07/99 San Francisco, The Fillmore
1805 Geary St, San Francisco
Capacity: 1,250
Support: MXPX

07/07/99 Los Angeles, The Palace
1735 North Vine, Hollywood
Capacity: 1,250
Support: Hepcat

11/07/99 Kinross, T In The Park Festival
Capacity: 52,000
Also appearing: Manic Street Preachers, James, Travis, Stereophonics

01/08/99 Japan, Fuji Rock Fest
Capacity: 100,000
Also appearing: Rage Against The Machine, The Chemical Brothers, ZZ Top

Setlist included:
Techno D-Day, London Calling, X-Ray Style, White Man In Hammersmith Palais, Tony Adams, Straight To Hell, Rock The Casbah, Forbidden City, Bankrobber, Yalla Yalla, I Fought The Law, Tommy Gun, Junco Partner, Brand New Cadillac, Diggin' The New

EUROPEAN SHOWS

The Crew
Chris Griffiths: Tour Manager ("Free Wheels" only)
Gary Robinson: Tour Manager
Justin Grealy: FOH Sound
Joe Campbell: Monitors
Dave Morris: Lighting Designer
Andy Boo: Guitar Tech
Roger Middlecote: Drums/FX

13/08/99 France, Free Wheels Festival
Base De Loisirs de Cunhlat, Clermont Ferrand
Capacity: 15,000
Also appearing: Chris Spedding, The Silencers, Nashville Pussy

19/08/99 Austria, 2 Days a Week Festival
Schollingstrasse, Wiesen
Capacity: 8,000
Also appearing: Rosarot, Tocotronic, The Offspring

21/08/99 Koln, Bizarre Festival
Von Hunefied Str/ Hugo-Eckner Str, Cologne
Capacity: 20,000
Also appearing: Catatonia, Toctronic, Bloodhound Gang, Paradise Lost

22/08/99 Portugal, Vilar de Mouros Festival
Vilar De Mouros, Pareda De Coura
Capacity 15,000

24/08/99 Dublin, Olympia Theatre   **SOLD OUT**
72 Dame St, Dublin
Capacity: 1,600
Support: None

25/08/99 Belfast, the Limelight   **SOLD OUT**
17 Ormeau Road, Belfast
Capacity: 800
Support: None

03/09/99 Munich, Kunstpark Ost
Grafinger Str, Munich
Capacity: 10,000
Also appearing: Lit, Silverchair, The Offspring

04/09/99 Bologna, Independent Days Festival
Arena Parco Nord, Bologna
Capacity: 15,000
Also appearing: Punkreas, Lit, Hepcat, Silverchair, The Offspring

Setlist included:
Forbidden City, Rock The Casbah, X-Ray Style, Straight To Hell, Diggin' The New, Yalla Yalla, Brand New Cadillac, London Calling, Tony Adams, Junco Partner, White Man In Hammersmith Palais, I Fought The Law, Tommy Gun, Techno D-Day, Bankrobber, London Calling

UK TOUR

The Crew
Gary Robinson: Tour Manager
Justin Grealy: FOH Engineer
Joe Campbell: Monitors
Kevin Moran: Systems Engineer
Nick Ayres: Lighting Designer
Andy Boo: Backline
Gordon White: Backline
Ross McNamara: Truck Driver

18/10/99 Nottingham, Rock City **SOLD OUT**
8 Talbot Street, Nottingham
Capacity: 1,700
Support: Little Mothers

19/10/99 Leeds, Town & Country Club **SOLD OUT**
55 Cookridge St, Leeds
Capacity: 1,800
Support: Little Mothers

21/10/99 London, Astoria **SOLD OUT**
157 Charing Cross Road, London
Capacity: 2,000
Support: Little Mothers

22/10/99 London, Astoria **SOLD OUT**
157 Charing Cross Road, London
Capacity: 2,000
Support: Medal

23/10/99 Norwich, UEA
University Plain, Norwich
Capacity: 1,470
Support: Little Mothers

25/10/99 Cardiff, University
Park Place, Cardiff
Capacity: 1,350
Support: Little Mothers

26/10/99 Wolverhampton, Civic Hall
North St, Wolverhampton
Capacity: 2,126 (Balcony closed)
Support: Little Mothers

28/10/99 Manchester, Academy　　　　**SOLD OUT**
Oxford Road, Manchester
Capacity: 1,800
Support: Little Mothers

29/10/99 Glasgow, Barrowlands　　　　**SOLD OUT**
244 Gallowgate, Glasgow
Capacity: 1,900
Support: Little Mothers

Setlist included:
Diggin' The New, Nothin' 'bout Nothin', Rock The Casbah, Quarter Pound Of Ishen, Brand New Cadillac, Tony Adams, Trash City, Nitcomb, Road To Rock 'n' Roll, White Man In Hammersmith Palais, Safe European Home, Yalla Yalla, Rudie Can't Fail, London Calling, Pressure Drop, Tommy Gun, Junco Partner, Straight to Hell, I Fought The Law, Bankrobber, X-Ray Style

AMERICA, CANADA AND EUROPE TOUR

The Crew
Gary Robinson: Tour Manager
Justin Grealy: FOH Engineer
Joe Campbell: Monitors
Nick Ayres: Lighting Designer
Andy Boo: Backline Tech
Gordon White: Backline Tech
Joff Lillywhite: Merchandise

01/11/99 Seattle, The Showbox
1932 Second Avenue, Seattle
Capacity: 700
Support: One Man Army

02/11/99 Portland, Music Millennium
801 NW 23rd St, Portland
Instore Acoustic: Joe

02/11/99 Portland, Roseland Theatre　　　　**SOLD OUT**
8 NW Sixth Avenue, Portland
Capacity: 1,250
Support: One Man Army

04/11/99 San Francisco, The Fillmore				**SOLD OUT**
1805 Geary St, San Francisco
Capacity: 1,150
Support: One Man Army, Pietasters

05/11/99 Anaheim, Sun Theatre
2200 East Katella Avenue, Anaheim
Capacity: 1,400
Support: Pietasters

06/11/99 Hollywood, House of Blues				**SOLD OUT**
8430 Sunset Blvd, West Hollywood
Capacity: 1,000
Support: Pietasters

07/11/99 Las Vegas, Hard Rock Hotel/The Joint
4455 Paradise Road, Las Vegas
Capacity: 1,600
Support: Pietasters

09/11/99 Denver, Ogden Theatre
935 East Colfax Avenue, Denver
Capacity: 1,400
Support: Pietasters

11/11/99 Minneapolis, The Quest
110 North 5th St, Minneapolis
Capacity: 1,600
Support: Pietasters

12/11/99 Columbia, The Blue Note
17 North 9th St, Columbia
Capacity: 1,000
Support: Southern Culture

13/11/99 Chicago, the Metro				**SOLD OUT**
1301 North State Parkway, Chicago
Capacity: 1,100
Support: Pietasters

15/11/99 Columbus, Newport Music Hall
1722 North High St, Columbus
Capacity: 1,400
Support: Pietasters

16/11/99 Cincinnati, Bogarts
2621 Vine Street, Cincinnati
Capacity: 1,460
Support: Pietasters

18/11/99 Detroit, St Andrews Hall
431 East Congress, Detroit
Capacity: 1,000
Support: Pietasters

19/11/99 Cleveland, The Odeon   **SOLD OUT**
1295 Old River Road, Cleveland
Capacity: 900
Support: Pietasters

20/11/99 Toronto, the Warehouse   **SOLD OUT**
132 Queen's Quay East, Toronto
Capacity: 1,800
Support: Pietasters

22/11/99 Boston, The Roxy   **SOLD OUT**
279 Tremont St, Boston
Capacity: 1,460
Support: Pietasters

23/11/99 New York, Roseland Ballroom   **SOLD OUT**
239 West 52nd St, New York
Capacity: 2,200
Support: Pietasters

24/11/99 Philadelphia, Theatre of Living Arts   **SOLD OUT**
334 South St, Philadelphia
Capacity: 810
Support: Pietasters

25/11/99 Conan O'Brien Show
Tony Adams, London Calling

02/12/99 Barcelona, Bikini Club   **SOLD OUT**
105, Deu i Mata St, Barcelona
Capacity: 800

04/12/99 Milan, Rollingstone   **SOLD OUT**
corso XXII Marzo 32, Milano
Capacity: 2,000
Support: None

07/12/99 Paris, Elysée-Montmartre   **SOLD OUT**
72 Bvd de Rochechouart, Paris
Capacity: 1,400
Support: The Hellboys

Setlist included:
Quarter Pound Of Ishen, Diggin' The New, Bankrobber, Nothin' 'bout Nothin', Rock The Casbah, X-Ray Style, Brand New Cadillac, Tony Adams, Trash City, Nitcomb, Road To Rock 'n' Roll, White Man In Hammersmith Palais, Yalla Yalla, Safe European Home, Rudie Can't Fail. London Calling, Pressure Drop, Tommy Gun, Junco Partner, Techno D-Day, Straight To Hell, I Fought The Law, Island Hopping, White Riot, Forbidden City, Shouting Street

2000

JAPANESE TOUR

The Crew
Gary Robinson: Tour Manager
Justin Grealy: FOH Engineer
Joe Campbell: Monitor Engineer
Gordon White: Backline Tech
Andy Boo: Backline Tech
Des Evlis: Backline Tech

16/01/00 Osaka, Zepp Osaka   **SOLD OUT**
1-18-31 Nankoukita Suminoe-ku Osakashi
Capacity: 2,000
Support: Knuckles

17/01/00 Tokyo, Akasaka Blitz   **SOLD OUT**
TBS Square 5-3-6 Akasaka, Minato-ku Tokyo
Capacity: 1,900
Support: Cobra

18/01/00 Tokyo, Akasaka Blitz   **SOLD OUT**
TBS Square 5-3-6 Akasaka, Minato-ku Tokyo
Capacity: 1,900
Support: None

AUSTRALIA AND NEW ZEALAND

Big Day Out

21/01/00 Auckland, Ericsson Stadium **SOLD OUT**
Maurice Road, Penrose
Capacity: 40,000
Green Stage
Also appeared: Foo Fighters, The Chemical Brothers, Beth Orton, Red Hot Chilli Peppers, Urban Pacifika

23/01/00 Queensland, Parklands **SOLD OUT**
Parklands Dr, Southport
Capacity: 45,000
Green Stage
Also appeared: Foo Fighters, The Chemical Brothers, Blink 182, Red Hot Chilli Peppers, The Cruel Sea

25/01/00 Sydney, Metro **SOLD OUT**
624 George St, Sydney
Capacity: 1,050
Support: The Monarchs

26/01/00 Sydney, RAS Showground **SOLD OUT**
Showground Rd, Homebush Bay
Capacity: 50,000
Green Stage
Also appeared: Foo Fighters, The Chemical Brothers, Nine Inch Nails, Red Hot Chilli Peppers, The Hellacopters

29/01/00 Richmond, Corner Hotel **SOLD OUT**
27 Swan St, Richmond
Capacity: 750
Support: Luxedo

30/01/00 Melbourne, RAS Showground **SOLD OUT**
Epsom Road, Flemington
Capacity: 40,000
Green Stage
Also appeared: Foo Fighters, The Chemical Brothers, Grinspoon, Red Hot Chilli Peppers, Shihad

04/02/00 Adelaide, RA & HS showground **SOLD OUT**
Goodwood Road, Wayville

Capacity: 25,000
Green Stage
Also appeared: Foo Fighters, The Chemical Brothers, Goldie, Red Hot Chilli Peppers, Testeagles

06/02/00 Perth, Bassendean Oval **SOLD OUT**
West Road, Bassendean
Capacity: 30,000
Green Stage
Also appeared: Foo Fighters, The Chemical Brothers, Primal Scream, Red Hot Chilli Peppers, Eskimo Joe

Setlist included:
Diggin' The New, Road To Rock 'n' Roll, Rock The Casbah, X-Ray Style, Brand New Cadillac, Nothin' 'bout 'Nothin, Tony Adams, Nitcomb, White Man In Hammersmith Palais, Straight To Hell, London Calling, Yalla Yalla, Rudie Can't Fail, Safe European Home, Pressure Drop, I Fought The Law, Tommy Gun, Bankrobber, Police On My Back, White Riot, Sandpaper Blues, Trash City, Nitcomb, Willesden To Cricklewood, Island Hopping, Techno D-Day, Forbidden City, Quarter Pound Of Ishen

31/03/00 New York, Bowery Ballroom
6 Delancey St, New York
Capacity: 575
Also appeared: Run DMC
*15th Anniversary party for *Spin* magazine

04/04/00 London, Poetry Olympics
Royal Festival Hall, London
Also appeared: Linton Kwesi Johnson, John Cooper Clarke
*Strummer and Cook

MAY 2000

The Crew
Neil Mather: Tour Manager
Justin Grealy: FOH
Pete Russell: Monitors
Nick Ayers: Lights
Andy Boo: Backline
Alex McCarten: Backline
Dave Fowler: Backline
Merchandise: Joff Lilywhite
Merchandise (Dublin): Jeff Skellen

01/05/00 Dublin, Olympia Theatre   **SOLD OUT**
72 Dame St, Dublin
Capacity: 1,200
Support: Neon

02/05/00 Sheffield, Leadmill
6/7 Leadmill Street, Sheffield
Capacity: 900
Support: Ten Benson

03/05/00 Newcastle, University SU
Kings Walk, Newcastle
Capacity: 1,200
Support: Ten Benson

05/05/00 Liverpool Royal Court Theatre
1 Roe St, Liverpool
Capacity: 1,796
Support: Ten Benson

06/05/00 Brixton Academy   **SOLD OUT**
211 Stockwell Road, London SW9
Capacity: 4,300
Support: Ten Benson, LSK

Setlist included:
London Calling, Nothin' 'bout 'Nothin, X-Ray Style, Road To Rock 'n' Roll, Rock The Casbah, The Harder They Come, White Man In Hammersmith Palais, I Fought The Law, Nitcomb, Tony Adams, Sandpaper Blues, Bankrobber, Safe European Home, Rudie Can't Fail, Yalla Yalla, Police On My Back, Pressure Drop, Hang On Sloopy, Straight To Hell, Brand New Cadillac, White Riot, Trash City, Tommy Gun, Junco Partner, Quarter Pound Of Ishen, London's Burning

08/05/00 *Later with Jools Holland*, BBC TV

09/05/00 *Later with Jools Holland*, BBC TV

30/06/00 Jesolo Beach Bum Festival
Arena Peaks, Jesolo
Capacity: 15000
Also appeared: Eels, Gene, Tiny One Silence, Reef
*Played as a five-piece band due to Antony Genn's absence

17/08/00 Leicester, The Charlotte   **SOLD OUT**
8 Oxford St, Leicester
Capacity: 390
Support: None

19/08/00 Stafford, V2000
Weston Park, Stafford
MTV Peoples sound.com Stage
Also appeared: Moby, Beth Orton, Feeder, Hepburn, Coldplay

20/08/00 Chelmsford, V2000
Hylands Park, Chelmsford
MTV Peoples sound.com Stage
Also appeared: Moby, Beth Orton, Feeder, Hepburn, Coldplay

Setlist included:
Brand New Cadillac, Rock The Casbah, X-Ray Style, Rudie Can't Fail, White Man In Hammersmith Palais, London Calling, The Harder They Come, I Fought The Law, Pressure Drop, London's Burning, Bankrobber, Tommy Gun, Police On My Back, Tony Adams, White Riot, Yalla Yalla, Diggin' The New

08/10/00 Astoria 2, Poetry Olympics
Charing Cross Road, London,
Also Appeared: Jah Wobble, John Hegley, Martin Carthy
*Strummer, Cook, Dogg

The Band
Joe Strummer: Guitar/Vox
Martin Slattery: Keys/Gtr/Vox
Smiley: Drums
Pablo Cook: Percussion/Vox
Scott Shields: Bass
Tymon Dogg: Violin, Classical

27/10/00 London, 100 Club   **SOLD OUT**
100 Oxford St, London
Capacity: 500
Support: None
*Jimmy Hogarth stands in for Scott

30/10/00 Birmingham, NEC (Supporting The Who)
*Jimmy Hogarth stands in for Scott

02/11/00 Manchester, MEN (Supporting The Who)
*John Blackburn stands in for Scott

03/11/00 Glasgow, SECC (Supporting The Who)
*John Blackburn stands in for Scott

05/11/00 Glasgow, SECC – (Supporting The Who)
*John Blackburn stands in for Scott

06/11/00 Newcastle, Arena (Supporting The Who)
*John Blackburn stands in for Scott

08/11/00 Birmingham, NEC (Supporting The Who)
*John Blackburn stands in for Scott

10/11/00 Sheffield, Arena (Supporting The Who)
*John Blackburn stands in for Scott

13/11/00 London, Docklands (Supporting The Who)
*John Blackburn stands in for Scott

15/11/00 London, Wembley Arena (Supporting The Who)
*John Blackburn stands in for Scott

16/11/00 London, Wembley Arena (Supporting The Who)
*Jimmy Hogarth stands in for Scott

Setlist included:
Minstrel Boy, Bhindi Bhagee, Bummed Out City, Gamma Ray, Rock the Casbah, Before I Grow Too Old, The Harder They Come, Brand New Cadillac, London Calling, Bankrobber, White Man In Hammersmith Palais, Straight To Hell, I Fought the Law, Folk Riot, London's Burning

2001

The Band

Joe Strummer: Guitar/Vox
Martin Slattery: Keys/Gtr/Vox
Scott Shields: Guitar/Vox
Tymon Dogg: Violin, Classical
Luke Bullen: Drums
Simon Stafford: Bass, Trombone

The Crew
Simon Foster: Tour Manager
John Nave: FOH Sound
Paul Menpes: Backline

Instore Dates

16/07/01 London, HMV
Oxford St, London
Capacity: 500

17/07/01 Leeds, Virgin
Albion Street, Leeds
Capacity: 350

24/07/2001 Conan O'Brien Show
Johnny Appleseed

24/07/01 New York, Virgin
Times Square, NY

25/07/01 Toronto, HMV
333 Yonge St, Toronto

27/07/01 Chicago, Tower
2301 N. Clark Street, Chicago

28/07/01 San Francisco, Amoeba
1855 Haight St, San Francisco

01/08/01 Los Angeles, Tower
8801 W Sunset Blvd, LA

02/08/01 Los Angeles, The Viper Room   **SOLD OUT**
8852 Sunset Blvd, West Hollywood, CA 90069
Capacity: 250
Support: None

04/08/01 Los Angeles, Greek Theatre
2700 Vermont, Los Angeles, CA 90024
Capacity: 8,000
Special guest to Brian Setzer

Setlist included:
Cool 'n' Out, Global A Go-Go, Shaktar Donetsk, Johnny Appleseed, Bummed Out City, Mega Bottle Ride, Bhindi Bhagee, Mondo Bongo, The Harder They Come.

GLOBAL A GO-GO
AMERICA AND CANADA TOUR

The Crew
Simon Foster: Tour Manager
John Nave: FOH Sound
Justin Grealy: Monitors
Mark McCann: Guitar Tech
Paul Knowles: Backline Tech
Andy Hurst: Lighting Tech
Chris Urban: Merchandise

03/10/01 Late Night With David Letterman
Johnny Appleseed

04/10/01 Washington, 9:30 Club   **SOLD OUT**
815 V Street, NW, Washington
Capacity: 1200
Support: The Players

05/10/01 Philadelphia, Theatre of Living Arts   **SOLD OUT**
334 South St, Philadelphia
Capacity: 810
Support:

06/10/01 Atlantic City, Trump Marina Hotel
Brigantine Blvd, Atlantic City, NJ 08401
Capacity: 550
Support: None

08/10/01 Hartford, Webster Theatre   **SOLD OUT**
31 Webster St, Hartford, CT 06114
Capacity: 800
Support: Monk, The Flames

09/10/01 New York, Irving Plaza   **SOLD OUT**
17 Irving Place, New York
Capacity: 1,000
Support: The Slackers

10/10/01 New York, Irving Plaza **SOLD OUT**
17 Irving Place, New York
Capacity: 1,000
Support: The Slackers

12/10/01 Worcester, Palladium
261 Main St, Worcester, MA
Capacity: 2,530
Support: The Slackers, The Explosion

13/10/01 Montreal, Spectrum
822 Sherbrooke Est, Montreal
Capacity: 1,200
Support:

14/10/01 Toronto, The Guvernment
132 Queens Quay East, Toronto
Capacity: 1,200
Support: Tom Wilson

16/10/01 Chicago, Metro
3730 North Clark, Chicago
Capacity: 1,100
Support: Ike Reilly

17/10/01 Seattle, Groundworks Benefit Concert
EMP 325 Fifth Avenue N, Seattle
Capacity: 15,000
Also appearing: Artis the Spoonman, The Wallflowers and Chris Whitley

18/10/01 Scottsdale, Cajun House
7117 E 3rd Ave, Scottsdale
Capacity: 1,200
Support: None

19/10/01 Anaheim, House of Blues
1530 S. Disneyland Drive, CA 92802
Capacity: 950
Support: John Doe

20/10/01 San Francisco, Fillmore **SOLD OUT**
1805 Geary Blvd, San Francisco
Capacity: 1,250
Support: Sean Kennedy

22/10/01 Los Angeles, Troubadour   **SOLD OUT**
9081 Santa Monica Blvd, CA 90069
Capacity: 500
Support:

23/10/01 Los Angeles, Troubadour   **SOLD OUT**
9081 Santa Monica Blvd, CA 90069
Capacity: 500
Support:

25/10/01 Los Angeles, Troubadour   **SOLD OUT**
9081 Santa Monica Blvd, CA 90069
Capacity: 500
Support:

26/10/01 Los Angeles, Troubadour   **SOLD OUT**
9081 Santa Monica Blvd, CA 90069
Capacity: 500
Support:

JAPANESE TOUR

30/10/01 Fukuoka, Drum Logos   **SOLD OUT**
1 8 25 Maizura, Chuo-Ku, Fukuoka
Capacity: 800
Support: None

01/11/01 Tokyo, Club Quatro
32 13 Udagawa-Cho, Shibuya-Ku, Tokyo
Capacity: 800
Support: None

02/11/01 Tokyo, Akasaka Blitz
5 3 6 Akasaka, Minatu-Ku, Tokyo
Capacity: 2,000
Support: Ska Flame

04/11/01 Nagoya, Club Quatro
8F Nagoya Parco, Higashi-Kan, Nagoya
Capacity: 500
Support: None

05/11/01 Osaka, On-Air
Big Step 4F 1 6 14, Nishi-Shinsaibashi, Chuo-Ku, Osaka
Capacity: 900
Support: None

11/11/01 Gran Canaria, Womad Festival

BRITISH AND EUROPEAN TOUR

The Crew
Simon Foster: Tour Manager
Paul "Champ" Knowles: Stage Manager
John Nave: FOH Sound
Darren Scully: Monitors
Mark "Brain" McCann: Guitar Tech
Andy Hurst: Lighting Tech
John Wynne: Dimmers
Ritchie Gibson: PA Technician
Joff: Merchandise

15/11/01 Brighton, Concorde 2   **SOLD OUT**
Madeira Drive, Brighton
Capacity: 540
Support: Wreckless Eric

17/11/01 Manchester, Academy   **SOLD OUT**
Oxford Road, Manchester
Capacity: 1,800
Support: John Cooper Clarke

18/11/01 Glasgow, Barrowlands
244 Gallowgate, Glasgow
Capacity: 1,900
Support: John Cooper Clarke

20/11/01 Birmingham, Academy
52–54 Dale End, Birmingham
Capacity: 2,700
Support: John Cooper Clarke

21/11/01 Dublin, Olympia Theatre   **SOLD OUT**
72 Dame Street, Dublin
Capacity: 1,500
Support: John Cooper Clarke

23/11/01 Bristol, Colston Hall
Colston Street, Bristol
Capacity: 1,886
Support: John Cooper Clarke

24/11/01 London, Brixton Academy   **SOLD OUT**
211 Stockwell Road, Brixton
Capacity: 4,272
Support: John Cooper Clarke

26/11/01 Paris, Elysée-Montmartre   **SOLD OUT**
72 Blvd Rochechouart, Paris
Capacity: 1,500
Support: The Hellboys

29/11/01 Thessaloniki, Ydrogeios Club
26th October 33, Sfageia
Capacity: 800
Support - None

30/11/01 Athens, Sporting
Aghios Eleytherios, Patissia
Capacity: 2,500
Support: Teenage Angst

Setlist included:
Cool 'n' Out, Global A Go-Go, Bhindi Bhagee, Rudie Can't Fail, Trash City, Armagideon Time, Shaktar Donetsk, Mega Bottle Ride, Tony Adams, Mondo Bongo, Johnny Appleseed, Bummed Out City, Police On My Back, The Harder They Come, Yalla Yalla, Pressure Drop,
I Fought the Law, Bankrobber, London's Burning, A Message To You Rudy, Island Hopping, Police And Thieves, Minstrel Boy, Blitzkrieg Bop, Junco Partner

2002

FIVE NIGHT STAND

01/04/02 Brooklyn, St Ann's Warehouse   **SOLD OUT**
38 Water St, Brooklyn
Capacity: 600
Support: The Realistics

02/04/02 Brooklyn, St Ann's Warehouse   **SOLD OUT**
38 Water St, Brooklyn
Capacity: 600
Support: Nada Surf

04/04/02 Brooklyn, St Ann's Warehouse   **SOLD OUT**
38 Water St, Brooklyn
Capacity: 600
Support: Radio 4

05/04/02 Brooklyn, St Ann's Warehouse   **SOLD OUT**
38 Water St, Brooklyn
Capacity: 600
Support: Dirty Mary

06/04/02 Brooklyn, St Ann's Warehouse   **SOLD OUT**
38 Water St, Brooklyn
Capacity: 600
Support: Stellastarr*

Setlist included:
Yalla Yalla, London's Burning, Shaktar Donetsk, Tony Adams, Rudi Can't Fail, Cool 'n' Out, Global A Go-Go, Police And Thieves, Junco Partner, Get Down Moses, Bummed Out City, White Man In Hammersmith Palais, The Harder They Come, Mega Bottle Ride, Johnny Appleseed, Pressure Drop, Police On My Back, I Fought The Law, Lose This Skin, Walk On The Wild Side, Blitzkrieg Bop, White Riot, Bhindi Bhagee, Armagideon Time, Bankrobber

08/06/02 London, The Fleadh
Finsbury Park, London
Capacity: 25,000
Also appearing: The Pogues

HOOTENANNY FESTIVAL AND SUMMER SHOWS

The Crew
Simon Foster: Tour Manager
John Nave/Chris Ridgeway: FOH Sound
Darren Scully: Monitors
Mike Timm: Guitar Tech
Paul Knowles: Backline Tech
Andy Hurst: LD
Jack Kane: Merch USA

04/07/02 Las Vegas, House of Blues
Mandalay Bay Casino, 3950 Las Vegas Blvd, NV 89119
Capacity: 1,800
Support: Flogging Molly

05/07/02 San Francisco, Shoreline Amphitheatre
1 Amphitheatre Pkwy, Mountain View, CA 94043
Capacity: 5,000
Also appearing: Reverend Horton Heat, The Blasters, X, Nashville Pussy, Tiger Army, King Bees, Lee Rocker, Original Sinners, Hank Williams III, Social Distortion

06/07/02 Orange County, Hidden Valley
Hidden Valley, Irvine Centre Drive, Orange County
Capacity: 7,500
Also appearing – Reverend Horton Heat, The Blasters, X, Nashville Pussy, Tiger Army, King Bees, Lee Rocker, Original Sinners, Hank Williams III, Social Distortion

07/07/02 San Diego, Embarcadero Park
Embarcadero Park South, East Harbour Drive, San Diego
Capacity: 4,000
Also appearing: Reverend Horton Heat, The Blasters, X, Nashville Pussy, Tiger Army, King Bees, Lee Rocker, Original Sinners, Hank Williams III, Social Distortion

11/07/02 London, Shepherd's Bush Empire
Shepherd's Bush Green, London
Capacity: 2,000
Support

12/07/02 Manchester, MOVE Festival,
Old Trafford Cricket Ground, Manchester
Capacity: 14,000
Also appearing: Ian Brown, Paul Weller, Shed 7 and Haven

13/07/02 Kinross, T In The Park Festival
Balado, Nr Kinross
Capacity: 52,000
Also appearing: Oasis, Badly Drawn Boy, Primal Scream and Haven

03/08/02 Cambridge Folk Festival   **SOLD OUT**
Cherry Hinton, Cambridge
Capacity: estimated at 20,000

Also appearing: Indigo Girls, The Waterboys (acoustic), Billy Bragg, John Prine, The Dubliners, Iris DeMent, Chumbawamba, Oysterband, Taraf De Haidouks, Kate Rusby Band, Altan, Eric Bibb, Blue Murder, Eliza Carthy and Martin Green, Alison Brown Quartet, Cara Dillon, Rory McLeod, Salsa Celtica, Chip Taylor with Carrie Rodriguez and John Platania, Brian McNeill, The Holmes Brothers, The Be Good Tanyas, Coope Boyes and Simpson, Malinky, Ezio, La Volee D'Castors, Fiddlers' Bid, Slide, Token Women, Horace X, Give Way, The Chipolatas, Ben Waters Band, Filska

Setlist included:
White Man In Hammersmith Palais, Bhindi Bhagee, Shaktar Donetsk, Police And Thieves, Rudie Can't Fail, The Harder They Come, Guitar Slinger Man, Armagideon Time, Mega Bottle Ride, Johnny Appleseed, Police On My Back, I Fought The Law, London's Burning, Bummed Out City, Tony Adams, Yalla Yalla, Quarter Pound Of Ishen, Cool 'n' Out, Bankrobber, Pressure Drop, Walk On The Wild Side, A Message To You Rudy, Junco Partner, Get Down Moses, X-Ray Style, Willesden To Cricklewood, 1969

JAPANESE TOUR

28/09/02 Fukuoka Zepp, Japan
2-2-1, Jigyohama, Chuo-ku, Fukuoka
Capacity: 2,000
Support: Jude, Thee Michelle Gun Elephant

29/09/02 Asagiri Jam Festival, Japan
Asagiri Arena, Fujinomiya, Shizuoka
Capacity: 8,000
Also appearing – Tortoise, The Boredoms, Pe'z,

01/10/02 Liquid Room, Tokyo, Japan
3-16-6 Higashi, Shibuya-ku, Tokyo, Japan
Capacity: 1,500
Support: Jude, Thee Michelle Gun Elephant

Setlist included:
Shaktar Donetsk, X-Ray Style, Rudie Can't Fail, Guitar Slinger Man, Bhindi Bhagee, Quarter Pound Of Ishen, White Man In Hammersmith Palais, A Message To You Rudy, Mega Bottle Ride, Get Down Moses, Tony Adams, Cool 'n' Out, 1969, Johnny Appleseed, Sanposuru Harajuku, I Fought The Law, Bankrobber, Police On My Back, Yalla Yalla, Coma Girl, Walk On The Wild Side, London's Burning, Armagideon Time

BRINGING IT ALL BACK HOME TOUR

The Crew
Simon Foster: Tour Manager
Nigel Fogg: F OH Sound
Darran Scully: Monitors
Mike Timm: Guitar Tech
Stumpy: Backline Tech
Rob: Merchandise

10/11/02 London, Royal Opera House
St Martin's Lane, London
Capacity: estimated at 3,000
Also appearing: Bryan Adams

11/11/02 Edinburgh, Liquid Rooms   **SOLD OUT**
9c Victoria Street, Edinburgh
Capacity: 600
Support: The Basement

12/11/02 Newcastle, University of Northumbria   **SOLD OUT**
Student Uni Building, 2 Sandyford Road, Newcastle Upon Tyne
Capacity: 880
Support: The Basement

13/11/02 Blackpool, Winter Gardens
Church Street, Blackpool
Capacity: 1,200
Support: The Basement

15/11/02 London, Acton Town Hall   **SOLD OUT**
Acton High Street, London
Capacity: 1,000
Support: Velvet Sisters, No Bitchin'

16/11/02 Newport, TJ's   **SOLD OUT**
16–18 Clarence Place, Newport
Capacity: 600
Support: The Basement

17/11/02 Bridgwater, The Palace   **SOLD OUT**
24–26 Penel Orlieu, Bridgewater
Capacity: 400
Support: The Visitors and Vibrakings

19/11/02 Portsmouth, Wedgewood Rooms   **SOLD OUT**
147b Albert Road, Southsea
Capacity: 400
Support: The Raveonettes

20/11/02 Hastings, The Pier
The Pier, The Seafront, Hastings
Capacity: 1,200
Support: The Raveonettes

21/11/02 Sheffield, Leadmill
6 Leadmill Road, Sheffield
Capacity: 900
Support: The Raveonettes

22/11/02 Liverpool, University   **SOLD OUT**
Stanley Theatre, 160 Mt Pleasant, Liverpool
Capacity: 400
Support: The Bandits

Setlist included:
Shaktar Donetsk, Rudie Can't Fail, Police and Thieves, 1969, Quarter Pound Of Ishen, Bhindi Bhagee, White Man In Hammersmith Palais, A Message To You Rudy, Mega Bottle Ride, Get Down Moses, Tony Adams, Cool 'n' Out, Johnny Appleseed, I Fought The Law, Bankrobber, Junco Partner, White Riot, Dakar Meantime, Police On My Back, Yalla Yalla, Coma Girl, London's Burning

Discography

ALBUMS

Rock Art And The X-Ray Style

Release Date: 2 November 1999
Format: CD
Highest Chart Position:
   British Chart: 71
   Billboard/Heatseekers Chart: 34
Label & Cat No: Hellcat 80424

1 *Tony Adams* 2 *Sandpaper Blues* 3 *X-Ray Style* 4 *Techno D-Day* 5 *Road To Rock 'n' Roll* 6 *Nitcomb* 7 *Diggin' The New* 8 *Forbidden City* 9 *Yalla Yalla* 10 *Willesden To Cricklewood*

Joe Strummer: Guitar (Acoustic), Guitar, Vocals, Mixing
Antony Genn: Synthesizer, Bass, Guitar, Piano, Strings, Programming, Vocals (bckgr), Beats
Scott Shields: Guitar (Acoustic), Bass, Guitar (Bass), Guitar (Electric), Vocals (bckgr)
Martin Slattery: Organ (Hammond), Saxophone, Melodica, Wurlitzer)
Pablo Cook: Percussion, Drums, Vocals (bckgr)
Ged Lynch: Drums
Smiley: Drums
Gary Dyson: Vocals (bckgr), Chant
DJ Pete B: Scratching
Dave Stewart: Guitar (Acoustic)
B. J. Cole: Pedal Steel
Richard Norris: Keyboards, E-Bow, Drum Programming
Ian Tregoning: Engineer

Recorded at: Battery Studios
Mixed: Richard Flack and Antony Genn
Produced: Antony Genn
Engineered: Richard Flack

Global A Go-Go

Release Date: 24 July 2001
Format: CD/LP
Highest Chart Position:
  British Chart: 68
  Billboard/Heatseekers Chart: 45
Label & Cat No: Hellcat 80440

1 *Johnny Appleseed* 2 *Cool 'n' Out* 3 *Global A Go-Go* 4 *Bhindi Bhagee* 5 *Gamma Ray* 6 *Mega Bottle Ride* 7 *Shaktar Donetsk* 8 *Mondo Bongo* 9 *Bummed Out City* 10 *At the Border, Guy* 11 *Minstrel Boy*

Joe Strummer: Vocals,
Antony Genn: Strings, Loops
Scott Shields: Bass, Guitar, Bongos, Drums, Organ (Hammond), Vocals (bckgr), Bells, Loops
Martin Slattery: Synthesizer, Bass, Flute, Guitar, Accordion, Organ (Hammond), Saxophone, Vocals (bckgr), Melodica, Dulcimer (Hammer), Wurlitzer, Drones, Fuzz Guitar
Pablo Cook: Percussion, Bongos, Conga, Drums, Tambourine, Whistle (Instrument), Bells, Noise, Harmonica (Glass), Bodhran, Shaker, Guiro, Screams, Cuban Percussion, Udu
Tymon Dogg: Guitar (Acoustic), Mandolin, Violin, Spanish Guitar
Roger Daltrey: Vocals
Richard Flack: Cymbals, Vocals (bckgr)
Chris Lasalle: Sequencing

Recorded at: Battery Studios
Mixed: Richard Flack
Produced: Scott Shields, Martin Slattery and Richard Flack
Engineered: Richard Flack

Streetcore

Release Date: 20 October 2003 (UK); 21 October 2003 (RoW)
Format: CD/LP
Highest Chart Position: N/A
Label & Cat No: Hellcat 80454

1 *Coma Girl* 2 *Get Down Moses* 3 *Long Shadow* 4 *Arms Aloft* 5 *Ramshackle Day Parade* 6 *Redemption Song* 7 *All in A Day* 8 *Burnin' Streets* 9 *Midnight Jam* 10 *Silver and Gold*

Joe Strummer: Guitar, Vocals
Scott Shields: Guitar (Acoustic), Guitar, Harmonica, Percussion, Arranger, Drums, Guitar (Electric), Programming, Vocals (bckgr), Producer, Engineer, Slide Guitar, Cowbell, Mixing
Martin Slattery: Organ, Synthesizer, Guitar, Piano, Arranger, Drums, Guitar (Electric), Programming, Sax (Tenor), Tambourine, Vocals (bckgr), Producer, Engineer, Mellotron, Chamberlain, Mixing, Wurlitzer
Tymon Dogg: Violin
Simon Stafford: Bass, Guitar, Trombone, Cello, Cornet, Vocals (bckgr)
Luke Bullen: Conga, Drums, Loop
Richard Flack: Programming
Cameron Craig: Programming
Josh Freese: Drums
Peter Stewart: Vocals (bckgr)
Benmont Tench: Harmonium
Tim Bran: Program

Recorded at: Rockfield, 2KHZ, Battery Studios
Produced: Martin Slattery and Scott Shields
Engineered: Cameron Craig

SINGLES

Yalla Yalla
Release Date: August 1999
Format: CD/12"
Highest Chart Position: N/A
Label & Cat No: Mercd523 Mercury

1 *Yalla Yalla* (Album Version) 2 *The X-Ray Style* (Live) 3 *Yalla Yalla* (Norro's King Dub) 4 *Time and the Tide*

Johnny Appleseed
Release Date: July 2001
Format: 7in
Highest Chart Position: N/A
Label & Cat No: 1057-7 Hellcat/Epitaph

1 *Johnny Appleseed* 2 *At The Border, Guy*

Coma Girl
Release Date: 6 October 2003
Format : CD/CD/7in
Highest Chart Position: 33
Label and Cat No: 1137-7 Hellcat/Epitaph
CD 1: 1 *Coma Girl* (Album Version) 2 *Yalla Yalla* (Live) 3 *Blitzkrieg Bop* (Live) 4 *Coma Girl* (Video)
CD 2: 1 *Coma Girl* (Album Version) 2 *The Harder They Come* (Live) 3 *Rudi, A Message To You* (Live)
7in single and limited edition numbered 7in picture disc single: 1 *Coma Girl* (Album Version) 2 *Blitzkrieg Bop* (Live)

Redemption Song
Release Date: 15 December 2003
Format: CD/CD/7in
Highest Chart Position: N/A
Label & Cat No: 1149-7 Hellcat/Epitaph

CD 1: *Redemption Song*, *Arms Aloft* and *Armagideon Time* (Live)
CD 2: *Redemption Song*, *Arms Aloft* and *Pressure Drop* (Live)
Limited edition numbered 7in picture disc single: *Redemption Song*, *Arms Aloft* and *Junco Partner* (Live)

Plus additional:

Give 'Em The Boot Vol II
Inc: *X-Ray Style*
Release Date: 23 November 1999
Format: CD
Highest Chart Position: N/A
Label & Cat No: Hellcat 80420

Big Day Out 00
Inc: *Forbidden City*
Release Date: 2000
Format: CD
Highest Chart Position: N/A
Label & Cat No: Shock BDO2000CD

Give 'Em The Boot Vol III
Inc: *Global A Go-Go*
Release Date: 12 February 2002
Format: CD
Highest Chart Position: N/A
Label & Cat No: Hellcat 80444

Black Hawk Down – Motion Picture Soundtrack
Inc: *Minstrel Boy* (Film Version)
Release Date: 15 January 2002
Format: CD/LP
Highest Chart Position: N/A
Label & Cat No: Decca 440 017 012

Free with magazines:

Unconditionally Guaranteed vol. 10 (free with *Uncut* 11/99): *Sandpaper Blues*
Uncut (free with *Uncut* 10/01): *Mega Bottle Ride*
Uncut UG 33-39 *White Riot vol. 1* (free with *Uncut* 12/03): *Long Shadow*
Uncut 2003 12B

Ultimate Songwriters (free with Q Magazine 10/04) *Redemption Song*
Radio Clash (free with Mojo 10/04)
White Man in Hammersmith Palais (Joe Strummer and The Mescaleros at 100 Club)

Special thanks to (without whose help etc):

Lucinda Mellor, Smiley, Pablo Cook & Laura, Andy Boo & Grub, John & Virginia Blackburn, Martin & Kirsty Slattery, Scott Shields, Luke Bullen, Antony Genn, Simon & Kate Stafford, Tymon Dogg, Jimmy Hogarth, Richard Flack, Gary Robinson, Simon Foster, Chris Shiftlett, Pat Gilbert, John Hatch, Tresa Redburn at Dept. 56, John Zimmerman, Terry McQuade, Nyle Shepherd, Ben Gooder, Bob Gruen, Anika Jamieson-Cook, Steve Lea, Guiseppe and Manuela Rivella, Jane Mingay, Christian Bilda, Simon at Trakmarx, Alisa Williams, Alex Hryshko, Philip Morton, Eva Sommerfield, Sukwoon Noh, Dave Maud & Elizabeth Dew, Juha Koivisto, Terry Currier & Rachel Landtroop at Music Millenium, Jack Rabid & Michelle at The Bigtakeover, Barbara Lang, Eric Aniversario, Jon Webb, Jane & Andy (the sink!), Nikola Acin, Richard King at The Blue Note, Iku Kaneko, Neil 'Lumpy' Lewington, Tami Peterson, George Binette, Simon Rose at KBXR. 102.3 FM, Jenny Lizak at The Metro, Larry Rudnick at Zia Records, Orion Eckstrom at Cajun House, Gina Migliozzi at The Palladium Worcester, Arlene Owseichik at The Fillmore, Ed Stack at Nightclub 9:30, Iossif Batsos, Gary Cormier at the Guvernment, Graham Jones.

I would also like to thank the people who showed faith in me and were a great encouragement and kept me going:

Michael Kozeluh (AKA Fivestring), Nate Ranger, Anthony Fenton, Ferruccio Martinotti, Riccardo Ferro, Mauro Zaccuri, John Shipley, Mark Gibson-White, Craig Thompson, George Baldacchino, Eeva King, Mick Wilson, Joe Swinford, Alessandro Zangarini, Antonello Del Mastro, Giorgio "Gigio" Bricca, Michael Clifton, Peter Shovlin, Laura Fitzgerald, Ben Hope, Frank LaVerda, Angie Piper, Shannon and Dawn, Jo Campana, Ashley Wildman, Mum and Stret, Dad and Sheila, Emma and Simon, Bruce Reid, Alex Cranmer, "The Great" Johnny King, Kevin Duffy and all at Mountsides, Brendan and Firoza, Derek Gill, Carol Cope.
All at Mount Pleasant Sorting Office (management excepted) for covering for me over the years and patiently listening to my tales!

Last but not least to my wife, Janet and "my girls", Amée and Ellie.

Sites worth catching

http://www.radioclash.it/
   Mauro's super Italian site
http://clashuk.tripod.com/index.htm
   Johnnytheglove at his best
www.gpjones.free-online.co.uk/
   Graham's Blackmarket Clash
http://www.lostinthesupermarket.com/aisle3/shields/ss.html
   Shannon and Dawn's favourite Glaswegian site
http://www.redangeljsmusic.com/
   Laura's lovely site
http://boards.gcuber.com/board/
   AKA Satch's Forum
http://www.strummernews.com/
   Tami's great site
http://cla5h.com/
   Sukwoon's wonderful site
http://www.jacksonunited.com/top.php
   Chris Shiflett's band
http://www.foofighters.com/
   Chris's day job. Say no more!
http://www.thehellboys.com
   Great band that supported The Mescaleros in Paris
http://californiasaga.com/
   Barb's great Beach Boys site
www.caughtinaction.co.uk
   Dave Maud's fantastic pics site
http://www.punkoiuk.co.uk/
   Rebecca's great site for up to the minute Punk and Oi news
http://www.trakmarx.com/
   Simon at his best
http:// www.bxr.com/
   KBXR 102.3 FM, Columbia, Missouri
http://www.themescaleros.co.uk/
   Zadie's Mescaleros site.
http://www.bobgruen.com
   Rock 'n ' roll photographer
http://www.baywell.ne.jp/users/isshi/default.htm
   Taku's splendid Clash site
www.strummerville.com/
   The Joe Strummer Foundation for New Music

http://www.primeticket.net/shows/joestrummer/
　Joe & The Mescaleros Live in Toronto
http://www5.ocn.ne.jp/~kanebon/
　Iku's Japanese site
http://www.strummersite.com/
　Home of The Mescaleros
www.proper-gander.co.uk
　John Zimmerman's site

Passion is a Fashion
Pat Gilbert
Published by Aurum
October 2004

The "definitive history of The Clash"